BRADFORD WILSON, PH.D.,
AND GEORGE EDINGTON, M.A.

First Child,
Second Child . . .

What Your Birth Order Means To You

PANTHER
Granada Publishing

Panther Books
Granada Publishing Ltd
8 Grafton Street, London W1X 3LA

Published by Panther Books 1984

First published in Great Britain by
Souvenir Press Ltd 1982

Copyright © Bradford Wilson and George Edington 1981

ISBN 0-586-06170-3

Printed and bound in Great Britain by
Collins, Glasgow

Set in Times

Bradford Wilson tried his hand at being a professional portrait painter, at ceramics and at jewellery-making before settling down to his career as a psychotherapist and psychologist. He became interested in the effects of birth order while doing graduate work at the New School for Social Research in New York, and although he spends part of his time writing, he still practises psychotherapy. His family has lived in Westfield, Massachusetts, since about 1628, but he himself has lived in New York since he was eighteen.

George Edington worked in market research and was a promotion writer for the now defunct *New York Herald Tribune* before taking a degree in psychology at the New School for Social Research where, like his co-author, he became interested in birth order. Since then he has worked for schools and in hospitals, and is currently employed as a psychologist in the South Bronx area of New York, working with black and Hispanic children, while preparing his doctoral dissertation.

To Harmon S. Ephron, M.D.
our teacher, mentor, guide, colleague
and very dear friend

Contents

Introduction

Most people register surprise when they become aware that many of their feelings and opinions about being the first, last, middle, or only child in their family are shared by others in the same 'birth order,' as it is called. For reasons that are by no means clear, the closely allied fields of psychiatry and developmental psychology have paid surprisingly scant attention to the strong influence this factor exerts upon the formation of our individual personalities.

It goes without saying that a person's gender, age, place of birth, gait, mode of dress, accent, occupation, etc., are all matters we take into account when sizing up a stranger. The fact that there are so many elements to take into account does not prevent any of us from wanting to know what makes other people tick; it seems a basic part of our human nature to gather information, put it together, and come up with conclusions. That some of these conclusions are erroneous and that they get perpetuated is, of course, a frequent and unfortunate outcome.

Birth order has the advantage of being easier to check out than most other kinds of data; we can ask people whether or not they have brothers or sisters on relatively short acquaintance without offending them. Some ordinal positions are more easily recognized than others (but you will be surprised at how your guessing improves with practice).

When we begin to study *how* people came to be the way they are, the going gets rougher. Weighing so many factors one by one can become very complicated. Even sheer luck seems to play a large part in what happens to us and how our personalities are shaped. Owing to the fact that no two people have precisely the same experiences, an encounter with two girls from the same family may disclose that one of them is athletic and outgoing; she gets on the girls' gymnastic team, goes to competitions, and enjoys meeting many other girls from distant places. Her sister, on the other hand, would rather stay at home, likes cooking, and is content with knowing only a small group of kids from school. Similarly, a young man may wonder 'How come my sister is such a *party* type while I prefer to stay home and work on my stamp collection?' And if he had had an introductory course in psychology, he would probably add 'After all, we both had the same parents, grew up in the same neighborhood, and went to the same school!'

To this we would say yes, but *you* had a little sister, and *she* had a big brother, so it wasn't exactly the same at all! Parents have different attitudes toward boys and girls; toward first-borns, last-borns, and children in between. An oldest child is likely to spend several formative years with happy parents who are in love with one another. A last-born child in the same family, however, may grow up with parents who barely tolerate each other and who harbor many years' worth of unexpressed grievances.

Ever since Freud, it has been generally held that during childhood our parents (especially mothers) are the most influential persons in our lives. They are the giants, the masters, the punishers, the dispensers of goodies. A nod of the head allows us to stay up a half-hour beyond our usual bedtime or to go on a trip with our school class. Few other adults (unless they actually take on a parental role) ever play so important a part in a child's life as do the parents. You may not have liked Miss Green, your teacher, but she was never the ultimate authority during your formative years. Teachers may point out our sins of commission in class but they don't have the continuing power over us that our parents do, and their authority most often ends at around 4 o'clock in the afternoon.

As it stands, most of us born into a nuclear family (that is, one consisting of parents and children) grow up regarding our mother (consciously or not) as the prototype of All Women and our father as the prototype of All Men. However, if things go reasonably well, we do change as we develop and certain new attitudes come to replace a number of outmoded ones that no longer work. We discover that there are a great many women and men who are admirable and even lovable without sharing our parents' virtues. Similarly, we can be relieved to discover a number of men and women who don't display some of our parents' less pleasant qualities.

An older brother or sister may function as a kind of straw-boss, meting out rewards and punishments to younger siblings, even though the Supreme Court in most families is Dad and Mum. At the same time, the younger sibs have ways of challenging that authority – if only on the grounds that it is for the most part temporary and does not usually carry the clout that characterizes parental authority. Of course the greater the age disparity (eight years or more) between the older and the younger sib, the more their interaction will resemble that of parent to child. Generally speaking, however, the very fact that brothers and sisters do not have the power of parents but are fellow children accounts for the lasting effect that relationships with them exert upon one's life. For they are fellow sharers in the family love and warmth, or fellow inmates of a prison or concentration camp, or perhaps fellow toilers in the family vineyard. While an only child's domestic intimacy is largely confined to his or her relationship with one or both parents, most other children experience their greatest intimacy with siblings. Here the word 'intimacy' does not necessarily imply deep affection, but refers rather to the acquisition of privileged information in the course of living together closely over a number of years.

G. K. Chesterton once observed that, although we make our friends on our own hook, God gives us our next-door neighbors (for better or worse) and we're stuck with them; the same holds true for siblings. *Many* a youngster has regretted asking for a baby brother or sister only to find that once their wish has been granted, the baby is here for keeps, and any dreams of sending it back to the hospital are forlorn and pathetic fantasies. One need not play with other kids in the neighborhood if one prefers not to, but there is rarely any choice when it comes to living (and often sharing a room or even a bed) with one or more siblings.

Willy-nilly, both life and reality require that we eventually come to terms with the impact which early household members had upon our lives. For some of us this may include, or even feature, such personages as boarders, relatives, a family friend, or even a servant or two. For we learn most of our assumptions about living with other human beings from what we experience in the bosom of our childhood family, whatever forms it took for each of us. It was there that we first learned how to negotiate compromises, to trade advantages, and to wheel and deal. It was there that we also learned how to defend ourselves, to take note (and advantage) of other people's weaknesses, to bide our time, and to seek redress of grievances.

There is a bit of folklore in most families to the effect that parents are obliged to love all their children equally, and in an effort to fulfill this ideal, mothers and fathers often lean over backwards to maintain a conspicuously equitable balance in the distribution of their favors. But the children in a multi-sib family are usually aware (perhaps without ever bringing it out into the open) of who is the father's favorite and who the mother's. It is a wise child indeed who keeps his or her own counsel in this regard, and avoids futile confrontations with parents who are not conditioned to handle such issues. Similar wisdom may, however, prompt some children to use that very same knowledge for the purpose of pressing an unfair advantage (or 'laying a guilt trip,' as American parlance would have it) upon a bewildered and unsuspecting parent. Equally effective are the child's requests as earnestly relayed via the parental favorite.

Saint Paul is quoted as saying 'Now I am a man, I have put away childish things.' It may be that some extraordinary people (like saints) do not carry their childish attitudes over into their adult lives, but the rest of us harbor a child within us all our lives long – a very precious child to whom we owe most of our capacity for joy and wonder. So far as that child's relations with siblings are concerned, early attitudes and beliefs are long-enduring.

Of course, such attitudes and beliefs occur on subconscious as well as on conscious levels. Very few people nowadays question the existence of subconscious mental layers which seem to possess purposes and hidden agendas of their own. Much current questioning of this concept arises from Freud's admittedly pessimistic view of the subconscious mind as being a potential enemy of the psyche that must at all times be monitored and kept in check.

It is our firm belief that the subconscious mind is always our friend; a loyal protector who never sleeps and whose motive is to protect us and to promote our best interests according to its own lights. This, of course, is where a lot of our most painful problems have their roots. Because, unfortunately, our subconscious can only order its priorities and shape its agendas on the basis of its 'inputs' – that is, the data it receives from conception onward. Feed it accurate data, and its 'programs' will prove to be creative and life-promoting; feed it warped, misguided, or phony data, and the subconscious will, with all the best intentions in the world, get us into what turns out to be trouble of one sort or another.

It is the great tragedy of the human condition that we make far-reaching decisions about ourselves too early in life – at age two or three or four. That is to say, much of the data by which we consciously and subconsciously order our lives got fed into our psychic apparatus before we were sufficiently developed or experienced to draw the conclusions necessary for our fulfillment in adult life. When you stop to think about it, it's truly amazing that so many of us are able to survive and prosper as well as we do!

The important thing to realize, though, is that our loyal friend, the subconscious, *can be re-educated*. Its power to resist such efforts is legendary, however, for the simple reason that, having learned its lessons in the school of hard knocks, it isn't about to put you in what it considers to be a dangerous situation if it can possibly avoid doing so. Persuading the subconscious that it's okay and safe to experiment, to try new ways of reacting and dealing with the world, is no easy task. Because it is our friend and has learned in a hard – and biased – school, its loyalty prompts it to take up postures which may have served us well in childhood but are now counterproductive, and to defend those postures with enormous energy and singleness of purpose.

It is not a simple matter to figure out the intricacies of birth order phenomena. One might regard it as a three-object problem, as it were; when mathematicians and engineers collaborated in launching a missile to the moon, they had to take into account that all three objects were in motion – the missile, the moon, and Earth itself – not to mention the influences exerted upon all three objects by the sun as well as the other planets.

Birth orders can get almost as complicated. Even if we limit our discussion to two-sibling families, we still have to take into account the ways in which father, mother, relatives, and society itself affect the perceptions, attitudes, and ways of coping that define one's personality. Knowledge concerning the regularities of birth order (like knowing about Western middle-class child-rearing practices) is of enormous help in the accurate assessment and prediction of personality variables. Generally speaking, nuclear families* within a given culture are enough alike so that the roles which accompany various ordinal positions (as birth orders are often called) resemble each other more often than not. For example it is reasonable to assume that most young couples are not very experienced at having children. Consequently the first-born is an object of more parental anxiety and attention than later-born children are apt to be.

Being the first, last, or middle in anything influences us in fairly predictable ways. Freud's onetime student Alfred Adler was the first psychologist to discuss birth order at some length in his treatise of 1908. Followers of Adler have, since that time, maintained a keen regard for and interest in the subject, which they have always considered a strong contributor to that end product known as 'personal life-style' (a phrase coined by Adler, incidentally). Freud, on the other hand, is peculiarly silent on the subject – an anomaly all the more significant in view of the fact that there were so very few aspects of the human condition to which his wide-ranging and creative curiosity did not address itself at one time or another.

* Nuclear families are composed of two parents and their children only. In the 'extended family,' parents, grandparents, children, cousins, uncles, aunts, in-laws, etc., all inhabit the same locality (sometimes even the same house) and enjoy fairly easy access to each other's households. Since members often look out for one another, each person may have many and varied parents and sibs at any stage of development.

There are those who maintain that the fourth, fifth, and sixth child will show the same fundamental characteristics as the first, second, and third child – and that the seventh, eighth, and ninth will do likewise, and so on. While this may be so, we are not in possession of the raw data upon which this assertion is presumably based. First of all, it is not nearly so easy as it once was to find families which contain nine or more surviving children. And secondly, locating and enlisting the cooperation of many such families and obtaining the kind of in-depth information about its members that might lead to meaningful conclusions would constitute a task of mind-boggling scope and magnitude. We can only conclude that the proponents of this theory must, in their zeal, have jumped to rather hasty conclusions based on what we consider insufficient evidence.

In addition to the bare fact of ordinal position, one's gender must be taken into account as an extremely important variable. Mothers and fathers are conditioned by their own upbringing to expect varieties and degrees of behavior in boys which differ from those of girls. And what's more, brothers and sisters are similarly conditioned in their anticipations and expectations – a factor which is all too frequently ignored by investigators in the field. It is no wonder, then, that birth order dynamics are at their most clearly discernible in families with only two children, where there are not so many sibs to further complicate the picture.

In the last decade or so, professional and popular articles on birth order have appeared with increasing frequency. Interest in the topic has progressed from a mere trickle to a high tide. Diligent and dedicated psychologists have made countless controlled studies and have investigated everything relating to birth order from thumb sucking to membership in religious orders. As the authors have read and explored this growing body of knowledge, we have been impressed by how rarely the findings are at variance with what we have been observing over the past twenty years. Research conclusions may differ in some of the details, but the biographical sweep which characterizes each birth order remains clearly intact – making up, as it were, a kind of 'lifescript' recognizable by its own distinctive stamp; its own list of assets and liabilities, advantages and disadvantages, joys and sorrows.

It is to the biographical sweep of each birth order that we will be addressing ourselves in this book. Although we have been in the practice of clinical diagnosis and psychotherapy for the past twenty-five years, we have resisted – successfully, we trust – the temptation to indulge in psychological theorizing or to offer interpretations of what we have observed. Instead, we will be offering a composite sketch of each birth order written in the second person singular, so that you, the reader, may get a sense of what it can mean to be born into a given ordinal position and what the world of other people can look like from that particular vantage point.

At the same time it is not our intention to give anyone the notion that this book purports to be the final word on the subject – or on any particular birth order. As in most areas of serious study, there is always more to be learned. It would have been very neat if our present state of knowledge had made it possible for us to cover the same topics for each birth order – occupational preference, friendship choices, fortunate (versus unfortunate) marital partners, relationship to employers, employees, authorities, etc. We enjoy nifty packaging as much as anyone else – but our data doesn't work out that way. In the case of certain birth orders much is known about occupational choice while for others no discernible patterns have thus far appeared. We see no point in resorting to speculation simply for the sake of uniformity.

Meanwhile, our composites will be drawn not only from readings but also from our own clients and personal acquaintances: some from remote childhood; many of them neighbors, relatives, and friends. Although you may find yourself taking exception to some of our observations concerning your own ordinal position, we believe that many of the descriptions to follow will bear a strong resemblance to persons of your acquaintance, and that such resemblance will *not* be 'purely coincidental.' At the conclusion of this volume, after you have had a chance to get to know the various birth orders, we shall reveal our own, so that you may decide for yourself what – if any – bearing this has had on our undertaking.

PART ONE

The Major Birth Orders

CHAPTER ONE

Only Child – General Observations

Perhaps the easiest birth order to spot is that of the only child or 'singleton' as you are sometimes referred to in the literature. By only child we include, of course, all those who are brought up with no other children in the household. You may have been one of seven or eight, but if you were entrusted to your grandmother or to a childless aunt and uncle at the age of six months, you were, for all intents and purposes, an only child. In any case, as such you are likely to have a way of speaking which reflects great self-assurance; a quality of cool command. Almost certainly you grew up assuming that center stage was yours by right, so that when you offer an opinion you naturally expect other people to listen. This doesn't mean, of course, that all of you are spellbinding speakers, but it does mean that most of you have a good feel for audience reaction and timing, both in public and with smaller groups of friends or family. As a child you took it for granted that the adults around you, especially your parents, would hear you out. Not for you the admonition 'Now don't all talk at once!' or 'I know you learned a new poem at school today, dear, but Buddy learned one too, and I promised I would listen to his first.' The mother of an only child may only sometimes half-listen but she seldom if ever says 'Hey you talk too much,' or 'Come on, loudmouth, why don't you let someone else talk once in a while?'

Like other first-borns, you were probably the recipient of considerable intense personal attention from your parents. They waited eagerly for your first intelligible words, your first attempts at standing, walking, and so forth. 'The eyes of The World are upon you' could well have been your motto since the day you were born. While being in the limelight has advantages, the drawbacks are axiomatic, especially when you are a singleton. You entered and left the scene on cue, were expected not to fidget or try to hog the show when others were on stage, and were expected to be a good listener as well as an exemplary performer. Unlike the first-born of several children, you rarely had contemporaries in the audience or onstage to play wicked stepsister to your Cinderella, or pirate crew to your Captain Kidd. The gallery to which you played was composed pretty exclusively of adults. If you also happen to have been an only grandchild as well as an only child, you got a double or even triple dose of adult attention during your growing-up years.

In addition to having grown up as the focus of much parental concern, it is more than likely that they, in turn, may have demanded a considerable amount of *your* attention. After all, parents have their problems, too – and it is often to their first-born child that they turn when they need advice, empathy, or tender loving care. In the case of a first-born eldest, however, they are apt to be more discreet and more selective about what they share because there is always the danger that the child may inadvertently 'leak' some top secret information to a younger sibling who may (also inadvertently) let it outside the family. You, however, can find yourself at a very early age being the repository of your parents' most poignant preoccupations – a state of affairs which, while admittedly flattering to you, can also be very burdensome. This holds especially true when each parent turns to you with problems which relate (directly or indirectly) to the other parent. While it is possible that you learned to say 'a pox on both your houses!' and refused to become involved, it is far more likely that you found yourself torn between loyalties and generally trapped in the role of Peacemaker. The most frequent outcome is that you learned to thread your way across the battlefield like a World War I ambulance driver, miraculously avoiding bombardment (nine times out of ten) from either side; your services were needed by both contestants, as you all knew full well – and neither could afford the risk of taxing your patience beyond endurance. Needless to say, this placed you in a position of wielding more power than any child can reasonably be expected to handle. And yet you did. But the price you paid is likely to have been costly: either you built a kind of 'armor' around yourself which tends to 'tune out' other people's grievances in a way which your associates regard as 'cold-blooded' – or else you become Everybody's Rescuer who agonizes over other people's problems (especially parents and others of their generation) and cannot resist your knee-jerk impulse to fly to their rescue, no matter what the wear and tear to yourself. Your only rival in this arena is the youngest child – owing to his/her need to prove self-worth by becoming indispensable to others. We can only affirm your basic right to defend your own space from intrusion by others who try to appoint you to be the arbiter of their disputes and the binder-up of their wounds. Believe it or not, you were not born to save humankind, and it is no come-down for you to let that cup pass now and then, and, yes, allow yourself to reach out for the attention which you so often extend to others in their time of need.

That your contact with grownups was probably much greater than the contact with your peers during your early years makes it likely that you are exceptionally comfortable with older people in your adult life. For whatever reason, most people from other ordinal positions tend to avoid the company of those whom they consider 'old,' as if to say 'I can't bear to gaze on what I myself may one day become.' This seems especially true of their attitude toward members of their own sex who are advanced in age; it seems far easier for them to form attachments to elderly members of the opposite sex. You, however, are at ease with both.

As a general rule, you present your point of view or your information without apology or boasting. Your enthusiasm for the subject is often quite contagious. You seem to derive solid and deep satisfaction from immersing yourself in whatever you undertake until you are almost an authority on whatever has captured your interest, which may be anything from horse racing to the mating habits of goldfish.

This capacity for total immersion is also often found in the older of two children when there is an age gap of six years or more between them. In that case, the older child was a singleton for those first few important years and therefore the center of parental attention for quite a long period. In this connection it's important to bear in mind that during the formative years (from birth to age seven), a year or two of *anything* is considered a long period.

You singletons not infrequently have several different interests going at once and often are thoroughly engrossed in *all* of them. A stranger meeting you for the first time may be impressed by your extensive knowledge of plants; then, a few months later, he or she discovers that you know all about the art of wine-making and have, indeed, made wine out of everything from raisins to potato peels. A year after that you may disclose the fact that you have actually published articles on the subject of Waterford glass, and so on.

The leisurely **way in** which these items of information gradually emerge **into** the open is not the result of any false modesty on your part. You take your interests for granted and are a little surprised that anyone should think them unusual, either alone or in combination. They are in all probability an outgrowth of your being left alone as a child to pursue your consuming interests unmolested. You may have grown up under a spotlight, so to speak, and were the center of much adult attention and concern, but, with only three people in the household, there inevitably were times during which you could all get away from one another and go off to 'do your own thing.'

When your parents entertained grownups like themselves, you were probably required to go off by yourself right after dinner to do homework, or whatever. With no age mates in the household (to help you get into the mischief that children will perpetrate in each other's company but not alone) you were often left with only a hobby or books for company and entertainment. If you were a bright youngster, such self-entertainment probably took the form of self-education. Perhaps because you were allowed (and encouraged) to do your own thing, that could have been so self-absorbing, and your attack upon it so single-minded that you may sometimes have appeared thoughtless or disrespectful of other people's interests – especially those which were inconvenient or in conflict with your own.

In any event, you had a lot of creative solitude which provided you with the kind of environmental enrichment that made possible your imaginative and innovative approaches to many events – at home or in your business and social life. Note, however, that you probably take this quality of yours for granted or else are less aware of it than you should be. Experts in childhood development regard environmental enrichment as crucial to the nurture of that elusive and cherished entity known as creativity. Children's TV programs like 'Sesame Street' and 'Play School' have as one of their goals the enrichment of young viewers' inner lives, thus leading to a more lively relationship with the world whereby the child gradually becomes more aware, more curious, more self-informed, and hence more creative.

Having to learn more about how to live alone and like it

than people with sisters and/or brothers, you probably also had serious difficulty in having to deal with more interruptions than other people. The oldest child in a family (especially if male) is often given private space which is considered sacrosanct by the rest of the family; 'Big Brother (Sister) is busy studying. You can empty the rubbish (mind the baby, set the table, feed the cat) can't you?' But for you, as a singleton, it was not that easy; you were the only child in your family, and so your pursuits more often got interrupted. Moreover, your parents were concerned lest they spoil you by exempting you from your household duties and other obligations, even for a single instance. This highlights a very special problem for you as a singleton: the parental *ambivalence* that prompts them to indulge you while at the same time leaning over backwards to see that they don't ruin your chances for survival in the 'sibling'-ridden world in which you will one day have to compete and work out viable transactions. Such a balancing act presents an enormous and perpetual challenge to the mothers and fathers of singletons, and they are bound to make a number of mistakes along the way. Having to deal with constant interruptions made it necessary for you to acquire far stronger powers of concentration than you perhaps appreciate. But this fortunate attribute has some unfortunate consequences: you are impatient and intolerant of others.

It is difficult for you to realize the sheer distractability of others; what you put your mind to invariably gets done come hell or high water. You are often perplexed by the way in which other people fail to do what they say they will do when they say they will do it! You have difficulty comprehending what you see as the carelessness and irresponsibility of anyone who can leave jobs half-completed and promises unkept or only partially fulfilled.

Although we are not aware of any research on the subject

as it relates to birth order, our strong impression is that your penchant for driving yourself very hard without realizing you are doing so increases the likelihood that you may be a 'Type A' person. This is the label that has been given to the sort of person who is an overactive deadline-meeter, who rarely takes rest breaks, who feels under constant pressure. Type A personalities appear to run a higher risk of encountering coronary or other cardiac problems in the course of their lives. If you belong to this category (as opposed to the 'Type B' person who is much more relaxed and takes life as it comes), you probably run to answer the phone or doorbell (instead of walking) and, like the White Rabbit in *Alice in Wonderland*, you feel as though you are perpetually catching up. You therefore probably won't pay the slightest attention when we suggest that you would do well to build regular rest periods into your busy day.

There is another aspect of your development that also comes under the heading of 'enrichment' (one that first-borns share with you to a certain degree): as an only child you spent a lot more private time with adults than most children do. You had more exposure to the thoughts, attitudes, and feelings of grownups than is generally experienced by younger children in a family, who are – aside from their contact with teachers – more limited to the intellectual environment of other children.

This enrichment, however, was counterbalanced in your case because it gave you an edge on the other youngsters of your acquaintance which they may not have taken kindly to. You probably could not understand how others in your own age group could be such babies, be so ignorant, or hold such uninformed opinions. While it might have given you a valid sense of sophistication, it also put a certain amount of distance between you and your peers.

Not having had little brothers and sisters, you were not

so often called upon as are oldest children to subvert your own viewpoint and to go along with conventional or family ways of doing things. Consequently you tend to be more impatient than other first-borns when you hear platitudes, canned opinions, clichés, bromides, political slogans, or just plain nonsense. You enjoy and appreciate original thinking – which makes you more daring than other first-borns; of all ordinal positions yours is the one most likely to break new ground in your thoughts and ideas. You have only one rival in this respect – the youngest child of three or more children (Ben Franklin and Christina Rossetti being cases in point). However, a youngest child's particular brand of independence is usually characterized by considerable protest and iconoclastic melodrama, whereas yours tends to be more cool and self-confident. This will be discussed at greater length in Chapter 8, which deals with the youngest child.

Another distinct advantage you had was that you were exposed at a tender age to a much wider range of environmental stimuli than most later-borns experience. Whether or not you were always able to appreciate the long train rides, theatrical events, carnivals, museums, weddings, and other events to which your parents probably subjected you, these experiences contributed a great deal to your mental and emotional development. It is known that children – as well as monkeys, dogs, cats, and laboratory rodents – who have had rich and varied experiences during baby- and toddlerhood grow up to be 'brighter' – more lively and more explorative – than those who were raised in a less invigorating environment. In short, you had more things to play with and more events to observe than most other children. Thus, without being aware of the fact, your powers of observation became sharpened at a very early stage in life.

These observational powers combine very neatly with

your capacity to await the right moment for taking action so that you probably excel at games which call for this watch-and-wait combination – poker, bridge, rummy, chess, etc. Having grown up as a little human tape recorder, you probably remember everything. Making note of which cards have been played is second nature to you. Singletons have been known to repeat whole conversations, and even to recite the lyrics of a new musical after a single exposure. Organizations and committees are doing themselves and their cause a great service indeed when they appoint you as their recording secretary, or editor of their newsletter, or fund-raiser, or whatever – because not only will you be precise and accurate in what you report, but you will also write and proofread your own copy down to the very last comma. In addition, the appropriate number of perfect copies will be reproduced and mailed out at the exact time they are due. Of all birth orders you are by far the most conscientious and reliable: you almost invariably do what you say you will do, when you say you will do it.

All those years of sitting around owl-eyed and pitcher-eared while the adults around you interacted, conversed, and exchanged confidences has made you a very astute spectator to the human scene. The noted anthropologist Dr Margaret Mead used to advise her students not to conceal themselves behind bushes or duck blinds when they wanted to observe people, but told them instead to mingle freely until they became 'part of the background scenery' and were no longer noticed. Many a child playing quietly with blocks on the floor or unobtrusively putting a doll to bed or assiduously rearranging a stamp collection has thus become privy to the kind of scandalous stories most parents wouldn't dream of sharing with anyone other than a spouse or a very close adult friend. And so it was with you most of the time. The direct result of such extensive exposure is that you generally manage to be head-and-shoulders above any other ordinal position when it comes to your agility in sizing up individuals and social situations with lightning rapidity and a high degree of accuracy. Since you are firm in your opinions and outspoken concerning your likes and dislikes (however hard you may bend over backwards to be fair) you can often startle associates with your instant likes and dislikes which you almost never revise. In the course of time, friends and fellow workers usually come to respect your shrewdness of observation, and will often seek out your guidance in the assessment of persons whom they find baffling or difficult.

There is, of course, a debit side to the ledger. Because you were included so often in adult activities as a matter of course, you are likely to be more touchy than other birth orders when it appears to you that you are being excluded. You have a strong need to be in the know and while this may be subconscious on your part, you have developed many subtle (and often not-so-subtle) ways of acquiring inside information. The admonition that 'children should be seen and not heard' did not prevent you from listening, figuring things out, and coming to a number of shrewd conclusions about the world around you.

Many (if not most) only children are born to parents who are somewhat older than the parents of other first-borns. Although there are probably medical factors involved here (discussed later in the chapter), the impact of this on your childhood should not be underestimated. Like the youngest child in a big family, you may well have parents who were around thirty-five (or over) at the time you were conceived, and who were probably starting to feel a little less energetic than they were willing to admit.

Moreover, your parents didn't have the help of older children to act as substitute parents; to watch and see that you didn't get into mischief or pick you up when you cried, and even to feed you if necessary. Even if they were able to afford one or more servants to take up the slack, their own inexperience lent anxiety to their manner of handling the demands and behaviors of a very small child.

If you observe a very young father with his three-year-old, you will probably notice a certain element of easy give-and-take going on between them; he treats the tot almost like a contemporary; much as an older brother might. While a father of thirty-five may have fun with his toddler, his sense of age gap is usually quite apparent, and he rarely if ever treats his child as though they were of the same generation. However kindly and fatherly his approach may be, it still carries a big label which reads 'I will put up with no nonsense!' To cite another example, a bright and curious four-year-old may have a need to go outdoors and come back in again a dozen times in a single day – behavior which a very young parent might scarcely notice. But an older parent is more likely to feel victimized, or else turn the whole thing into some kind of senseless power struggle ('Make up your mind, once and for all – indoors or outdoors – and I intend to see that you stick to it!').

There is a possibility that your parents recognized their own impatience and went to great lengths to be tolerant and understanding – an attitude which you doubtless discovered (as children so often do) so that you may have become quite expert at putting them on the defensive and keeping them there for your own advantage. If that was the case, then the more successful you were in such maneuvering, the more likely it is for you to now expect (and even demand) that your present-day efforts should prove equally triumphant – whether inside or outside your present-day family. In short, you may have come to expect that people will anticipate your needs and understand the whys and wherefores of your conduct whatever the context: romantic, occupational, social, etc.

It is this mixture of expectation and demand, more than

any other factor, which gives you the often unfair reputation for being spoiled. Add to this your unquestioning confidence in your own opinions, and the combination thus produced can be formidable indeed! If the shoe we have described above just happens to fit you, don't despair; you don't have to wear it! You could, after all, use your unusual talents for experimentation in the service of paying more attention to the needs and feelings of other people, and listening to their side of the story more than you've been accustomed to doing.

In social situations the singleton can usually be recognized by the qualities of self-sufficiency and self-containment. As a rule, you had scant opportunity during childhood for learning how to compete and how to share. No one ever gave you 50p with the admonition to share it with a sibling, nor did you ever watch with vigilant eye to make sure that no sibling got a minutely larger slice of cake than you. Lacking such formative experiences with siblings, you may now find yourself holding back from what you perceive as childish or undignified behavior when you encounter it in adult life. Free-wheeling participation in group 'nonsense' – which members of other birth orders often enjoy and even seek out – is not for you.

In point of fact, you seldom feel truly comfortable with the competitive hurly-burly which goes on openly (or covertly) in many social gatherings or work situations. You most often feel truly at ease in settings where the ground rules have been made perfectly clear beforehand. Competition is not your strong point. At your place of work you may find yourself being secretly puzzled by all the squabbling over coffee breaks and jockeying for the boss's favor that seems to go on so incessantly. Underline 'secretly' because you generally keep such thoughts to yourself – unlike those men and women who loudly proclaim that they are 'above such pettiness' (and who are apt to be first-borns from families harboring at least three sibs). They find such goings-on irritating, whereas your reaction is more apt to be one of genuine puzzlement.

On those relatively rare occasions when you find yourself caught in an overt altercation with one of your peers, your instinctive reaction is to seek out the person in authority. If you don't obtain satisfaction from this quarter, you may go over that person's head to an even higher authority, and so on clear up to the top of the ladder, if need be. Friends and fellow workers (as well as your playmates during childhood) may view such behavior on your part as 'not cricket' – when and if they ever discover it – but to your way of thinking it's simply the direct action the situation seems to call for: getting the facts, putting your own opinion on the line, and insisting that arbitration be accomplished with swiftness and dispatch. Under such conditions you find it difficult to see how anyone could regard your behavior as reprehensible, and you take conscious pride in this propensity of yours for insisting that matters be quickly brought to a head.

Others may wonder why you are so secretive about these things if you really believe that you are doing the right thing. Our considered opinion is that the answer can usually be found in your underlying fear and avoidance of face-to-face confrontations, especially in group settings where the possibility of being ganged up on can be very anxiety-provoking. It is important to remember that, as a child, any time you came into conflict with your environment your adversaries were almost invariably adults with a considerable amount of worldly experience at their disposal – literally 'giants' so far as you were concerned. It is a rare child indeed who can successfully stand up to persons three times taller and heavier who present a united front against his or her puny wishes and opinions. It's not surprising, therefore, that many singletons become quite expert in the use of divide-and-conquer strategies. You are apt to be more adroit than most people in seeking out a private heart-to-heart conference with each of your adversaries during which you obtain commitments which you may consciously or subconsciously use later on in such a way as to pit them against one another. When this happens, you seem honestly surprised to find yourself at the center of a storm of controversy (and perhaps being cordially disliked by all parties concerned).

Children in general are amazingly resourceful when it comes to pressing their hard-won advantages, and singletons like yourself apply the divide-and-conquer principle very effectively to extract *half* a promise from each party and then (by means of subtle argumentation which would do credit to Socrates) combine them so that they could be legalistically construed as a *whole* promise from both. For this reason you often make a superb debator and may even be a lawyer (a professional Ambrose Bierce once playfully defined as 'one skilled at circumventing the law'). You generally excel at thinking on your feet and take justifiable pride and pleasure in your own capacity to never (well, hardly ever) find yourself lacking a snappy retort – another reason why people enjoy having you on their side.

As for sharing – the other major problem with which you have to struggle – well, it's no simple matter. If sharing were like the childhood chant 'one for you and one for me,' that would be one thing, but in your case the difficulties are far more subtle, touching upon the deep importance which personal independence has for you. Remember that yours is the most self-sufficient of all birth orders, and this makes you view anything which might lead to your feeling obligated or indebted to others as a severe threat to your own sense of self-reliance. For this reason you insist upon such rituals as the splitting of restaurant bills and other shared expenses down to the last penny. It doesn't seem to cross your mind that others might construe this as a sign of distrust on your part, when actually it is merely another facet of your passion for independence.

This awkwardness which you encounter with regard to the ins and outs of sharing is a touchy subject. We realize that you are seldom aware of its effect on many important facets of your life, and that you are inclined to be offended by any assertion that you could possibly be handling so crucial a topic with less than your usual aplomb. You may feel that we are accusing you of gross mismanagement. Not so. We merely wish to point out that there are times when you feel so convinced about the correctness of your own viewpoint that you can close your eyes and ears to the fact that other people may be feeling bulldozed by you.

Our hunch as to the origin of this problem is that it derives largely from the experience of gift-giving when you were little. When there is only one child in a family, gifts to that child are likely to be more expensive than when the gift budget has to be divided among several children. In multi-sib families, moreover, two or more youngsters can chip in on a combined gift of greater size or significance than any one of them could afford alone. You had no such resources available to you, and as a result you are apt to be a far more watchful (and touchy) score keeper than most people in matters of reciprocity – a characteristic which can often put a crimp in the flow of transactions between yourself and the world. This may also apply to the exchange of personal favors. Having developed your personal lifestyle at an unusually early age, you are inclined to show less tolerance than most people when it comes to having the routines disrupted by the needs, demands, or competitiveness of others. While you, like anybody else, can lend money or permit someone the use of your car or your living quarters, you are most likely to do so when it won't inconvenience you very much or for very long.

As your parents' one and only, however, you may have had an 'embarrassment of riches'; not only your parents but grandparents, other relatives, and family friends may have showered you with lots and lots of gifts on any and all occasions. Realizing that your playmates (not to mention your cousins) weren't as fortunate, you may have felt guilty in your abundance and tried to assuage it by giving away some of the overflow. This would hold especially true if your parents, teachers, and Sunday School instructors had imbued you with moral imperatives about sharing the wealth. If such was the case, your parents may have become alarmed. 'How,' they might have asked, 'would Uncle David and Aunt Mary feel if they found out that you gave away their present?' There may even have been some lectures against buying friendship – a forerunner of feelings that 'all they're after is my money!' It is more than likely, then, that you became quite chary about giving and receiving gifts. 'Neither a borrower nor a lender be' is a rule of thumb which you are very apt to observe in your social transactions. Singletons usually grow up with a lingering sense of obligation from being so often on the receiving end of adult favors which they could never hope to reciprocate adequately.

Only children seldom have to share the praise of parents with other children – and, of course, never with a sibling. This has given you a certain egocentricity which often causes you to be insensitive to the fact that other people also need appreciation and affirmation. No one has ever said to you 'Be nice to your little sister, she didn't win the prize in school that she was so hoping to get.' This is not to say that you are a totally indifferent person; just that you can sometimes be obtuse about other people's legitimate need to be given credit or receive praise. Conversely, however, you did not have anyone with whom to share the blame or bear the burden of guilt for wrongdoing, so that you tend to be more conscientious than most people and more harshly self-critical than any other birth order. It also means that you can be something of a pushover in your readiness to accept rather obvious flattery, and are easily wounded and extremely vulnerable to criticism as well.

You have a perfectionist's need to be above reproach, and this facet of your nature often puts you under considerable strain. The word 'perfectionistic' has two major meanings, each of which embodies a quite different emphasis. You can, for instance, be perfectionistic in the sense that you are determined to be *the best* at everything you undertake. Or, you can try to be *complete and thorough* in everything you undertake simply because you are prone to a sense of worthlessness whenever you are accused of not measuring up; the emphasis in this kind of perfectionism is on avoiding any kind of criticism.

While on the subject, we make note of our impression that male singletons are characterized more by the first kind of perfectionism which has its roots in the 'need for achievement' (as it is often called in social science terminology); while female singletons incline toward the latter, avoiding criticism. In any case, both of you tend to be extremely tidy and well-organized in your habits. Living and working areas are usually immaculate and efficiently laid out, and you do your chores punctually and thoroughly – for you are an excellent planner with a highly developed time sense. Having accustomed yourself at an early age to organize life's various routines in a manner creatively tailored to your own individual needs, you have a tendency to take it for granted that your way of doing things is the only way. For this reason it can become quite difficult for you to live with other people unless they are willing to let you manage things; compromise in such matters is not your forte, to say the least. Bones of contention constantly appear and have to be dealt with, and if your partner also happens to be a singleton then both of you have your work cut out for you!

Returning once more to the subject of competition, as a singleton you can expect to find yourself in a bind whenever you have to deal with what psychologists call 'sibling rivalry' whether with other adults (as discussed earlier) or with children (your own or others'). In coping with interpersonal friction so alien to your own experience – especially the ferocity which can transpire between children – you need to resist your strong temptation to put your foot down and arbitrarily *forbid* any wrangling in your presence.

Much the same reaction to children's open expressions of rivalry (especially when shrill or disruptive) often characterizes the parent who was the older of two sibs, particularly when the age gap was about six years or more. Here the parental cry is liable to be something like 'Why can't you kids agree? – the way I did with *my* brother (sister); *we* never carried on like that!' One good reason for this presumed state of affairs is the large difference between their ages. But note also the word 'presumed.' Parents who grew up with sibs closer in age, on the other hand, are apt to take most kinds of interpersonal bickering pretty much for granted, and to consider it a natural part of the human condition. While keeping an eye out for behavior which is patently unfair or downright dangerous, their attitude is more often one of 'Okay, kids, if you're going to fight, go and do it out of doors (upstairs). I can't hear myself think with so much pandemonium!' Understandably, the parental situation gets much more complicated when one parent is a singleton and the other grew up with siblings close in age. The former will probably consider his or her opposite number uncaring, while the latter is apt to be appalled by the other's readiness to butt in.

On the plus side of only-child parenthood, you are more likely than others to show a high degree of respect for your children's goals, encouraging them to carve out their own niches in the world. Having learned how to convert solitude into an asset, you generally retain a lifelong capacity for self-amusement, for the steadfast pursuit of pet projects, absorbing avocations, and the like. Owing to that special brand of thoroughness at which you seem to excel, it's not at all uncommon for you to develop considerable expertise in something that began as a hobby. You often convert these into actual careers or lucrative occupations in their own right. As a parent, therefore, you generally maintain a healthy respect for your children's hobbies and fascinations, and will defend their rights to indulge in even the most far-out or seemingly absurd interests.

A corollary to what must seem like an endless chain of problems associated with competition are those which confront you when you yourself get entangled in an open fight of any sort. As we pointed out earlier, your childhood situation was often analogous to that of an embattled pygmy outnumbered by giants. Because of this, you come to anticipate either of two diametrically opposed outcomes: a) you would be utterly and humiliatingly defeated by one or more of the adults; or b) one or more of them would capitulate completely so that you could emerge with total victory. In the first case you would come out of the fray with an exaggerated sense of helplessness and defeat, while in the second instance you would experience an inflated and grandiose concept of your own power.

Neither alternative provides much in the way of a foundation for understanding the realities of what a genuine fight is all about. If your parents were the kind who believed that adults should have a firm policy about raising a child and stuck to it adamantly (so that you couldn't win, *ever*), you learned to avoid head-on confrontations at all costs. If they were the sort who gave up without struggle, you probably acquired the unrealistic expectation of winning forever. In the latter case, it would be easy for you to have become something of a bully or a poor sport or a bad loser, or perhaps all three. In any event, quarreling, hostile digs, and angry verbal sparring appear far more deadly to you than to most people, especially when the antagonist is a friend or loved one. The vehemence involved can be very threatening to you, since it is hard for you to believe that an honest-to-goodness shouting match need not necessarily signify the end of the world or lead to a state of irreversible enmity.

As a rule, you are reluctant to expose your innermost feelings: emotional revelation is not your cup of tea, although at the same time you are not the least bit shy about giving your opinion about almost everything under the sun. People are so startled by the contrast between these two characteristics of yours that they often mistakenly accuse you of duplicity. A more likely explanation for your emotional reserve is that your childhood silent observations convinced you that most people are pretty careless when it comes to keeping secrets, and that a great deal of interpersonal friction is caused thereby. Mothers of only (and oldest) children are often more than eager to broadcast their child's quaint sayings and clever deeds without sufficient regard for the youngster's right to a certain degree of privacy and confidentiality.

The price you pay for your understandable reticence is that others often harbor unspoken doubts about your sincerity. Even though they may feel sheepish about it, they find themselves holding you somewhat at arm's length without quite knowing why. In order to protect your private feelings, you developed a noncommittal public face which unfortunately combines with your native self-sufficiency in such a way as to convey an out-of-sight, out-of-mind attitude to many of your acquaintances.

Thus far we have mentioned some qualities of being an

only child, many of which are shared by first-borns. We would like to call your attention to one important set of differences you may not be aware of – the various possible reasons why you are your parents' only child.

The most common reason for your being a singleton involves problems of conception. This may arise from a variety of medical factors ranging anywhere from a low sperm count in the father to more complex physiological limitations on the part of the mother. More often than not, your parents married comparatively late in life – at age thirty or beyond. Add to this the probability that your mother had experienced at least one unsuccessful pregnancy prior to your successful conception and birth. The result is that you, more than the children of any other birth order, are apt to be saddled with at least one predecessor whom you experience as a competitor (ghostly though he or she may be) of awesome stature.

If the child who preceded you was of the opposite sex from your own, you may have grown up saddled with the dilemma of whether or not to stand in for the deceased infant of opposite gender and thus try to assuage your parents' sense of loss. This predicament may well have taken place at an *unconscious* level, but it still involved you in the question of how far you should extend yourself in an effort to fulfill your parents' buried fantasies about the deeply mourned son or daughter who would have been the first-born embodiment of their love and caring for one another.

It is hard to imagine a heavier burden being placed (however unintentionally) upon any child, and it is one of the many reasons why we feel that yours is probably the most difficult and complex of all birth orders. If the 'phantom' sibling was of the same sex, then you may have had the distinctly unpleasant feeling that your role in life was to be a stand-in for the *real* star of the show; a kind of second fiddle who could never live up to all the good qualities with which one or both of your parents endowed that long gone (but by no means forgotten) first child. Staking out your inherent right to be your very own person, therefore, fell upon your own small shoulders in a way that seldom characterizes children born into any other birth order. Consequently you have either learned to be individual and indeed have become your own person, or else you experience an enormous amount of confusion in this area. We would add that for you singletons there never seems to be very much space between any two alternatives you get confronted with, regardless of their exact nature.

We mentioned before that your mother and father were probably older as parents go – which suggests that by the time you reached the very difficult preteen age of ten or eleven or twelve, your parents were well into their forties (an emotionally difficult period for many adults), and were therefore in no mood to handle or perhaps even comprehend the myriad problems you were being confronted with at that time. Parents in their twenties when their children are born generally have a lot more sheer physical energy at their disposal with which to take on the various crises and issues which assault them and for which older parents have far fewer resources.

Although the late cartoonist Al Capp is quoted as once having said 'What ten-year-old kid wants a forty-year-old *pal*?' the other side of that coin might read 'What forty-five-year-old going through midlife crisis wants to cope with the problems of a ten-year-old kid?' There are, of course, a number of older parents who are able to bridge the generation gap successfully, but they are few and far between. In any event, the severe drop in energy level which most people experience at middle age makes it likely that your parents gave short shrift to a lot of those childhood growing pains which younger parents would not only have empathized with but also would probably have actually enjoyed – if only out of nostalgia for their own youth. A thirty-two-year-old father may still enjoy going out to play ball with his twelve-year-old son; a fifty-two-year-old father is far more likely to regretfully shake his head and plead his bad back, his bum knee, or the loss of his pitching arm. Certainly, both parent and child suffer from such losses of togetherness, but this also helped you develop your characteristic perseverance and you learned to seek satisfaction elsewhere.

A possibility which pertains almost exclusively to first-borns (and singletons, of course) is that you were conceived (though not necessarily born) out of wedlock. While this has become increasingly acceptable in our society, the fact remains that until recently it was pretty much frowned upon. If your parents were already engaged or otherwise firmly committed to marrying each other, your sudden entry upon the scene probably brought minimal problems. If, on the other hand, your parents weren't ready to seriously entertain the idea of marriage and were unable to seek an abortion for financial, religious, moral, or whatever reasons, then they may have submitted themselves (and you) to what is traditionally termed a 'shotgun wedding' to legitimize their offspring. Such pressured arrangements sometimes end in divorce or annulment – in which case the child is reared by a single parent (who almost invariably is the mother).

Shotgun wedding or otherwise, there is also the happy possibility that your parents may have so successfully worked through their dilemmas that you were welcomed with open and cherishing arms, and the only reasons for not providing you with brothers and/or sisters were purely medical ones. A woman's most difficult pregnancy and delivery are apt to attend the birth of her first-born, and when this event involves grave medical problems, she may decide (or be advised) not to risk a second pregnancy. And in this connection it must be recognized that this medical factor alone is by far the most common reason why you have no younger sibs.

Then, of course, there is the matter of financial readiness. While you may not have been an 'accident' in the usual sense of the word, your parents may nevertheless have been assailed by anxiety-provoking second thoughts and misgivings, once they recognized the various economic burdens imposed by your entrance upon the scene. In some cases this can lead to such a prolonged spate of reciprocal blaming and bickering that both parents end up firmly resolved not to take that particular 'trip' again – ever; and they didn't.

Still further friction can sometimes arise when one or both parents had problems attendant upon the arrival of their own younger brothers and/or sisters. If either of your parents was an older child who felt 'dethroned' or outright rejected when a new baby entered their family, your arrival might well have revived in them some old feelings of anger, resentment, guilt, and jealousy – all arising out of a fear that they will be replaced by the newcomer in their spouse's affections. These and other frightening or morbid anticipations, we might add, are almost invariably experienced (on an unconscious level at least) by all parents of first-borns, and may well crop up regularly whenever a subsequent baby is in the offing. We are seldom aware, as children, of exactly what we feel, let alone why, and as adults we can often replay these undigested emotions, with all the accompanying confusion, and bewildering anxiety. And so it is not surprising when a husband accuses his pregnant wife of neglecting him, or she accuses him of being self-centered and uncaring. Under such restimulative circumstances it is very easy for both parties to behave without much insight into the underlying reasons for their persistent feelings of hurt and resentment.

While tradition the world over may permit pregnant women a certain latitude when it comes to being temperamental during gestation, there is rarely an allowance made for psychological problems which may arise on the part of the father. We would make note of the role played by what Ashley Montagu called 'womb envy' (the counterpart of what Freudians call 'penis envy' in women) during this very trying period in the life of novice parents-to-be; i.e., a man can often feel overshadowed by the awesome reality of a woman's capacity to give birth, and can become pretty envious. We have read that at least one American Indian tribe has learned to cope with this particular problem by creating a custom whereby the man imitates each and every symptom that his pregnant spouse goes through – even to labor pains and the final spasms of delivery.

The reasons why you are an only child can be many and complicated and are apt to produce more problematic than pleasant outcomes. However, a final word is in order. There is one positive aspect to keep in mind: despite the various handicaps which characterize your ordinal position, you are nevertheless more able than anyone else, in our opinion, to preserve a basically positive outlook on life, regardless of how problem-ridden it may sometimes appear to be. A relatively even disposition seems to accompany this optimism, along with your special brand of humor – which involves a keen sense of the absurd, arising from your steadfast awareness of the ridiculous contrast between things as they are and things as they ought to be. This makes you a delightful companion, both to your close friends who are apt to be other singletons and oldest children and who understand you, and to others who perceive you as a fascinating if unpredictable individual.

CHAPTER TWO

Only Girl

If you belong to this category, you are probably the most independent of all people in this book. As we observed in our general discussion of the only child, it is more than likely that your parents were over thirty when you were born – which carries with it more than a normal share of advantages and disadvantages. Students of infant behavior have noted that female babies tend to be less fretful than males and are more responsive to parental soothing. It's therefore not surprising that older parents find a little girl easier to keep pace with. So it often happens that much of the energy which parents normally devote to curbing a small child's rambunctiousness gets converted into more verbal and instructive channels when an only girl child is involved. To put it another way, older parents have a tendency to concern themselves with calming down a little boy's exuberance whereas a little girl's verbalness is generally viewed as less challenging. In your case the emphasis is likely to have been on drawing you out and encouraging you to articulate your experiences. You soon learned how to attract and sustain their interest while they in turn acquired the habit of encouraging you to reach for ever higher standards by which to evaluate yourself.

Whether you are still trying to live up to this kind of perfectionism or gave it up years ago, chances are that you have been pursuing either course with a vengeance – because you rarely if ever do anything by halves. 'All or nothing' is more typical of you than of any other ordinal position. However, the first is the more likely alternative as you continue to maintain high standards and long-range goals. Although you make exceptions, which we will discuss later on in this chapter, you are not averse to setting similar standards for those around you – which can get a bit rough on them, despite your (somewhat self-righteous) assurances that 'I never demand from others more than I do from myself.' As for the long-range goals, you seem to have become goal-oriented very early on, and have probably never been without at least one. Having different, often equally important, goals can produce a subtle kind of confusion, however, and you bring yourself up short from time to time and ask 'Will the real Me please stand up?'

Children with two or more siblings rarely encounter this problem because, as a rule, children in larger families get type cast, voluntarily or not, into certain roles, such as Family Artist, Family Brain, Family Clown, Family Athlete, etc. Even in those families that share a talent or interest in common – for music, say – one child may specialize in the cello, merely because a brother has already claimed the fiddle, and a sister is custodian of the piano. Of course less complimentary designations are equally possible – such as Crybaby, Black Sheep, Tramp, Con Artist, etc. Being an only child, you are spared the pitfalls and limitations which are part and parcel of such gratuitous and compelling group feedback. At the same time, however, you lacked contemporaries with whom you could share your family's value system and the pressures which it placed upon your shoulders. So that in a sense you were on the receiving end of more parental and familial hopes and fears than most children fall heir to. We would even go so far as to say that of all singletons or first-borns yours is the hardest row to hoe. Siblings, after all, do manage to take some of the pressure off a child's back – either out of competitiveness, or compassion, natural predisposition, or by sheer default. In your case, however, none of the roles had any takers, and it was left up to you to sort them out –

and to assess each one's importance to the meaningful adults in your environment, *and* to weigh the probable gains and losses in accepting certain ones and rejecting or downplaying others. This is by no means an easy position for a little girl to find herself in.

In our culture, a variety of familial hopes and expectations are invested in the first-born (or only) son. You, as only child, inherited them all. And the earlier your parents realized there would be no other offspring, the more roles you were expected to adopt. An exception to this is the familial or cultural milieu in which the sole destiny pictured for a daughter is that of making a 'good' marriage. Even in this case, however, a number of expectations which would ordinarily accrue to the first-born son do, nevertheless, get unconsciously foisted onto the only daughter. (And unconscious expectations are much more powerful than the ones we are aware of – and consequently have a chance to deal with.)

And so growing up as an only girl made for special difficulties in arriving at a coherent picture of yourself and your place in the scheme of things. Because while male singletons are generally encouraged to think in terms of what they will do in this world when they grow up, female singletons undergo more pressures relative to who they are – not only when they attain maturity, but step by step along the road of childhood as well. The parents of an only child are analogous to a gardener with a single tree or shrub to care for: they give it more attention than it needs or wants in order that their efforts might produce a perfect specimen. More often than not you responded to such pressures by trying to live up to parental hopes and expectations, whether these were explicit or merely inferred. Consequently you early became more self-conscious about your behavior than most other children, and you took what you perceived to be your parents' wishes very seriously.

Having been reared in the singleton's goldfish bowl, you have (out of sheer self-preservation) probably acquired more skill than you realize in the delicate arts of glib speech and wearing a poker face so that nobody can guess the true state of your inner self. You became adroit at deliberately playing cameo roles with all the finesse of an accomplished drama-school graduate – a skill which carries the disadvantage of leaving other people to grapple with doubts about your sincerity and who you really are, deep down. Some people may even accuse you of being phony. They don't understand that this is simply your polite way of protecting your privacy.

We live in a world nowadays which seems increasingly fond of violating personal space, but you are somehow able to hold your own more tenaciously than anyone else. Unlike your male counterpart (who didn't have to fend off so many invasions of his privacy) you are generally a scrupulous respecter of other people's boundaries. For this particular reason anyone who gets really close to you learns to trust you totally over the years – although it goes without saying that there are not many who do get all that close. You 'do not suffer fools gladly, nor hardly anyone else at all' – as *Time* magazine once said of the redoubtable Lady Astor.

Knowing the value of privacy and discretion, you are a good listener and you almost never blab. Above all, you pride yourself on your integrity and you can even be a bit pompous about it. Your utter dependability is another source of pride, but has drawbacks in that it makes you vulnerable to other, less exacting people who take their promises and commitments more casually. You can be quite touchy about the subtleties of confidentiality, even to the point of feeling betrayed by minor lapses which most other people take for granted.

Tolerance is not exactly your forte – except when dealing

with those who are your acknowledged subordinates. Being the custodian of much private information (acquired usually by knowing when to keep your mouth shut and your eyes and ears wide open), you have it in you to be a very astute politician whose influence is likely to be most powerfully felt behind the scenes – because singletons are apt to be long on candor and short on tact.

Despite this tendency to be headstrong, only girls frequently make excellent teachers. This may seem contradictory in view of what we've said concerning your impatience with people less capable than yourself, but what we mean is that you have scant patience with persons who only *claim* to know what they're doing. In the case of those who openly acknowledge their limitations, you are apt to be most encouraging, supportive, and forbearing. For this reason you are most often a very nurturing mother – your major drawback in this arena is the unrealistic expectation that your children should be able to love each other and not fight.

The only child's inability to fight is doubled in you; you had no brothers and sisters to quarrel with and, being a girl, seldom had to defend yourself in the playground or changing room. Only children often indulge in fantasies about sisters and brothers, but most often these are unrealistic daydreams of pure harmony, love, and mutual support – with no room for bickering, quarreling, grudges, or vendettas. Imaginary sisters, after all, never borrow your best blouse and then spill ketchup on it, nor smile bewitchingly at your boyfriend, nor do imaginary brothers mock your cosmetic rituals or inform you that your cherished aspirations are all a bunch of crap.

In Chapter 1 we touched upon a number of possible reasons why you were the only child in your family, but we did not mention that for a female singleton with a single mother, a most painful reason can be her mother's

assertion that she never wanted children in the first place –
i.e., that you were an accident. Chances are that this is far
from an accurate statement on her part, but a woman who
feels abandoned by her spouse and left to care for a lone
daughter (instead of a son – who gives some hope of one
day being the socially required man in her life, the head of
the family) may harbor some very bitter feelings about her
plight – and is not always able to restrain herself from
occasionally spilling them to her daughter. This is most apt
to be true if your parents were parted (by death, but
especially by divorce or separation) when you were aged
seven or younger. Even if your mother was able to work out
a gratifying love relationship soon afterwards, your interactions with her most likely contained subtle tensions. Not
being aware of the legal strictures which award child
custody to the mother in cases of marital discord, you
probably harbored a fantasy that your mother had
somehow managed to drive your father away from you and
the home. This was a far less painful conclusion to reach
than that of attributing your father's absence to a lack of
caring on his part. Whenever one parent leaves home, a
child's deep-down, often unspoken reaction is almost
invariably 'He (or she) didn't love me enough to take me
with him (or her) or to stay at home for my sake' – or, still
worse, 'There must have been something about *me* which
brought about this calamity.'

Once we emerge from the womb, it takes us a long time
to give up the notion that we are the prime movers in our
environment. It is by no means easy for us to acknowledge
that our mother or father (or anyone else close to us, for
that matter) could possibly be happy or unhappy for
reasons that are not directly attributable to us – our
character, our behavior, our virtues, our failings. Who else,
after all, could possibly be all that important? And so it is
that it takes at least seven years (under fairly optimal

conditions; otherwise it takes much longer) for a child to face the unflattering fact that parents are often influenced by *other* persons and situations in their lives. When a parent (either deliberately or inadvertently) implies that the child was indeed responsible for this unpleasant state of affairs, or permits a child's fearful and guilt-ridden imaginings to go uncorrected, then the myth of the Almighty Me persists unchecked – perhaps far into adulthood – with unhappy consequences for all.

Unlike a male singleton, who is more apt to seek out and successfully find a father substitute in the world – somewhere, somehow, sometime, you probably became intimately entangled with the travails of a beleaguered mother who, more often than not, had to struggle with the twin problems of earning a livelihood and arranging for baby sitters, child-care centers, afterschool programs, and the like. Your efforts to establish a secure place for yourself in her world may have involved considerable friction and confusion between the two of you as you both strove to find legitimate space for yourselves while at the same time struggling to define and allocate blame for the painful aspects of the situation in which you both found yourselves.

Having thus become acquainted with a particularly formidable kind of woman-to-woman rivalry at a very tender age, you are less trusting of your women friends' good intentions than most women are, and are hence more apt to have a greater turnover in the 'female best friend' department. While you remain surprisingly flexible when it comes to your male best friend's lapses from interpersonal rectitude, you have a relatively short fuse when it comes to the women in your friendship circle, and are likely to bolt at the first sign of anything which can be remotely construed as bad faith on their part.

You have, as we've already noted, a way of playing your emotional cards close to your chest; life in the goldfish bowl taught you to keep your own counsel as the only safe way to avoid too much intrusion by other people – which, incidentally, suggests that you may not take too kindly to this 'intrusion' of ours, and will find yourself disagreeing with much of what we have to say about you. Even as we say it, we realize that such an assertion on our part must sound unfair to you – even when we're wrong about you, we excuse ourselves by saying 'Of course you disagree with us, that's just part of your nature as an only girl!' We hope you'll give us an A for effort in our sincere attempt to portray you even though you don't accept all we have to say.

You tend to be a person of strong and well-thought-out opinions arrived at through a relentless kind of logic which you often attribute to your father's teachings. Indeed, if anyone is so slipshod as to say in your presence that the sky is blue, you are quite capable of objecting in no uncertain terms, on grounds that one can't make such sweeping generalizations, 'Why, I've seen lots of days when the sky was actually gray (or pink or black or purple).' What is more, you are more often right than wrong. This comes about because you make it your business to explore thoroughly any subject which engages your attention so that by the time you finish you're a genuine authority on it. You are, in short, accustomed to doing everything to the best of your ability, and although you display an admirable degree of tolerance toward people who admit to being less perfectionistic, deep down you do not have the kind of respect for them which you reserve for people as meticulous as yourself.

While the majority of singletons manage to surpass all other ordinal positions when it comes to do-it-yourself pursuits, you are more apt to practice at being a Jack-of-several-trades, and wind up mastering them all. At the same time you show yourself more willing than your male counterparts to accept help from others (bumbling though it may be). This derives more from your overall sense of efficiency than from any inclination on your part to delegate responsibility, which is not exactly your strong suit. But this willingness often entails a paradox that your friends, family, and fellow workers find perplexing – i.e., your penchant for putting up with distinctly substandard performances on the part of those whose job it is to lighten your workload. They regard it as being out of character, because it hampers your well-known efficiency; annoying, because you generally refuse to accept any advice about it; and somehow endearing, because it demonstrates that you are, after all, fallible. Thus it is by no means unusual for you to patronize a dry-cleaning establishment which fails to remove spots, a hairdresser of distinctly mediocre abilities, or a household help most of whose work has to be done again (by you, of course) afterwards.

What seems most puzzling about this odd state of affairs is that you often allow the situation to go on and on long after anyone else would have called a halt. We think that part of the reason may lie in that steadfast loyalty of yours; a less flattering cause might be your strong reluctance to accept any kind of criticism, however kindly or caringly presented. For you to recognize and correct matters would, to your way of thinking, constitute an open admission of two flaws which you consider highly reprehensible: inefficiency and poor judgment.

You share this overtolerance for failures and foibles on the part of subordinate persons with a large number of male first-borns, who are permitted to be flexible about such things – but not with female first-borns, whose role is more often that of nursemaid, tutor, and overseer to younger sibs (either by self-appointment or by parental edict). Having taken a large part in the training of her sibs, the oldest girl is apt to insist that helpers and tradespeople really know their onions and require minimum surveillance. You are aware that your standards are unusually high – and this can entice you to the conclusion that, outside the small circle you consider your peers, most human beings wallow in such ineptitude that it's just not worthwhile trying to assess relative degrees of incompetence. And so you console yourself with the notion that any help is better than none. (As clinical psychologists we might also speculate that perhaps this is an unconscious way of indulging – vicariously, that is – a lingering wish to let some aspects of your personal world be a little less perfect, a little less up to scratch.)

Otherwise it is more typical of you to see things through from start to finish all on your own without quite realizing that life could be quite a lot less hectic than you might think. 'If I want something done right, I'd better do it myself,' seems to be your slogan, and you'd rather type a letter yourself than give it to somebody else and later have to spend precious time proofreading it and correcting the mistakes. Again, we don't want to imply that you are a carping or nit-picking person who goes around finding perpetual fault with people and things (a trait characteristic of many youngest children). You are far more diplomatic than that, and when you are angry you are more than likely to choose your audience with utmost caution.

At the same time you are highly vulnerable to criticism from others, even when it is presented with extreme tact. Your reaction can sometimes be out of all proportion to the event as you carry on like someone who has been publicly violated or stabbed in the back by an otherwise trusted friend. Such conduct is particularly startling to those who don't know you very well because they have accustomed themselves to regarding you as the epitome of self-assurance; unassailable and unflappable. The last thing in the world they expect is for you to behave as though you were being attacked for purely personal reasons. Although you're a good sport about losing games, money, and horse races, you're apt to cry 'foul!' when you're in the wrong.

We mentioned in Chapter 1 that among singletons the need to measure up involves an understandable need for appreciation and praise, although it is difficult for others to perceive this, owing to your habitual air of self-confidence and aplomb. Folk wisdom maintains that 'others regard us the way we regard ourselves'; your innate self-respect is almost palpable and does not prompt others to reach out and pat you on the head; and the people who ask for praise are more likely to receive it. A rather heavy price to pay for appearing so strong, but there it is. Everything you can comfortably do to reveal your own underlying humanity will go far toward remedying this unfortunate state of affairs.

Your abiding wish to be thought of as a socially worthwhile and contributing person sets you apart from most male singletons, who are not only less philanthropic than you, but also less inclined to join causes unless they have direct and concrete relevance to their own personal concerns. Owing to the fact that you're not so hard-headed as your male counterparts when it comes to giving of yourself you probably invest more time and effort than you can realistically afford to organizations and movements which ultimately fizzle, through no fault of your own. When this happens, you are usually an exemplary good sport about it as you chalk up the whole fiasco to experience, and promptly donate your considerable energies to the next project. For you are rarely without a project for very long – mastering a new skill (or teaching it), or learning a new dance, or trying out a new cuisine, or taking up a new hobby – and your high standards and fine concentration usually insure that you do it well.

CHAPTER THREE

Only Boy

It will probably come as no great surprise to you when we note that of all male ordinal positions, people are most likely to perceive you as a Mother's Boy. It goes without saying that they never intend this designation as a compliment. At the same time there is a germ of subtle truth in it which requires us to give it a little more respectful attention than it usually receives. After all, you certainly did not choose to get yourself painted with that particular brush, and we'd like to offer some observations which may help you to shed whatever aspects of it may have been causing problems in your life.

Like most singletons, your mother and father were probably older than the general run of parents at the time of your birth – in their thirties or older. Add to this the various other factors which go along with being your parents' only child (see Chapter 1) and we can see several pertinent facts emerging. It is important, first of all, to recognize that a man who is thirty-five or over is considered by most adults to be still in his prime while a woman of the same age is apt to regard herself – rightly or wrongly – as heading over the hill. She feels that her safe years for child-bearing are fast drawing to a close, and may also be starting to worry about her desirability as a love partner generally. Your mother may have had good reason for concern, especially if your father was beginning to worry about his approaching 'twilight years' and starting to do any of the things that men sometimes do in their forties – like eyeing other (and usually much younger) women. Whatever the reasons, a mother can feel tempted to channel many of her emotional needs regarding males into the relationship that grows up between herself and her son. Some women are aware of this tendency and staunchly resist it, while other women gradually succumb to it.

If your mother was a resister she may have tried to preserve a safe distance between the two of you. She may have bent over backwards in seeing to it that nobody could ever accuse her of coddling you, with the sad result that she may have withheld comfort or sympathy at crucial times when you needed it most; when it really would not have proved damaging to your character. Or perhaps she was excessive in her zeal to insure that you would always be able to stand on your own two feet. So she cut your ties to her apron strings and sent you out into the world while you were still very young. If you were brought up in this kind of atmosphere, the chances are that you now display an exaggerated tendency to go it alone and rarely permit yourself to need other people's advice or consolation. A small child's idea of what his parents expect is almost invariably a caricature of what the adults really say or mean at that time – and the younger a child is when such 'learnings' take place, the wilder and more fantastic the distortions are apt to be. Consequently you are the most prone of all birth orders to put up a brave, stoic front while keeping your deepest hopes, fears, and opinions to yourself. Your interpretation of the parental admonition to go out into the world most often gets translated into a personal lifestyle which evolves into such things as taking long walks by yourself, or finding a library where you can read to your heart's content. It may take the form of quiet visits with a favorite aunt or uncle or other adult who is in tune with you and allows you to be your own kind of person – with no questions asked and no answers required.

You have a strong (and almost unique) pull toward persons who are not only your own elders, but often the elders of your parents as well. This need to be close to older people most often takes the form of a very special and deeply meaningful attachment to one person – a favorite great-aunt, perhaps, or grandparent, or one of their contemporaries. Girl singletons are apparently better able to feel comfortable with children their own age or younger at a much earlier stage in their lives than you are. As you progress through adulthood, however, your friendship preferences usually balance out to include men and women across a whole range of age levels. But because you established an easy rapport with older people during your growing-up years, you have never lost your exceptional tolerance for old age and all that the term implies.

Your closest friend among your peers is usually also a singleton, although he may sometimes be an oldest boy. Your loyalty in such relationships is deep and abiding. More often than not, your friend is called an 'odd fish' or a 'loner' by most of the people who know you both. But no matter – he is your friend and comrade and probably the only person with whom you reciprocally share what Carl Rogers has dubbed 'unconditional positive regard.' There are no ifs, ands, or buts when it comes to exchanging sympathy, companionship, and moral support.

Occasionally it happens that your father is the boon companion of your childhood years. This may be particularly the case if he is of a rather withdrawn disposition – a man who is inclined to be baffled, nettled, or thrown off base by the 'emotional female' side of your mother or one (or both) of your grandmothers. Under such circumstances he may form a strong – though largely silent or even monosyllabic – rapport with you, whereby he makes you his Strong Right Arm. You in turn do all in your power to be worthy of his trust. When this happens your mother may feel left out – and have several reactions: she may plunge into outside activities or withdraw into psychosomatic aches and pains. Or, she may take a back seat and enjoy the obvious harmony which exists between the two important males in her life. Of course, your mother also has a seldom-used fourth option – to become fiercely jealous and to do all in her power to win you away from the husband whom she now considers a formidable rival for your affections.

This brings us to the likely source of an Only Boy's reputation for being a Mother's Boy. It is an established fact that long before children start talking (in the formal sense) parents and infants exchange countless 'verbal' messages from birth onward – in the form of mutual cooing, getting baby to say da-da, etc. Life in our industrial society being what it is, the mother usually spends far more time with a newborn babe than the father does. In addition, females are apt to be more verbal than males, so that a lot more vocalization is likely to have transpired between you and your Mum than between you and your Dad. This is especially true inasmuch as mothers of singletons are apt to have striven for motherhood over a longer period of time than most women do – and perhaps with some painful derailments prior to your birth (see Chapter 1). Again we must point out that the parents of singletons are usually verging on middle age (the 'devil of midday,' as the French call it). This usually means that they are afraid and have a need to clutch at and cling to life's joys in a way which is generally incomprehensible to persons under thirty. Thus there may have been any number of reasons for your mother's need to hold you close. For a number of decades it has been stylish in psychoanalytic circles to revile the so-called 'possessive mothers' of this world, but it's time to call a halt to this kind of sexist lack of compassion. After all, it is no easy task to be a wife and mother in any society, and being the mother of an only child is particularly challenging. It is easy to understand, then, how a mother who knows that she will bear no further offspring and who may be going through a transitional phase in her marriage might unwittingly establish a very symbiotic relationship with her child.

If your mother was widowed or divorced she may have remained a single parent (by choice or otherwise) for a good part, if not all, of your childhood. Whatever the reasons for her continued 'single' status, it would have taken an enormous amount of courage and insight for her to resist the temptation to reach toward you as her main source of spiritual comfort and moral support. Perhaps she succeeded to a remarkable degree; perhaps she did not.

Whether your mother was or was not successful in balancing her dependency needs, there was nonetheless *your* green-eyed monster to contend with. Your ordinal position is characterized by a very relentless kind of jealousy which is a source of anguish to you and consternation for those close to you. Unlike your female counterpart, the only girl, you are more prone to focus your intense feelings on one individual, and during childhood it was very easy for you to make your mother the main object of your possessiveness. One reason for this is the fact that when separation or divorce are involved, custody is awarded to the child's mother; you, now the man of the family, experience a special relationship to your mother – you feel responsible for her (not usually characteristic of the role of an only girl alone with her mother).

Singletons are more at the mercy of their passionate involvements than other birth orders. Realizing how vulnerable you are, you learn to conceal it – so well, in fact, that many people perceive you as an unusually independent loner who never gets caught up in the kind of dramatic emotional storms which plague the rest of us. Small wonder they are set back on their heels when they get a glimpse of the underlying passions beneath your generally calm surface! It's a pretty good guess, therefore, that your

attitude toward any men in your mother's life was at best
ambivalent. You may have genuinely needed and wanted a
father figure (who had added value as someone who
lessened Mum's interference in your activities), but at the
same time you probably harbored a fair amount of
resentment at the idea of another male invading your
territory. The upshot was that if you were left alone with
your mother for any protracted period of time during your
childhood, neither you nor she had an easy passage. Mutual
dependency, isolation, possessiveness, and jealousy thrive
readily in such a climate – unalleviated and undiluted by
the presence of siblings or by even one other person in the
household.

Which brings up another of your vulnerabilities: your
difficulty with regard to what might be called 'group
relations.' A group, by definition, must consist of three or
more persons, and the sum of its mutual interactions is
greater than the sum of its parts. It is very difficult for an
only boy to experience the special give-and-take of most
group interactions, whether he grows up with only one or
with both of his parents. Unless, of course, one or both
parents is sociable and gregarious and therefore able to
provide him with rich and vibrant social experiences. From
what we've seen, however (and it's something we can't
explain) the parents of singletons tend to be reclusive, with
the result that your childhood environment could hardly be
described as a kaleidoscope of unforgettable characters.
Being a boy, this had a particularly stultifying effect. Your
female counterpart had a much easier time of it in this
department, since girls in our culture are encouraged to
enlarge their social relationships.

Your verbal skills, however, give you the potential for
developing as many one-to-one friendships as you desire.
Again, unless your family environment encouraged group
relationships, you are probably inclined to keep it that way;

one-to-one. You are less inclined than any other ordinal position to 'share' your friends – even to simply introduce them to one another; it's almost a rule that you don't want them to engage in independent relationships which exclude you from the interaction. Bob hears about Nancy and Nancy hears about Bob, but if you have any say in it, 'hearing about' is as far as they get. It would appear that you live in dread lest any pair – or combination – of your friends might get together in a manner which could leave you in the lurch, possibly because you experienced your parents as forming a team that left you out.

Your consummate skill in keeping your friends separate is such that most people who know you are only vaguely aware that this is your game. As a single male you can get away with it because our society doesn't expect bachelors to be much good at social choreography. If and when you ally yourself with a love partner – we say 'if and when' because you and your female counterpart are the most likely of all birth orders to remain single – you relax as a rule, and the two of you may become well known for the social gatherings over which you preside with extraordinary grace and gusto. Why? Because your possessiveness is now totally invested in your *partner*, and it is now safe for you to allow various friends to work out whatever they wish to establish with one another; their togetherness is no longer a threat to your ingrained need to be the center of the known universe.

You may have been taken aback by our assertion that you are, in effect, the bachelor birth order. We must again point out that the major disadvantage of being a singleton lies in the very special and difficult problems which relate to matters of competition and sharing. Both of these problems are magnified out of all proportion in the growing-up years of only children. Sharing and competition, after all, are central to any love relationship. There is a whole gamut of partnership arrangements that any two individuals eventually have to work through in the course of their collaboration. Singletons often find it more than they can cope with to even own a pet – be it a goldfish, turtle, or dog. A cat – maybe. (Cats are very self-sufficient and don't usually demand the kind of emotional care-taking that other animals do, even though they may be very apprecia-tive of any extra strokes they receive from their owner.) Your female counterpart is much more flexible than you are in this department. This is not to say that she does not have a lot to learn when it comes to group relations (see Chapter 2), but she is more inclined to create situations in which her friends can get to know each other, and is more willing to take on the task of helping to make another person happy.

Having had no steady peer competition during child-hood, most singletons are certain of their audience and of their 'right' to be heard. And this makes you more prone to egocentricity than other birth orders. There is a certain tendency on your part to indulge in monologues, and you sometimes get monotonous and start to lose your audience. This tendency is not ordinarily shared by your female counterpart, probably because girls in most cultures are encouraged to develop their social awareness more than most boys are. They have a keener sense of audience reaction and rarely have to be reminded by the chair that their time was up ten minutes ago. On the other hand, you are considered to be the most skilled at early language development of all ordinal positions, and when you speak, you are frequently a spellbinder – often without under-standing why. Our guess is that during your toddler years you flabbergasted your parents, relatives, and other adults by being precociously articulate. So you grew up assuming that everyone else would be equally fascinated by the style and content of your utterances. Well, no matter; you're generally correct in this assumption. You have a real gift for exposition, anecdote, and repartee – enjoy it!

There has been a lot of popular talk about 'narcissism' in recent years, much of it claptrap. What the term really refers to is the fact that each of us is born into this world with a completely and naively self-centred orientation. We experience our own self as being at the very center of the known universe; everything and everyone else revolves around *us*, and we regard them solely in terms of whether they gratify or frustrate our needs. If they gratify us we feel good about ourselves; if they thwart us our self-esteem – our sense of worth – takes a plunge. Gradually, if all goes well, we enlarge the boundaries of our self-involvement to include a sense of empathy and concern for the welfare and happiness of the people close to us. During this time we gradually form an image of ourselves which we will probably carry with us for most of our lives. At first our self-image is totally dependent upon the feedback we get from those around us. If it's basically affirmative we feel lovable/beautiful/vivacious – on top of the world. It it's negative we feel unlovable/ugly/drab – in the pits. In either case it is a long, slow process but eventually the self-centeredness of the infant gives way and we arrive at the point where the feelings, hopes, fears, and basic importance of other human beings have a genuine place in our scheme of things.

What has that got to do with you? Everything. As a singleton, the world of your family of origin continued to revolve around you and your needs for years on end, far past your infancy. Lacking sibs, you had little in the environment to encourage you to outgrow the narcissism with which you – like the rest of us – came into this life. While only girls are more inclined to team up with a series of female peers, it was easier for you (as a male) to seek refuge at home where you could continue to be the unchallenged center of your parents' attention. Thus, you may not have outgrown your own narcissism adequately right up to the present moment. It's easy enough to test this out – the earmarks of such a posture are easily recognizable. Do you rarely think to ask others how they feel or what's going on in their lives? Do you often fail to anticipate the repercussions which your own actions may have upon the lives of others? At the same time do you often perceive the behavior of other people solely in terms of whether or not it is complimentary to your image of yourself? When you feel complimented are you a glutton for flattery? And when you feel insufficiently appreciated or downright insulted do you react with a kind of righteous rage and implacable vengefulness which may continue unabated for years? In fact, you are more prone than any other ordinal position to nurse a grudge brought on by injured narcissism. If this tendency gets out of hand you may find yourself in a state of increasing social isolation as you place heavier and heavier demands upon your remaining friends and associates either to take sides in your disputes or else to repeatedly indulge (hopefully thereby to repair) your punctured self-esteem.

Much of the foregoing can be remedied or at least softened by taking a little time each day to imagine what it might feel like to be in somebody else's shoes. Pick somebody – a coworker, love partner, newspaper vendor, bus driver, – and spend five minutes trying to sense what it might be like to be that person and to be living his or her life. You will enlarge your own horizons and through expanding your sensibility you will enable other people to better appreciate your own unique qualities – wit, articulateness, loyalty.

CHAPTER FOUR

Oldest Child – General Observations

Since you are generally the first offspring to result from your parents' closeness to one another you can expect to have much in common with the only child, whose profiles have been presented in the three previous chapters. We therefore suggest that you read them before proceeding further into this chapter.

Note please that we said 'generally the first' because it occasionally happens that the oldest child had one or more predecessors whose ghostly presence can sometimes exert a powerful unseen influence upon the surviving siblings. If this was so in your case, pay special attention to the discussion of this matter on page 41. Note also that we refer to your parents' 'closeness to one another': we don't presume that they were necessarily 'in love'. They may not have been married for the usual reasons. Their union may have been a shotgun arrangement demanded by one or both families or by some important individual whose counsels were grounded in secular or religious values. We mention all the ifs, ands, and buts because we feel that you, of all people, should appreciate our scrupulous attention to factual detail. For you are, basically, a Guardian of Traditions – when you aren't kicking over the traces, that is. We'll elaborate on that in the two chapters which follow this one.

In the meantime let us reassure you that we are well aware of the sheer variety of lifestyles which characterize your birth order. Of all ordinal positions yours is by far the most written about – yet one of the least understood. It is our educated guess that most of the voluminous work done

on comparisons between first-borns and later-borns has
been overseen by persons who were themselves 'successful'
first-borns. And not surprisingly, when people do scientific
research on themselves or their own class or kind, it is
extremely difficult to screen out biases and preconceptions.
The point is that the great majority of clinical investigations
into your ordinal position have almost invariably described
you in terms which can be summed up by that oft-used
phrase 'most likely to succeed.'

If you are one of the 'successful' oldest children, read on;
you will recognize yourself somewhere in these pages. If, on
the other hand, you feel that your life history departs from
this traditional model, take heart. We have a thing or two
to say which will be congruent with *your* experience as well.

There are certain common denominators which characterize the 'lifescripts' of almost any oldest child. Fore-
most among these is the bold-faced fact that you were
'dethroned' (to use Alfred Adler's expression) by the birth
of the children who followed you. The dethronement may
have been temporary, but the really glorious part of your
reign as your parents' one and only was at an end. The
wider the age gap between you and the next-born, the more
traumatic and challenging for you was his or her entrance
upon the scene, regardless of how intelligently or compas-
sionately the adults around you may have tried to prepare
you for the impending confrontation. No matter that you
probably had pestered Mum and Dad beforehand with
pleas for a little brother or a little sister whom you could
play with, treasure, protect, and love. Once the die was cast
and you had your wish! . . . Well, it's hard to imagine any
child in this world who wouldn't have second thoughts
about having made such a rash commitment. Coming to
terms with your sibling, then, was a necessary and major
adjustment in your life.

Unlike first-borns who remained singletons, you now

found yourself in an eyeball-to-eyeball confrontation with a rival, a competitor for Mum and Dad's attention and concern. Although your parents may have been very understanding and careful to include you in their preparations for the new arrival, this, nevertheless, was probably a very difficult period in your life as well as theirs. When parents bring home a second child and the first child feels anxious or threatened thereby, it becomes a hard game for the parents to win. If the newcomer was of the same sex as yourself, the question in your mind (subconscious perhaps, but there nonetheless) was 'If I was an adequate boy (girl), then why did they have to go and have a second one?' On the other hand, if the baby was a member of the opposite sex, the question became 'Wasn't I good enough? Why did they have to go and have one of those?'

It must have been a very busy time for you in those days. So many decisions to make! – so many possible courses of action! – so many crossroads to negotiate! Should you try to compete with the tiny upstart by suddenly reverting to your own infancy and developing feeding or toilet problems which might effectively snatch back the limelight? Or would it be more dignified to find more subtle ways of upstaging him or her – by being brighter, more lively or more talented? Would it perhaps be even more worthy of your status as first-born to simply withdraw into the silent aloofness of injured vanity? At such times, dark and savage fantasies of outright mayhem can sometimes put in an appearance. Perhaps you decided that it would be more appropriate to befriend the newcomer, to be a third parent, serving as guardian, mentor, and guide to your younger sib. In that way you could kill the kid with kindness, thus making him or her dependent upon your ministrations while at the same time bestowing upon yourself the aura of solicitous and benevolent know-how.

Needless to say, this last alternative is probably the most

workable solution, and the one most often picked by first-born children the world over. A close runner-up (generally frowned upon by Judeo-Christian cultures because it lacks magnanimity) is that of tyrannical ruler over all younger siblings in a spirit of 'might makes right.' This view of things is embodied in Machiavelli's treatise *The Prince*, which was highly regarded by Renaissance heads of state who were by law and custom mostly first-borns. If you belong to this category, we suggest that you read Machiavelli's remarkable book; you will find much about yourself to recognize in its pages.*

As we pointed out in our discussion of the only child, first-borns are usually included in adult activities at a much earlier age than are later-borns. Unlike the singleton, however, your good fortune suffered a partial eclipse when you got old enough to be left in charge of one or more younger siblings – an adult activity that you did not necessarily relish. Unless you were one of those who 'conquered by caring' you probably resented minding the baby and, at least in the back of your mind, that resentment may still continue. During childhood it certainly often occupied center stage as you found yourself being cajoled, seduced, persuaded, or ordered outright to help, guide, and generally supervise at least one child younger than yourself. It is, alas, the general custom among fathers and mothers of multi-sib families to leave the oldest to baby-sit the younger children at as early an age as possible. The parental fantasy that a cozy game of Monopoly goes on during their absence is as popular as it is self-deceptive and unlikely. More often than not, kids get down to the nitty-gritty of settling old scores and all hell breaks loose, the masks of innocence

---

* We might also point out that in the old days, when a Turkish Sultan came to the throne he typically had *all* his brothers strangled. There might have been as many as forty or fifty!

being carefully replaced as soon as the parental key is heard in the lock.

Before any sibs came along, your parents may have taken you along on their evenings out and initiated you into an array of experiences which most children don't encounter until much later in their young lives. You probably attended a movie, went to (and got lost in) a department store, were present at a wedding, ate in a restaurant, stayed up past midnight, sat through a concert, visited a museum, and perhaps even waited quietly and patiently in a bar while the grownups around you went through that seemingly endless ritual known as 'having a drink'. You undoubtedly resented being left behind with the babysitter after the next sib was born, but at the same time there may have been a certain compensation in impressing the babysitter – not to mention the baby – with your worldly sophistication.

When you became old enough to be the babysitter yourself, you may have enjoyed the authority and/or prestige. But chances are that once the novelty wore off, you found it an oppressive and unfair burden. The oldest child is apt to be constantly derailed as personal projects play second fiddle to 'more important' family business. Pressure is put on the oldest to follow the rules and the routines of family and society, lest a bad example may be set for the little ones or the family equilibrium be upset by 'newfangled ways' of doing things. Minding the younger children is one area where the rules are apt to be quite rigid, with little room permitted for innovation. Consequently even though you (as a first-born) are often voted Most Likely to Succeed, your success is apt to be accomplished within the framework of what is already known, rather than in the staking out of new territories: you are better at advancing the ball than inventing a new ballgame.

Now let's get back to your role of caretaker and your

general resentment thereof. To greater or lesser extent, you enjoyed playing the role of Noncommissioned Officer; oldest children are often designated to carry messages from Command Headquarters to the troops below. And while you seldom had a part in making the laws, you could fully savor helping to see that they were carried out. This undoubtedly contributes to your aforementioned conservatism. Nevertheless, you felt cheated of the time and energy being taken away from your personal pursuits. One thing is fairly certain; whoever was in your charge was probably aware of your annoyance, and aware as well of the fact that you were a mere straw boss and not a real authority – that your decisions and commands did not carry the weight of a bona fide adult. No doubt they missed few opportunities to try your patience, until you finally pulled rank and did things that were hostile or even sadistic – things you may feel guilty about to this very day. But be reassured; in our experience younger siblings have been proven to be more forgiving of you than you are of yourself. These little 'mice' know quite well how outrageously they sometimes played 'while the cats were away,' and they rarely grew up resenting your occasional (or perhaps frequent) loss of temper. They are aware that they asked for it.

If you had more than one younger sibling it is more likely that when your parents were invited out they could not include all the kids, and you were probably the one they took along (unless you grew up in one of those rare families where such matters were settled by drawing lots). To be sure, some expeditions may not have been your cup of tea. In that case, you doubtless felt quite put upon and envied anyone fortunate enough to remain behind. The other children, in turn, envied your inclusion – despite your insistence that they should rejoice at being spared carrying out family responsibilities. It is difficult for you to appreciate how much most later-borns yearn for the kind of status that you have always had and taken for granted. Little do they understand how 'uneasy lies the head that wears a crown.' They could not guess your secret fears about being outshone, outmoded, or otherwise permanently deposed. The larger the age gap between you and the next-born, the more certain you are apt to be about your 'rightful place in the world,' and the more likely you are to reflect those characteristics discussed in connection with the only child.

Unlike the singleton, however, you oldest children have almost invariably been included in the Councils of the Elders for as long as you can remember. Not only is it likely that one or both of your parents confided in you what they were unwilling or unable to share with one another, but probably at least one sibling also turned to you for advice or t.l.c. But to whom were you able to turn in time of need without feeling humiliated or degraded or diminished? Having been backstage in the lives of your parents – having seen them in their underwear, so to speak – it was not as easy for you as it would be for a later-born child to believe that your parents were all-seeing or all-powerful, let alone all-wise. Granted that growing up does involve certain experiences which can be regarded as universal – the sudden recognition of one's capacity to procreate and of the mortality of one's grandparents, to name only two – there were bound to be important differences between the problems of your generation and those which your parents faced when they were growing up. If you are now in close contact with children or adults who are your juniors by twenty years or more, you will grasp the truth of this statement and realize, perhaps, how perplexing your problems may have seemed to your folks. Conceding to them the greatest good will, you must have found many occasions on which their advice was less than adequate and you had to play it by ear. Out of sheer self-preservation you

learned to be conservative and generally keep a low profile
in going about things: it is not characteristic of you to call
attention to yourself in situations where you have not yet
had time to learn the ropes.

The greatest result of whatever success you had in
working out your problems was that from observing you,
your parents probably learned enough to render them
considerably more helpful to their later-borns. You too
were able to make use of your experience for their benefit as
you emerged from your struggles armed with hard-won
wisdom. You then had the option of sharing your know-
how with the later-borns and thus protecting them from the
kind of pain you underwent; or saying 'Tough luck for
them; if *I* could go it alone, so can they – now it's their
turn!' While the latter choice may sound cruel to an
outsider, it has its foundations in a very human reaction to
what the oldest sibling experiences as a bitter and severe
overload in the 'helping younger sibs' department.

The designation of oldest child is in some ways more of a
function than it is a bona fide birth order. If you happened
to have been chronically ill or handicapped, for example,
it's almost certain that a younger sib assumed the prerogatives and caretaking responsibilities of primogeniture. This
can also happen when one or both parents are seriously at
odds with the oldest child (for whatever reason) and look to
another child to serve as confidant and Good Right Hand.
In such a case the two children swap roles, regardless of
gender. (You will find a discussion of that situation in
Chapter 7.)

While we are still on the subject of your liabilities as
oldest child, by far the most universal drawback was that
you were seldom permitted to be just a child. You were
constantly being nudged by your nervous and inexperienced (albeit enthusiastic and doting) young parents to
take the next step along the road to maturity before you

were truly ready for it. Perhaps they even kept a book for the first year or two in which they carefully recorded each of your milestones – first smile, first sit-up, first intelligible word, first step, etc. Each accomplishment was hailed as a momentous occurrence that primed you for the next event in what may have felt like a never-ending steeplechase. If you had to wait more than two years for the next sibling to arrive and take some of the pressure for achievement off your shoulders, it was already too late. The 'eyes of Texas' had been upon you, and you were already hooked into the success game like other first-borns the world over.

A result is that you were probably encouraged to set up and pursue life goals at a very early age. And, with or without the custodial functions involving younger sibs, you were probably provided with everything you needed in the way of time and space (within the limits of the family budget) in order to get on with your preparations.

Even as we say this we realize that exceptions and variations take place around this theme. Among certain ethnic groups, for instance, any education or training which threatens to make the oldest child 'superior' to his or her family of origin is firmly and ruthlessly discouraged. In other groups, oldest girls are given academic encouragement more often than oldest boys. In such cases the pressures to excel may take other forms. As the first-born and Guardian of Tradition, you may have been expected to act as custodian of various family properties – land, investments, business, china, heirlooms, etc. Or you may have been pressured to follow in your mother's or father's footsteps in choosing a career. Or there may have been strong pressure to live out Mum or Dad's secret and not-so-secret dreams – at the expense of your own fulfillment.

The upshot of having been pretty much deprived of your childhood is that you grew up being somewhat of a 'heavy,' with a 'life is real, life is earnest' outlook on things. This, in turn, has fostered the kind of self-critical perfectionism which can often give rise to strong feelings of depression as you turn your hostile and aggressive emotions inward without realizing it. You are reluctant to seek help when you are puzzled or distressed – something that later-borns do easily. You consider it okay for them but not worthy of anyone occupying your position in the world. Instead, you tend to bottle up your problems and mull them over at great length. You are the prime worrier of the birth order zodiac and you often appear to go around carrying the weight of the world upon your shoulders.

This derives from a major disadvantage that accompanied your membership in the Council of Elders – namely that you now and then became privy to some frightening or dreary information about which you could do nothing. You would have preferred to remain ignorant like the other children had you been given the choice. At the same time you were probably admonished to keep it secret, so that you had nobody to whom you could unburden yourself, and you felt that you were indeed carrying the world on your back. The oldest is often the one child in the family who knows about such matters as the terminal illness of another family member, or a parent's criminal activity, or the fact that the household finances are a disaster area. If these were family secrets which the adult world was willing to share with you, what skeletons, you must have asked yourself, still lurked behind the cupboard door?

Small wonder, then, that being in the know is usually so important to you. Unlike singletons (who are treated as *the* child of the family, and learn to acquire information by dint of careful observation and putting two and two together), you often feel angry and helpless when people don't voluntarily let you in on what's happening. You have the heightened regard for other people's privacy typical of singleton and oldest children, but you are apt to experience secretiveness on the part of those close to you (family, intimate friends, lovers) as a definite affront. You most often attempt to handle it by feigning indifference, but you sometimes give vent to feelings of desperation or jealous rage.

A certain significance attaches to the sex and physical build of the next-born in the family. It doesn't take a very great leap of the imagination to realize that a shy oldest girl being succeeded by a charismatic younger brother or a frail oldest boy being followed by an aggressive younger sister could fade into the background. Add to this the possibility that the next child may have had a closer family resemblance to one or both parents (physically, temperamentally, or otherwise) than you did, so that the groundwork may exist for a genuine and lifelong feeling of dethronement. A painful outcome of that sort receives precious little attention in the literature which deals with the oldest child. If you had the misfortune to suffer through such an experience, there were two major choices open to you. You could assert yourself in ways that would attract negative attention, rather than suffer the indignity of being shunted aside in favor of the usurper – i.e., you could become a problem child. Or you repair quietly to the sidelines and there obtain whatever relief is to be found in watching your successor perform.

In short, being the oldest child does not automatically guarantee that your life will be crowned with laurels nor that you will emerge as the most 'successful' of your parents' offspring. However exalted the oldest child's position may have been at the outset, such pre-eminence can remain quite precarious until the youngest of the siblings gets to be around four years old.

If all went well up to that point and your coronet was still not askew, chances are that from then on your supremacy was assured. Otherwise you had best make other arrange-

ments if you haven't already done so. By this we mean that
you would do well to quit trying to recapture the good old
days by continuing to seek status in your family's eyes.
Instead, you would do better to follow the example set by
the middle child (see Chapter 7); look around you and find
kindred souls outside the family who will appreciate you
and back you up with their loving support. To do so does
not make you a quitter, by the way. It is a wise person who
can recognize where his or her own interests lie. Trying to
swim against the current will only exhaust you and add to
your sense of outrage and frustration. We will have more to
say about the vicissitudes of the displaced (or maverick)
oldest boy and oldest girl in the next two chapters. For the
time being, suffice it to say that genuine dethronement is no
laughing matter, and a great deal of courage and resourcefulness are required in order to cope with it successfully.

Of all birth orders, you are by far the least comfortable in
the company of your age mates. Rather, you tend to prefer
people considerably older or younger than yourself. Your
closest friends are likely to be either first-born or last-born
children in their own families. However, you – like
singletons – have a stronger desire for privacy than most
people, and are more able to actually enjoy being alone. At
the same time, you have a propensity for settling down with
a permanent love partner in whom you invest whatever
needs you have for closeness and companionship while
letting the rest of the world go by.

Making virtues out of necessities is a well-known
strength of your ordinal position, but this also means you
tend to take on too much in the self-sacrifice department.
Putting one's perceived duties ahead of all else is a socially
acceptable way for a young child to gain and hold on to a
sense of personal importance, but making oneself into an
adult packhorse for everybody else's excess baggage can
become a burden. We strongly suggest therefore that you
learn how to say no. It will make you nervous and anxious

at first, but with a little practice you will be surprised how easy it gets. It may puncture your vanity to discover that your dependants can do more things for themselves than you had ever dreamed possible, but you'll get used to it. Then you'll have the challenge of working out what to do with all the spare time that will become available to you!

We do understand how difficult it can sometimes be to drop the reins of power after struggling so hard to acquire and hold on to them in the first place. At probably no time in your life was there more at stake than during your first several years in school – when you had to leave your castle each morning to do battle with who-knows-what giants and dragons, leaving one or more younger sibs at home in charge of your terrain. Small wonder that the oldest child is more likely than any other ordinal position to suffer from school phobia and/or morning nausea. Apart from any habits you may have acquired when you were a singleton, it also helps to explain your tendency to hang around the house when you got home from school. It throws light on your reluctance to enter very heavily into after-school activities that would keep you away from home for too long. Generally speaking, you are not apt to be a joiner – unless you are the organization's founder or it meets at your home base. When you do join clubs and other organizations your creative leadership is usually highly admired.

You comprehend the uses of power and handle it with skill and aplomb. Regardless of whatever inner fears and misgivings you may wrestle with, other people find it easy to put their confidence in you. More often than not, they perceive you as a person of experience, know-how, and self-confidence. It's almost impossible for them to even imagine just how much you do fret and worry about things, but – believe it or not – if they should happen to find out, they usually appreciate your humanity in not being perfect. All that now remains is for *you* to appreciate it.

CHAPTER FIVE

Oldest Boy

As a group, you oldest boys have been the envy of younger-borns – both male and female – since time immemorial. This is because you have always been first in line for everything – inheritance, family titles, property, education – that carried with it the splendor of rank, importance, and prestige. You have been, in fact, the Crown Prince. If you were not the result of a shotgun or pressured marriage discussed in the previous chapter, then it's likely that your parents were very much in love with each other at the time of your conception. Children brought into being under such happy circumstances are known in folklore as 'love babies,' and are believed to be born with basically contented and pleasant dispositions. You probably got a pretty solid reception into this strange and confusing world.

Occasionally, an oldest boy is born to parents who have an unhappy relationship with one another or who weren't really prepared or willing to have children. In the days before family planning, many a young couple hoped that no children would arrive before they were on their feet financially and could move out of their tiny one-room apartment into more comfortable quarters. Whatever the specifics, if you were the oldest child who arrived too soon, you were bound to sense (as infants somehow always seem able to do) the uncertainty of your welcome. And that meant that the very beginning of your life was hedged with insecurity.

Usually, however, your arrival was marked with considerable fanfare, and you learned to wear your princely crown with regal assurance and poise. What most of your younger siblings probably fail to realize is that your exalted position as the Crown Prince has not always been everything it's cracked up to be. In the first place, your parents were probably inexperienced when you came on the scene. They were undoubtedly adoring and attentive novice parents, but they were also *nervous* parents. Your mother consulted *her* mother, your Great Aunt May, her six best friends, and Dr Spock (or her generation's equivalent of Dr Spock). Perhaps Mum didn't realize that newborn babies can't be expected to smile right away, so she was afraid that you might be retarded. She and Dad may not have known that boy babies take longer to talk than girl babies, and so they wondered if you had perhaps been brain-damaged while getting yourself born. The number of things that parents of first-borns can worry about is amazing!

What they probably didn't know is that you first-born males, as a rule, rank higher in verbal skills than children in any other ordinal position – even first-born girls. This is thought to come about through the combination of two factors. First, being more physically active than girl babies are apt to be, you may have given your parents – especially Mum – more frequent cause to talk to and interact with you. Second, mothers generally hope that their first-born will be a boy – for reasons which may be psychologically or socially determined. In either case, mothers tend to show more devoted attention to a first-born boy and to do those things – verbal and nonverbal – which set the stage for language acquisition later on. Having thus been encouraged to communicate and to understand words at a very early age, it is not surprising that your birth order is traditionally pre-eminent in the fields of academic and literary endeavor.

At the same time this means that you were also encouraged to give up prematurely the kind of pictorial and imaginative thinking which characterizes mental activity before children acquire speech. For this reason, perhaps, your creativity usually finds its most comfortable expression in modes and formats which already exist – rather than inventing new ones. This is not to say that you lack imagination *per se*: some of your private day dreams would probably put both Walter Mitty and Henry Miller to shame. But you aren't inclined to share your private make-believe with anyone else, even your closest confidant (if you ever had one you could really trust).

You tend – far more than your female counterpart – to be deeply supportive of tradition, law, and the continuity of customs and rituals; in George Orwell's book, *1984*, Big Brother symbolizes – with apparently no strong disagreement from the reading public – the rigid upholder of law and order, allowing no deviation from the letter of the law by his error-prone sibs.

As the guardian and upholder of family and societal values, you prefer to live and work within well-established and relatively traditional structures. You are not an iconoclast, and your innovations are more in the nature of synthesizing tried and true factors, each of which has already achieved respectability. When you do embark on uncharted waters or risk doing something that might look ridiculous or 'far out' to others, you are completely prepared and equipped beforehand or have come to unshakable convictions. Sigmund Freud (himself an oldest brother) who braved the derision of the entire Vienna medical profession is a case in point. His studies had led him to inescapable conclusions, and his sense of duty would not let them lie unspoken.

Your tendency to be more conforming than most of your peers can make you experience considerable uneasiness in the presence of people your own age. It is, after all, one thing to be Crown Prince in your own family, but quite something else to be the third-kid-in-the-second-row of your first grade class. You may have been the object of much love, attention, and respect at home, but in the larger world you can often feel like a fish out of water. You are apt more than any other birth order to choose only one or two close friends, and they are also likely to be other first-born males. Not surprisingly, next to only girls, you are the most inclined of all ordinal positions to be a loner. Girls, however, don't usually mind and may even prefer a state of solitary independence, whereas you oldest boys can occasionally be overwhelmed by excruciating feelings of isolation and loneliness.

In groups, you are at your most self-confident when working or playing with people considerably younger or older than yourself. And, of course, you are likely to function at your very top level when you work in solitude or in collaboration with one very close friend or associate. Under such circumstances you are in your most inquisitive, most planful, most concentrated, and most productive frame of mind. Nothing can distract you from a project once you have put your mind to it.

In your infancy, when Mum and Dad were not running to the book or calling their doctor to check on the most minor detail of your sleeping, breathing, eating, and toilet habits, they were secretly hoping you might turn out to be a genius. Your younger sibs may have envied you all the attention you received, but they do not, to this day, know what it meant or how it felt to be the object of so much loving scrutiny. Like other Crown Princes the world over, you really would have liked a bit more privacy, a little more room in which to make your own mistakes and to explore your own world without being constantly under observation.

In one of Noël Coward's plays a character cries out in desperation, 'You're so good to me and I'm so *tired* of it all!' The oldest boy often knows exactly how that feels. As a

French nobleman explained to Benjamin Franklin while they both witnessed Marie Antoinette giving birth to the dauphin, 'A prince's life is never private – he is born in public, lives in public, and dies in public.' To the doting parents, their first-born child is a thrilling novelty – the living proof of mother's womanhood and father's manhood; their fledgling family; their hostage to fortune and their stake in the future; heir to all their hopes, fears, doubts, and imaginings.

Younger children in your family may have envied you for being privy to the Council of Elders, imagining you to be in the know about everything important to the family. What they didn't know – and seldom discover – is that you often pay a heavy price for your place at the top. Both parents often unwittingly lean on the oldest boy for their own emotional support – a heavy burden. At the same time, when you have gone to them with urgent personal concerns of your own, you have often found them stumped for answers, owing to their inexperience as parents.

So you frequently have to struggle through personal problems all on your own and, as a result, you are later able to come up with viable answers for your younger siblings. In immigrant families it has almost always been the oldest boy (rather than the oldest girl or the parents) who most quickly learns the new language and customs, explores the new social environment, and is eager to pass along his hard-earned knowledge to the rest of the family. Indeed, for any family that moves to a new part of the world (a different continent, a new town, or six blocks away in the same community), it is generally you, the oldest boy, who acts as go-between, pathfinder, and guide. This Daniel Boone role may have given you genuine pleasure because you truly enjoy passing along your hard-won wisdom. This is one reason why the oldest brother makes an excellent teacher more often than the oldest sister. The latter was so overburdened with caring for younger sibs (whether she wanted to or not) that she either wants out thereafter or has her capable hands full in dealing with her own offspring.

In a family with three or more children, you probably grew up functioning as a kind of father substitute, but in special ways. For instance, if your family was poor or lived in a tough neighborhood, you may have acquired the role of street fighter and physical protector to your sibs, even when the odds against you were tremendous. Or you may have been the only child sent on errands involving money transactions, since, as the oldest and a male, you were the one considered best able to safeguard the cash and to fend off marauders. In this way your identification with 'grown-upness' made it more difficult for you to feel like one of the children than it would be for the oldest boy in a smaller family. A certain social anxiety and sense of not belonging in your own age group is likely to be a lifelong characteristic of yours.

As an oldest boy, you have a most enviable attitude: you expect the adult world to take you seriously rather than making light of you and your concerns. As a rule, you never on any account allow yourself to be trifled with by subordinates. 'Subordinate' in this context refers to anyone more than a year younger than yourself. Your reflexive reaction to attempts on their part to con, manipulate, or push you around is to withdraw the hem of your garment, so to speak, and assume a dignified aloofness. If the yapping and snapping continue, you know how to let fly a thunderbolt which will send your tormentors heading for cover. If all else fails, you know that you can convene a Privy Council of the Elders (from which all youngers will be pointedly excluded). You do not usually enjoy summoning up your royal prerogatives, but there are occasions when you feel it your painful duty to do so. It's almost as if you were born keenly aware of your responsibilities. While you the material, spiritual, and psychological welfare of those entrusted to your care (not to mention trying to keep them in line and out of your hair).

What is truly noble (in the best sense of the word) about you is your continuing and loyal willingness to come to the aid of an unhappy or beleaguered sib. You may often feel anxious and uncertain about your own effectiveness in this regard, but you bravely try to conceal your fears while obeying your strong sense of duty. Sometimes you can overextend yourself to the point where too large a proportion of your adult life is taken up with pulling your siblings' chestnuts out of the fire. It's one thing to invent games to quiet their fears during a thunderstorm when you are all children, but it's another, say, to take over one sib's mortgage and to be forever on the phone listening to the family hypochondriac's endless medical adventures.

When your other sibs were born, you may have resented them for attempting to dethrone you, but at the same time it was a relief not to have to be constantly on stage. The only serious drawback to this was that when it came time to drag yourself off to kindergarten, you had to leave a baby of two or three in charge of the fort. More likely than not, you wet your knickers on your first day at school and went home in a state of ignominy which you can still recapture vividly. The next day you may have thrown up during the morning break – and for many days thereafter. Sad to say, school phobias are most common amongst oldest children generally, and oldest boys in particular. Whatever your early school experiences were like, you eventually learned to get along well enough. You did your homework and probably earned better marks than your sibs.

In relation to love partners you are usually slow in learning the ropes, and are inclined to be passionately monogamous. In your anxiety and your bewilderment

about sex and love you probably turned to your parents for
guidance and found them surprisingly unhelpful in matters
of the heart. You probably found their outlook outmoded,
and their tongue-tied advice woefully inadequate. You
therefore learned once again to endure your anguish in
solitude and silence, breaking it only to confide in one or
another of your buddies – who are usually either equally
uninformed and unsure or else are not romantically
involved at the same time you are. For an oldest boy the
most difficult relationships in the world to negotiate are
usually those involving females of his own age. Even having
two or more younger sisters doesn't seem to help very much
– they, after all, are kid sisters, and aren't usually
considered valid in your eyes as full-fledged women. Much
of your difficulty in the love/romance department has to do
with your tendency to be overly possessive, which in turn
arises from your loner qualities. The fewer close relationships a person has in his life, the more he is apt to invest
emotionally in a 'one and only.' This may seem very right
and proper to your way of looking at things, but when this
happens your chosen love partner is saddled with the
enormous burden of living up to your requirements – many
of which may be basically unrealistic. As a result, you may
have to suffer a number of heartbreaks before you acquire
the flexibility needed to modify some of your more extreme
demands.

When it came to formal education, your elders took it for
granted that you would seek their advice. It was also taken
for granted that whatever training you planned together
would be duly arranged for if at all possible. It was a
foregone conclusion that you would take any endeavor
seriously and do your best to be worthy of their investment in you: no playing truant, no playboy boozing, no
student high jinks, no houseparty weekends for you. If you
had to choose a competitive sport, it most likely stressed

individual performance (like fencing, swimming, or athletics) rather than teamwork.

Occasionally, the enormous pressures for success placed on the oldest boy – either deliberately or subconsciously – backfire. To put it succinctly, you either knocked yourself out in your efforts to fulfill all the expectations heaped upon your shoulders – or you threw the rule book out the window and (especially if you had a younger brother) passed the Olympian torch down the line to one of your sibs. Let him hold it aloft and run with it! In this case you may have settled on a modest but stable way of being in the world, saying in effect, 'Don't count on me for stardom.'

A very painful option sometimes chosen by males in your ordinal position is that of total abdication. It happens more frequently than statistics would indicate, or than your near and dear ones would ever care to admit openly. Something seems to crack under the pressure of so many seeming demands for you to achieve perfection, and so by way of protest you may wind up being almost a caricature of failure. When this happens alcoholism, drug addiction, delinquency, and general 'losership' can characterize your lifestyle. Boys in your birth order can become problem children who remain a source of embarrassment and concern to everyone who loves and cares about them. Johann Sebastian Bach's oldest son, Wilhelm Friedemann is a case in point. He was the favorite, and we can easily guess at the pressures upon him. Wilhelm Friedemann composed a few works of merely acceptable quality, after which he apparently handed the torch over to his oldest surviving brother, Karl Phillip Emanuel. Wilhelm ended up a tormented ne'er-do-well who peddled untold pages of his father's manuscripts for booze money – with the result that many major works are now lost to humanity.

We note in Chapter 13 that the younger brother of an older sister often goes through a maverick period of storm

and rebellion during his teens and twenties. Your ordinal
position can be a close runner-up when it comes to kicking
over the traces – once you decide to go that route. True, this
kind of behavior is less frequent with oldest boys, but when
it does occur, it seems harder for you to outgrow. In the
language of clinical psychology this is called 'acting out.'
That is, you act out your protest instead of talking it out
with someone or otherwise coming to terms with your
submerged resentment and outrage or with your conviction
that you have 'failed' as a model of perfection. It's almost
as though you were announcing to the world, 'Okay, then,
if I can't measure up to your satisfaction as the Crown
Prince, I'll turn myself into the Crown Flop and see how
you like that!' We have observed that this state of affairs
happens most often with those of you who have at least two
younger brothers born within a few years of you, especially
if one of them was able to compete successfully with you on
your own turf.

Otherwise, you are generally the kind of fellow most apt
to be regarded as a pillar of society by all and sundry. You
provide and protect most of what is lasting, durable, and
stable in a world which appears to be changing at an
accelerated pace with each passing day. Your behavior is
predictably steadfast, and you take justifiable pride in the
fact that your word is your bond. You let the world know
that you can be counted on to do what you say you'll do
and to meet all deadlines punctually. You pay your bills
promptly whenever possible, balance your bank account
regularly and correctly, and keep your appointments come
hell or high water. (During the power blackouts in New
York, our clients in your ordinal position steadfastly
climbed ten flights of stairs to get to psychotherapy sessions
and invariably had their cheques made out and ready at
precisely the last session of the month.) In short, you are a
very responsible person; mainstay, confidant and Adjutant

General to your parents; shield and buckler to your younger sibs. But deep in your patient, dependable heart, you carefully conceal a secret wish to frolic in a pile of raked-up leaves – the way the kids always did. We suggest that you find yourself a pile of leaves (a haystack or a waterbed will do) as soon as possible and let yourself roll around in it – just once. Who knows? – it may get to be a habit!

CHAPTER SIX

Oldest Girl

No need to tell you that the role of Big Sister is not all it's cracked up to be. Later-borns and singletons (especially females) may envy what they regard as your unassailable prerogatives, but they really don't know whereof they speak. In addition, you probably get sick and tired of the thoughtless but widespread notion that you share the same advantages as your male counterpart. The fact of the matter is that you are denied many of the rewards of primogeniture and, into the bargain, get stuck at a very early age with all sorts of burdensome responsibilities which you certainly never ask for. You did not, after all, ask to be Mother Hen, Everybody's Nanny, General Director of Traffic, or Mum or Dad's Good Right Hand. You might have felt honored or flattered when these functions first landed in your lap. But once the novelty wore off – as it does with so many things during early childhood – you probably felt weighed down with more responsibilities than you had ever contracted for. Your younger sibs doubtless make the wrong-headed assumption that you were *born* in charge of the busy world around you. A sibling has to be extremely empathic indeed to recognize how complicated was the route by which you gradually arrived at your ultimate position of seemingly unquestioned authority. We shall explain later why we use the word 'seemingly.' Right now, suffice it to say that you had to deal with some very heavy challenges – and often enough found yourself in the paradoxical position of staunchly defending a job which, truth to tell, you didn't relish all that much.

People don't generally realize how stealthily and in what roundabout ways many of your duties were acquired. We discussed in Chapter 4 the manner in which first-borns are pressured by the environment ('encouraged' is your parents' word for it) to take one hurried step after another along the road to adulthood. You probably received your reward (a smile, a pat on the head, even a hug) for a performance well done, but this doesn't alter the fact that much of what you were able to accomplish involved a kind of jumping through hoops in hopes of pleasing your parents and/or other important adults in your household. To put it another way, you did not instigate many of the behaviors for which your world rewarded you. If, for example, somebody overheard you babbling 'ah-ah' in your crib, we will bet our last penny that in no time flat it was, 'Say Ma-ma! Say *ma, ma* . . . There! Didn't I tell you? She can talk! She just said her first word – *Mama*!' Not content with that, they then pushed for 'Da-da,' and so forth. This is apt to be the childhood lot of all first-borns, in our culture, anyway – achieve or run the risk of disappointing those whose faces must always be made to shine upon you if you are to be granted any peace. Having the one-to-one attention of adults, learning to command language early in life, and being an achiever are all plus factors. What we are noting here is that your progress was pushed and your development hurried – not always to your advantage.

If all goes well – if you don't either rebel or opt out under the sheer weight of it all – then you will have graduated step by inexorable step to a pinnacle of lofty status wherein you discover that you yourself have become the trainer who cracks the whip commanding yourself day in and day out to measure up (or pack it in), to excel (or fall by the wayside).

It is a perfectly understandable fact of human nature that when we feel pressured and pushed around, our first reaction is to look for somebody else whom we can manipulate, dominate, and manage – yes, even push around and bully. Show us a bully or a nag and we'll show you a person who has been bullied or nagged. This involves the third of those three basic human motivations: to obtain 'goodies'; to avoid pain and danger; and to 'get even.' The rewards which you were given for good performance satisfied your need for 'goodies' as well as allaying your fears concerning the pain and danger of rejection or banishment if you failed to please those in charge. As for the third motivation, destiny provided you with siblings to whom you could pass along some of the various pressures that beset you – if you so desired. We don't mean to imply that you were necessarily righting the imbalances to your life in a cruel or hostile way. It's just that the managerial tactics of a very little girl who takes her younger siblings in tow can often be a lot more painful to them than she could be expected to realize. If you are, from time to time, surprised or shocked at the stored-up vehemence that a younger sibling will occasionally express, that's probably where it's coming from. 'Look here,' he or she might shout, 'stop being a backseat driver! I'm old enough to know what I'm doing. You always were a loudmouth!'

Whether take-charge duties were foisted upon you or acquired through your own initiative, they increased far more then even you were aware of. Unlike your male counterpart, you were given little opportunity to carve out private space. Being a girl, you were expected to interest yourself in all sorts of domestic goings on, and in particular all of the various activities which attended the arrival of a new baby in the home. This is, for better or worse, the way society conditions its girls to learn the skills of house-keeping and motherhood – so that they can eventually find a husband, be fruitful and multiply. Mum – and perhaps other adult females as well – can be counted on to act as ubiquitous role models who give you your first conception of being 'feminine.' It is upon the basis of this intimate and protracted mother–daughter collaboration that much of your later personality development rests – and differs in important ways from that of the oldest boy. While he may (for whatever reason) choose to take upon himself certain equally burdensome responsibilities at a tender age, he is rarely encouraged or expected to do so until around age six or seven, as part of his preparatory training for adulthood. Minding the children is but one of the many kinds of hurdle he faces on the long obstacle course leading to full, adult status. It is proffered to little girls, however, as a desirable lifestyle from the moment they are given their first dolly to play with – probably while still in the cradle. The oldest girl, however, is generally not taught the various other managerial duties of life with an attitude that anticipates her having to support herself (or others) in the adult world. (Black American families appear to be an exception: due to post-slavery economic and social conditioning, greater emphasis is often placed on the education and training of oldest girls.) Thus, you are less likely than an oldest boy to have any clear notion of when, where, or how all your arduous childhood duties and responsibilities are ever going to pay off in adulthood.

Generally speaking, the basic assumption (whether openly stated or not) was that you would eventually get married and your future fulfillment would be assured. This would be especially true if one or more of the siblings immediately following you were males, as parents are inclined to postpone any career plans for their oldest girl when boys arrive on the scene. Otherwise they may have looked on you as an 'ace up their sleeve' in case their prayers for a son and heir went unanswered. Waiting for them to finalize their dreams for you must have made you feel very like a reserve sitting on the bench, half dreading and half looking forward to a possible turn to play. Perhaps you couldn't stand the suspense and made up your own mind to aim for marriage or a career or both. If you were followed by girls, there was more leeway for you to make career plans provided your family was not of the persuasion which insists that 'a woman's place is in the home' taking care of house, spouse, and kids. In that case your career plans may have been regarded as downright treason and you may have knuckled under to family coercion and gone the domestic route against your own inclinations. Otherwise the pressures for you to marry are likely to be eased when you have younger sisters who can take up the slack, supplying grandchildren and (if you come from an all-girl family) surrogate sons in the person of sons-in-law.

Well, what about romance and love partners, while we're on the subject? Here you are apt to share many of the same problems that beset oldest boys in the 'close relationship' department. On the whole you feel more comfortable and at ease with members of your own sex. Male peers (especially oldest boys) are apt to be as much of a puzzlement to you as you are to them. One might think that a certain mutuality of childhood experience as oldest children would draw you together and make for something like instant rapport between you. It happens quite often when two youngest children (of either sex) get together, but is quite rare for first-borns who are not singletons. We believe this is due to the fact that while you do have much in common – i.e., responsibility, perfectionism, high self-expectations, introversion tendencies, etc. – the differences between you are far more crucial to the development of your respective personalities than are the similarities. He's more inclined to be silent, and to govern by striking a posture of clear and cool command. So he may experience you as manipulative and overly concerned with a host of things which he looks down upon as trivia unworthy of his attention. To you, however, they are matters which your experience has taught you can 'reap a whirlwind' if not attended to and nipped in the bud.

Similarly, you are apt to find him stubborn, with a one-track mind, and unwilling to let himself perceive (let alone do anything about) the nuances and intricacies of personal interaction. You are acutely aware of these at the emotional level, and also able to articulate them skillfully. He may be more verbally skilled than other birth orders (see Chapter 5), but this is largely in the field of ideas and theories. You, on the contrary, have no equal among ordinals when it comes to giving precise voice to an emotional point of view.* Eventually you both discover, to your mutual bafflement and disappointment, that if your relationship is to become a mutually gratifying one, it will require a certain brand of patience in which you may both be rather lacking. If either one of you had opposite-sexed siblings, then you were probably accustomed to having them follow your dictates with a minimum of back talk. But if, on the other hand, you had only sisters (and he only brothers), then opposite-sex peers most likely come across to both of you as pretty much of an enigma. In that case, we can predict that both of you will get along best with those members of the opposite sex who are younger than yourself and who were also later-borns in their own family of origin. (Our male-dominated society being what it is, we hardly need add that such a pairing goes best when the male is an eldest and the female a later-born.) Even when you do get together with a male who happens to be a later-born (whether or not he is the same age as yourself) you may find

* History isn't very clear on the subject, but Shakespeare's Macbeth and his wife apparently were first-born children and certainly appear to be a good illustration of what we mean – he with his gloomy philosophical eloquence ('Tomorrow and tomorrow and tomorrow creeps in this petty pace from day to day') and she with her alertness to the emotional nuances of the environment ('The raven himself is hoarse that croaks the fatal entrance of Duncan under my battlements . . .').

him quite sensitive to what he will term 'domineering' behavior on your part.

As a rule, your keen awareness of power and its applications will stand you in good stead when it comes to the 'selection' of a love partner. We place the word in quotation marks out of deference to the fact that one's choice in love partners is largely subconscious and involuntary. Whoever your love partner turns out to be, there is always the danger that he may be of a pliant disposition and will prove unable to give you much in the way of emotional support when it comes to your turn to lean on somebody. Because even you – believe it or not – have a right to be frightened, unsure of yourself, and in need of a helping hand now and then. In sad truth, second only to the younger sister of a brother (see Chapter 17) you have the roughest time of any female birth order in the love department – even though you may be the first girl among your siblings to get married (a point of honor, be it noted – once you have decided you want matrimony).

But what if you don't decide to go that route? Well, that all depends on how the lines were drawn in the 'family constellation'* you grew up with. If you were not unduly close to either of your parents, you may have chosen to make your own way in the world and have a career. In that case you probably left the nest at the earliest opportunity – that is, when there were no juvenile sibs left at home for you to take care of. Women in your ordinal position frequently make excellent politicians, doctors, managers, counselors, therapists, etc.

If you were emotionally close to one or the other of your parents (most often Dad), then that may have become your career. Our society harbors a surprisingly large number of

---

* A useful term, coined by Walter Toman, who wrote the first popularized book on birth order (see Bibliography).

unmarried first-born females whose major occupation is that of being a kind of pseudo-wife to Dad. This is likely to happen when the mother passes away and the oldest daughter stays on to raise the children and take care of Dad, or if she is widowed or divorced and it seems more sensible to return to the nest than to try hacking it on her own. It may also occur when she is an unattached career woman and then Mum passes away – leaving Dad as lonely and at loose ends as she herself has felt. In any event, such a household usually consists of you, Dad, and perhaps an unattached younger sibling or two; Mum is almost never in the picture.

This brings us to a final topic without which this chapter would not be complete. In the preceding chapter we mentioned oldest boys who 'fail' in their mission as heirs to whatever throne the significant adults had in mind for them. We talked about several of the ways in which these males may seek to escape their plight. But the ways in which societies treat with and respond to male and female children can differ widely, and produce adult personalities and biographies which are correspondingly different.

A profligate male is considered socially acceptable in many circles (and sometimes even secretly envied) – provided he isn't a rotter. A profligate female is most often regarded with contempt, unless she is armed with considerable money, power, or invulnerable prestige. Of course you could opt out of your lifelong role as oldest girl and hit the burlesque circuit (in which case you'd be more likely to function as an independent performer rather than just another body in a chorus line), but your family and most of your friends would be horrified.

Or, like the rebellious version of the oldest boy, you might seek to drown your pain in drugs or alcohol (as a way of simultaneously venting anger as well as various pent-up dependency needs which you could never legitimately express within your family circle), but again, that is more the style of your male counterpart. You are more likely to become depressed or baffled or both – at which juncture you often have the good practical sense to reach out for help from your friends or even from a younger sibling. Since you may consider it the end of your world to be the help*ee* rather than the help*er*, you probably suffer a severe sense of disorientation when you decide to seek assistance. Your world seems turned upside down, and the resulting sense of panic may sometimes cause you to wonder if you are going crazy. Your friends and family have never seen you in such a state, so they most often react with alarm and rush lovingly to your aid – provided you can pocket your pride long enough to let them know of your distress. Unfortunately, you don't always do this, but are inclined to wait until you are in truly dire straits. In extreme cases, your friends or family may rush you into the nearest hospital – where the staff may or may not be helpful in restoring your lapsed self-esteem. At this point you have subconsciously turned the tables on your world; now you are the one in need of t.l.c. – and people are knocking themselves out to take care of you. Don't be so proud and headstrong that you have to turn yourself into a disaster area in order to obtain your fair share of those necessary comforts. All of us need the support and solace of others in order to survive (let alone thrive) in a world of many stresses and strains – even you.

In conclusion, your capacity to be in charge of yourself and others is a strength in which you take valid and justifiable pride. At the same time your reluctance to let anyone else assume cherished responsibilities (or share the power and prestige that accompany them) is your greatest liability. We invite you to relax and modify as many of your efforts at control as you possibly can; let go, sit back, and listen to the music – your own and others'. You won't be sorry!

CHAPTER SEVEN

Middle Child

Before discussing the middle child, a few words need to be said about ordinal positions generally and some of the problems we encounter in determining just where someone really belongs in the family lineup. We are bringing these issues to the fore at this point because it happens that of all the ordinal positions dealt with in this book, 'middleness' is the most difficult to define, let alone describe or generalize about in any meaningful way.

It is easy enough to say who the middle child is when there are only three children in a family, all fairly evenly spaced out and of the same sex. But suppose they are not evenly spaced, or suppose there is a boy followed by a girl, followed by another boy? In most American families the ideal is 'a boy for you, a girl for me . . .' The third child may feel superfluous, and inherit all of the 'fifth wheel' feelings with which we will be dealing in this chapter.

If there are four or six children in the family, two of them are in the middle. Or you may come from a family where there was an oldest boy followed eight years later by two other children who were fairly close in age. Strictly speaking, the second child is the middle one, but in actual fact he or she is more likely to be treated like another oldest child in relation to the later siblings. It is self-evident that the middle child of three boys will have quite a different growing-up experience from that of a boy who finds himself between two sisters – or a girl who is flanked by brothers.

There is yet another factor to which we would like to call your attention, namely the possibility that while you are the middle child numerically, you may have inherited (or been assigned) the mantle of an oldest or a youngest child. For example, the first-born in a family may suffer from a serious handicap that requires special handling, and therefore he or she is automatically exempted from both the status and the responsibilities normally assigned to the oldest. Or perhaps he or she opted out on the role so that you were free to take over as heir to the parental throne. A third possibility is that you were by nature a more assertive (charismatic, competitive, practical, competent) personality, so that it seemed quite fitting and proper for you to wear the crown which usually rings the brow of the first-born. In this manner, Louisa May Alcott (second-oldest of four girls) was the one who took things in hand and spent her adult lifetime supporting her indigent father and other family members by dint of the blood-and-thunder detective stories which she published under a pseudonym until her famous book *Little Women* became a best seller.

Again, still supposing that you are a middle child of three, your younger sib may have been handicapped or otherwise not a full participant in the family life, so that your place in the scheme of things was more like what we would expect for the younger of two children. By now you can see how complicated it becomes merely to locate yourself in the family constellation. To summarize, then, if you were indeed a stand-in for an oldest or youngest child in your family, we think you might find it more useful and more pertinent to consult those chapters in this book which deal with the ordinal position you stood in for.

So here we are, trying to write a chapter about you, and at the very outset there is a problem about where you belong. Already you may feel that you are being shunted about and lost in the shuffle – and are about to put the book down in disgust. But that's the story of your life, isn't it? Far more important than any technical definition of 'middlehood' is this type of subjective experience which characterizes it – the lifelong and never-ending search for belongingness. Because it is often the fate of your ordinal position to feel like a fifth wheel; an extra; a leftover who lives in dread of being completely bypassed and upstaged by elder and younger sibs – and anyone else in your environment. Nevertheless, even while you want to find a place in the world where you truly belong, you also have a maverick streak which can cause you to deliberately thumb your nose at many of the ground rules and conventions upon which your acceptance may actually depend. It sounds like a paradox and, as in the case of most paradoxes, these two seemingly opposite tendencies really represent the two sides of the selfsame coin. On the one hand you yearn for a stable role in the scheme of things; on the other you have learned the value of being an outsider, able to divorce yourself from many of the assumptions and ideas which most people take for granted. You end up, then, wanting to be part of 'the club,' scoffing at its sacred cows, but still feeling sadly left out.

To you, the family looked like a 'heads you win, tails I lose' situation. You might have enjoyed being in the middle sometimes, but often enough when you reached for the rewards of being a younger child, you got rebuffed on the grounds that you were too old, and when you sought the status of an older child you were told that you weren't old enough. This was a very bewildering and frustrating situation which you often despaired of ever sorting out, although, as we will point out, you learned to cash in on it. Neither camp would accord you full membership, and consequently you grew up feeling displaced and disregarded within the family framework.

As we often observe in this book, a useful way of looking at things is to posit three central motivations of the human psyche: 1) to obtain rewards and 'goodies'; 2) to avoid pain and danger; and 3) to get even – an eye for an eye and a tooth for a tooth. How do these apply to you? Well, let's begin with your behavior *vis-à-vis* your family. One thing that characterizes you as a middle child is your tendency to leave home early on in life. By this we don't mean that you tie up your belongings in a bandana on the end of a stick and run away, but that you make friends at school or in the neighborhood at a much earlier age than your brother(s) and sister(s). Many a mother of a middle child has been heard to say 'I only see that child at meals and bedtime – apparently other people's homes have more to offer than ours does!' By this same token, you find a gang of your own outside of the family, and you seldom if ever ask your siblings to join it along with you. It may be an athletic team, a clique or club in school, a group that just hangs out together – but you experience it, as does your family, as yours and not theirs.

In terms of our threefold (and admittedly simplistic) scheme of human motivation you firstly obtain your rewards and goodies by accepting value systems which lie outside your family's view of things. Secondly, you avoid the pains and dangers of being totally at the mercy of your family's yardsticks of propriety and 'right' behavior. And thirdly, you get even with your family and its dratted dos and don'ts by giving yourself the right to choose other groups (and their yardsticks) to measure yourself by. Of course the big drawback in this maneuver is obvious: it adds considerably to your family's tendency to experience you as an outsider. Whether or not they challenge you openly on this score – and they usually do – the feeling is always there. Your sense of distance can evolve into a deep feeling of rootlessness and is a painful aspect of your life which you rarely – if ever – share with any other human being. There is an important corollary to the emotional distance which you create and preserve between yourself and the external world. It is your great reluctance to become passionately involved with anything or anyone. By this we mean that you're more objective and matter-of-fact than most people are able to be when it comes to the major commitments of your life. You may interest yourself in a number of things – but you are not prone to become seriously excited about any of them. In dealing with people, you tend to have many acquaintances but few whom you would care to call real friends. You can be conscientious and careful in your work, for example, but you rarely get really turned on about it. You may admire many people but hero-worship none of them.

This very fact serves to hide your Achilles heel – i.e., an excruciating vulnerability which you feel too proud to confess to yourself, carefully building a protective wall around yourself and your feelings. Like the Great Wall of China it may keep attackers at bay, but that same wall prevents a lot of sympathetic persons from entering and enriching your world.

This façade of toughness gives you the false appearance of seeming thick-skinned, although nothing could be further from the truth. Your feelings are more easily hurt and slower to heal than most people's (with the possible exception of the only girl). Your characteristic talent for turning your weaknesses into virtues is an asset in this case. You find comfort in the realization that although your self-protective wall may cost you the joy to be found in warmth and closeness to others, you are thereby spared many of the painful aspects of intimacy.

All this is not meant to be a criticism of you. It behoves us all to admire and respect the resourceful ingenuity which every small child uses in an effort to make some kind of sense out of its environment and to survive in a puzzling and seemingly crazy world. A toddler's clever solution to a staggering dilemma may not always serve the requirements of adult life, but that gives us no reason to denigrate it.

Every psychological strategy is a useful tool to have in our 'kit'; we get into trouble only in misapplication. It took a lot of sheer courage for you to declare independence from your family at so young an age, and by doing so to be labeled an 'outcast.' But there was a drawback: the same feelings of hurt which prompted your withdrawal from the family may still govern much of your daily interaction with other people. Those feelings gave rise to your exaggerated need to be a very private person whose deepest feelings can only be guessed at by others. At the same time you invariably show a similar respect for another person's privacy, and as a matter of principle never ask questions no matter how much your curiosity or interest may be aroused.

Your sensitivity to slights causes you to have a very short fuse when it comes to tolerating or empathizing with the thoughts and feelings of others. All of us cope with life in two major ways: either we give back what life has handed us – in spades – or else we swing too far in the opposite direction. In other words, the adult who had to walk two miles to school and back each day can take up either of two positions – 1) he or she can assert, 'If I could do it, then anybody else can,' or 2) he or she can maintain that nobody should have to go through such travail, and then do everything possible to protect others from similar suffering. We call these two alternatives the 'hot potato choice' – i.e., one either passes the hot potato along, or one tries to cool it down. You are most apt to be a potato-passer; if somebody gives you one punch you will make it your business to give them two punches in order to even the score, no matter how long you have to wait. To your way of thinking, this is purely a matter of justice and fair play. For you are almost allergic to anything that smacks of favoritism or of unequal or discriminatory attitudes, even though you yourself can sometimes be quite prejudiced without really intending to be.

As human beings we all have basic needs our environment doesn't necessarily fulfill. When this happens, we often respond by becoming the source of supply to others who are expressing our own unfulfilled need. Thus a hungry person with strong emotional taboos about eating might become a professional cook. Somebody who keeps a tight rein on aggression might choose to hang out with a person well known for his or her pugnacity. The fact that your childhood family often neglected to provide enough of the care, love and warmth that you so desperately needed produces in people of your birth order a characteristic yearning to be needed – especially by those less robust than yourself. It is one of the factors which makes you a good person to work for or to study with, which we will discuss later on. It is also part of your need to have impact upon the world of other people.

Because your basic reticence combines with your underlying vulnerability, you give the appearance of being a person who is deeply modest and self-effacing by nature. We know better. Your fantasies of eventually being 'discovered' and catapulted to greatness lie just beneath the surface. You dream continually about having impact upon others, as a friend, enemy, teacher, lover, critic, pundit, or all six – and then some.

You are fiercely loyal to concepts, values, causes, and individuals, once you have espoused them. You learned at a very early age how to be a majority of one – and usually a silent one at that. Caught midway between the oldest and the youngest child, you generally came to recognize the futility of trying to vie with them for the rewards which their own ordinal positions brought them; to you it looked like the oldest child could do no wrong and the youngest could always count on somebody (whether cheerfully or reluctantly) to pull his or her chestnuts out of the fire. At the same time you also clearly recognized the drawbacks inherent in the other two birth orders: the tragic sense of responsibility which dogs the footsteps of the oldest, and the wild feelings of helplessness and futility which are often the lot of the youngest. In your heart of hearts you seem to have made a secret compact with yourself which said 'a plague on both your houses!' – and off you went.

'Where did you go?' somebody might ask. 'Out,' is your reply. 'What did you do?' 'That's for me to know and you to guess at!' For you are the most secretive of all the ordinal positions, believe it or not. In other chapters we have noted that the younger brother of an oldest girl (and his older sister as well) receive high honors when it comes to keeping their own counsel. But their reasons for being secretive differed from your own (see Chapter 13). Yours is a 'burned child' reaction to a world which you experienced as paying less attention to you than it did to the others. It's as though you were saying 'You never showed interest in where I was coming from – so don't expect me to confide in you now.' Small wonder that you are one of the rarest persons to seek out the services of anyone in the helping professions. Not only do you not wear your heart on your sleeve, but you have also become accustomed to suffering your private pains in silence. In this way you get even with a world which seemed to be giving you short shrift – sharing neither joy and triumph, nor pain.

While on the subject of your emotional life, we have several further observations to make. When anyone incurs your displeasure you are capable of dropping them from your life. You have, that is, the rare ability to terminate any relationship without ceremony once you decide to do so. Since you are not accustomed to expressing (and so haven't learned much about how to modulate) your emotional transactions, you are apt to pick one or the other of two extremes: you either drop the contact altogether without a word and without a backward glance, or you deliver a carefully rehearsed diatribe which the recipient experiences as being far more brutal than you could ever have imagined. Like the youngest child, you invariably underestimate the impact which you exert upon others. At the same time you have the rare ability to stand aside and objectively evaluate your ongoing relationships.

This doesn't mean that you're lacking in feeling. Toward those who behave themselves you can maintain a steady contact based on little more than mutual nostalgia, while your loyalty to longtime peer friends might be called legendary. Peers, after all, constituted the real family of your growing-up years – even when you had one or more blood relatives with whom you felt some degree of closeness. As for those who do not behave themselves, your motto seems to be 'Friends (or relatives) in need are a pain in the neck – get rid of them!'

Let us at this point return to that major aspect of your experience as a middle child – the feeling of middleness. Your elders regard you as their junior while your juniors look up to you as one of the seniors. More often than not, you have learned very early in life to cash in on the best of both these worlds while adroitly avoiding the pitfalls – and mishaps – of each. Thus as a 'junior' you know how to wear a mask of innocent passivity which encourages your elders to expect less of you than they otherwise would. At the same time, as an 'older child' you know how to claim the prerogatives of that ordinal position when it suits you best. This unusual resourcefulness often earns you the reputation of being an opportunist or a manipulator, but it spares you the struggles and heartaches which you associate with the extreme ends of the birth order spectrum. In other words, there can be great safety in a middle position.

Of course, knowing how to be all things to all people constitutes the stuff of which adroit politicians are made. But you are not good at political wheeling and dealing;

your aforementioned short fuse, combined with your basic suspicion of other people's motives, cramps your style, and you're not good at hiding it. Try as you might, outright pretense is not likely to be your strong suit. When you attempt being cagey, it is then that you are apt to be at your most transparent and obvious. We think this is largely due to your iconoclastic, maverick underpinnings, which are seldom pronounced enough to make you an outright revolutionary, but are a sufficiently important part of your make-up to raise strong doubts in the minds of political cronies.

This stance of being a conservative revolutionary is precisely where your middleness exerts its most important influence upon your life. You saw youngest children thrashing about, wearing their hearts on their sleeves. You saw the ominous risks which confront oldest children. So you learned early on to play your cards close to your chest. Paradoxically, however, when you blow your cool and abandon (or are forced to relinquish) your middle-of-the-road position you may find yourself behaving – to your horror – more like a screaming youngest or a beleaguered oldest than you had ever thought possible. Much of your lifestyle is geared towards making sure that such a dire state of affairs never – repeat, never – comes to pass so long as you have anything to say in the matter. You prefer to file away your grievances and hope that they won't lead to an emotional outburst. Generally speaking, you seldom forgive and you *never* forget. The explanation for your stiff upper lip and holding of grudges lies in the fact that your capacity to be different from the rest of your family made you look like a radical in their eyes. But, like most adolescents, who also put all their eggs in the one basket of peer-group approval, you have a lifelong need to fit in so far as your age mates are concerned. In their company you tend to run with the pack, to make sure that nothing you do or say will ever make you an outsider in *their* eyes.

Children in a family have a way of staking out territories for themselves with a tacit agreement not to trespass across the carefully defined boundaries. Thus one child may become the Family Musician, another the Family Athlete, another the Student, another the Comedian, etc. But sometimes this can be very damaging, as when one or another becomes the Dumbbell, the Oddball, the Misfit, the Black Sheep, etc. Owing to a very human tendency to see everything as either black or white, such designations tend to be polar opposites in nature and to get attached to the two opposites already there – oldest and youngest. If the oldest child is a bookworm, the youngest must become an athlete or whatever the particular family sees as diametrically opposite to studious. When it comes to you – the middle child – they often draw a blank or else fall back upon titles which have a distinctly negative quality; the Enigma, the Outsider, the Loner, etc. This helps to account for your lack of family loyalty, and for your persistent peer loyalty.

Questioning family values is par for the course during our teen years; few children between the ages of twelve and eighteen give much of a fig about the feelings or opinions of adult family members – it's the feedback from peers which carries the day. Then, at some point (usually prior to age thirty) a compromise is worked out whereby both forces get into some degree of balance, and we then use our family values along with our own experience to structure and deal with the world. In your case this compromise phase is apt to get postponed – perhaps throughout your entire lifetime. It's as though you decided to quit the family circle and its views at an age when most children are still very dependent upon their relatives for emotional support and guidance. We don't doubt that the capacity to outgrow one's family is a major cornerstone of genuine adulthood – nor do we doubt that your capacity to make your way in the larger world before your sibs dared to venture out constitutes a unique strength. This strength, incidentally, is characteristic of your birth order and yours alone. But to outgrow something carries the implication of a *productive transition* from one state of being to another which offers greater freedom and helps provide opportunities for self-fulfillment. Your abandonment of your family was probably just that – an abandonment; in a sense, a quitting of the field and you may not have quite outgrown the hurt that prompted it. It's as though you are saying, 'I'll never quite forgive you for the noncitizenship which you imposed on me.' It is this lingering resentment more than anything else which contributes to your quick readiness to righteous rage, the short fuse mentioned earlier which can sometimes affect your social relationships outside of the family.

Your youthful exodus from the family, however, has given you some advantages not enjoyed by many people in other ordinal positions. The ability to contact others on an easygoing and informal basis makes you a comfortable person to be with in any situation which is not emotionally laden. You are an enthusiastic team member. What's more, your freedom from the kind of dependent neediness that so many of your peers wallow around in confers upon you an aura of romantic and sexual charisma which others find to be quite magnetic. Emotional independence is, after all, a rare commodity in our world, and most people gravitate toward you as an embodiment of this enviable asset.

Although you'd sooner die than openly admit it, you are very prone to embarrassment. Able as you are to deliberately violate conventional standards, you don't want to make any clumsy moves which others could attribute to stupidity or lack of sophistication on your part. Although you may feel free to overdress or underdress where you work, you would feel more humiliated than most people if you (or anyone intimately associated with you) were to publicly slip up on a matter of ritual – whether it be a wedding, funeral, graduation, initiation, or other ceremony. You tend to be a stickler for the rules once you have entered a given arena, and while you are able to interpret them to your own advantage, you make it your job to know the rule book forward and backward. For this reason people in your birth order are frequently effective lawyers and union reps, and you function well in any milieu where the bylaws are clearly spelled out.

Getting back to your romantic life. It is our observation that despite your reputation for experimentation in this area, you are probably the most basically monogamous of all birth orders. Like the only child, once you settle in with a love partner, it is usually for keeps. Friends, relatives, and acquaintances may be skeptical, but you almost always surprise them. Meanwhile, whatever may be unpleasant about the partnership in your view will never get known beyond your own doorstep. Living with another person is not something you take lightly – popular rumor to the contrary. Once you decide to set up housekeeping with someone, it's pretty certain that you have checked it out diligently beforehand and have a clear picture of whom and what you are getting involved with. It is part of your 'burned child' experience to be very cautious when it comes to anything which resembles a close, ongoing involvement.

Forming an intimate family of your own devising has, more often than not, been a dream of yours since early childhood. Like most ideals which are formed at that time, however, this particular one may produce in you a low tolerance for anything in that family setup which runs counter to your way of doing things. You may not be aware of it consciously, but you tend to be overly touchy in matters of interpersonal conflict when it comes to persons whose loyalty is important to you. Put another way, you are inclined to regard any disagreement as a betrayal of your trust, and to deal with it accordingly. You have, that is, a penchant for picking up your marbles and quitting the game when things are not to your liking. Here again, you go on your way with never a backward glance.

We've talked about your being a 'burned child.' It seems to be at the root of your unusual ability to compartmentalize your close relationships more skillfully than most people. You hedge your bets, as it were, by keeping the various facets of your life separate – along with the people that go with them. Thus your personal lifespace may include a close friend, a relative, a central love partner, a favored child – but you are likely to keep each in ignorance of exactly what the others mean to you. This is the way you want things, and those closest to you know from experience that it would be an exercise in sheer futility to ask questions or otherwise attempt to infringe your privacy.

You long ago decided to be the center of your own adult environment. You did not relish taking third (or fourth or fifth) place in your childhood family, and you don't expect to repeat the experience in your own bailiwick. Consequently you carefully maintain the upper hand wherever possible, and you discourage any challenge to your ascendancy. When you are not in a position of outright command, you tend to keep a low profile, to camouflage yourself by fading into the woodwork. At such times other people hardly know you are there, but in all likelihood you are very much there – quietly doing your homework and biding your time until the day when you suddenly come into your own and people have to recognize that you have carved out a clearly defined place for yourself in their world.

As a parent, teacher, or supervisor you generally display a fine gift for being patient and tolerant towards the weaknesses and limitations of those under you. (The fact that you are not inclined to put up with much back talk from your family and close associates has nothing to do with the forbearance you are able to exercise in other departments.) You rarely show impatience in your treatment of subordinates or those less capable than yourself – provided, of course, that they show no signs of trying to steal your thunder; you will not put up with anything which you perceive as phoniness or one-upmanship. Otherwise *noblesse oblige* is your preferred style.

Childhood is, at best, a very perplexing and ambiguous experience. As we point out elsewhere in this book, it is no easy job for a child to sort out the avalanche of data with which he or she is inundated each and every day of each and every year. Even so, most of us manage – sooner or later, for better or for worse – to find some sort of niche for ourselves in the family scheme of things. You alone of all birth orders are subject to more than your own fair share of childhood's confusion and pangs. While we have tried to point out that you probably reaped some advantages which accrue to the status of oldest and youngest in the pecking order, we are keenly aware of the fact that by and large the debits far outweighed the credits. Whatever you have been able to acquire for yourself in this life is the result of your persistence in the face of adversity and confusion. You make good use of your capacity to keep your eye on the ball while walking a high wire without looking up or down or sideways.

We would suggest, however, that when you have achieved your major objectives it might be a good time for taking a backward glance, so as to digest your past experience in the light of your present-day knowledge and awareness. You will find that, just as you have grown and changed, so have all the others who took the same long march away from childhood. People do take you seriously – as they always did, believe it or not – so that there is no realistic necessity for you to regard life as a potential battle between those who zap other people and those who get zapped. There is more room for mutual charity and reciprocal give-and-take than your upbringing prepared you for.

Finally, owing to your early experience with your peer group, you middle children often wind up having a curious combination of social awareness: you are anxious to do the polished and proper thing and at the same time are obtuse about some of the more mundane amenities of day-to-day living. A middle child who does not care for pepper, for example, may neglect to make sure that pepper is available for visitors and dinner guests. Or, if you prefer tea to coffee the chances are that the second beverage will be tacitly banned from your household. Even though you are not known for excesses of empathy or generosity, you are nevertheless apt to be the most popular of all ordinal positions – well liked, attractive, and sexy – and while there are many who consider middle child to be the least fortunate of birth orders, one must admit that it does have its compensations!

CHAPTER EIGHT

Youngest Child – General Observations

Your birth order is characterized by a burning desire to make an important contribution to the world you live in. Accustomed as you were to having your opinions treated with less respect than those of your sibs – or so you felt – one of your most cherished fantasies is to experience the exhilaration that comes with applause and public acclaim. Not only are you inclined to make backbreaking efforts to reach this goal, but you are also often outraged when you think your exertions are not sufficiently appreciated. By the same token, you tend to be a pushover for praise in any form. As many of your elders have long ago figured out, even a minimal pat on the head (not to mention 'We're all counting on you!') is enough to inspire a redoubling of effort on your part. It is our considered opinion that the legendary Sisyphus was in all probability a last-born who was busily rolling a stone up a hill again and again and again long before he started doing it in Hades. For this reason it is very difficult – once you've started rolling – for you to know when to quit. If, for instance, you paint a picture, somebody has to hit you over the head when it's done – so that you won't go on and on, far beyond the stopping point. Ditto when you write books, articles, music, or stories; the final sentence is never finished. If you undertake to remodel a house, the last nail never gets hammered in.

Most youngest children are engaging show-offs who have a rare gift for enjoying the limelight. Unlike the only child, however, you have a much more alert sense of audience reaction, and are able to make a graceful exit when your time begins to run out. What kind of attention you reach out for is an important consideration, and depends on your conditioning. Some last-borns become very adept at charming the world in various ways, while others grow up with a feeling that the only way they can gain anybody's attention is by making a mess; by being a problem child or a pest or a rebel who enjoys sticking a tongue out at the Council. If you are a typical last-born, you have a fair share of both the charmer and the rebel in your make-up, and other people are often caught off guard by the fact that you can be endearing one minute, and hard to deal with the next.

Another aspect of this two-sided element in your nature resides in the fact that you can cherish a deeply felt yearning for full membership in 'the club' (be it professional organization, social club, honorary society, political party, or whatever), but once you have gained admittance it's not at all unlike you to find some reason for resigning – usually in a fit of impatience or annoyance. Sometimes it looks almost as though you're saying 'You made me work so hard to get in: now it's my turn to put you in your place.' Again, you are more likely to behave this way when you feel that your contribution is either being criticized or not recognized sufficiently.

This duality is so central to your make-up that it deserves further elaboration. You will probably let yourself recognize at least some of its manifestations because you have developed the habit of introspection, owing to the fact that the world presented a far more confusing picture to you than it did to youngsters at the first-born end of the scale. In the vocational arena, for instance, you may feel like God's gift to your employer and fellow workers one day and like a hopeless loser the next. In the romantic/sexual sphere you may see yourself as Helen of Troy or Casanova on one occasion and a total flop on the next – even with the same partner. Or a powerhouse of energy at one moment and a stretcher case the next. You get the picture; your existence is a kind of seesaw, and nobody is more puzzled or more distressed by this trend than you yourself are.

Life is more of a kaleidoscope for you than it is for any other ordinal position, but there is one very essential remedy which you – like anybody else who has this problem – can build into your life: namely, establishing a set of modest but regular routines. By this we mean such things as retiring and getting up pretty much at the same hour every day (except weekends and holidays, of course). Or fairly regular eating hours; whether you have three conventional meals a day or prefer to 'nosh,' it helps to set fairly regular times for such activity. Ditto for such matters as balancing your finances, performing regular household tasks, renewing your driver's license, changing the goldfish water, getting a twice-yearly dental checkup, watering your plants, writing personal letters, etc. Such routines are especially helpful during emotional crises – unemployment, the breakup of a love affair, the severe illness or death of a loved one. In this way you can build into your life certain stable and relatively unchanging structures which will go far toward offsetting the ebb and flow of what the Japanese, who are keenly aware of how essential these quiet 'rituals' can be to one's physical, emotional, and spiritual wellbeing, refer to as the 'floating world' of everyday life.

Another important area where you, as the youngest child, probably had difficulty is what we might call 'information processing.' We learn about the world by comparing our own perceptions of it with those of other people. We learn what to notice and what to ignore, we learn how to group things and how to distinguish them. It's a lifelong process which all people share in common. It can be a process charged with great excitement or poetic insight, as when a parent finds a novel method for explaining certain feelings to a child, or the child describes his or her own world in a fresh way. But the basic fact of the matter is that this business of processing is of extraordinary importance – for every child's ultimate development is at the mercy of the feedback that he or she receives from the world.

It is one of the ironies of human existence that we make so many long-term decisions about the nature of the universe and our place in it at a stage of development when we have neither the wisdom nor the experience to make such decisions. A child learns a lot of useful information about how to prosper and survive from his interactions with others, but he also acquires a lot of *mis*information. As a youngest child you acquired a lot of your misinformation from other children. An only child or an oldest child usually feels more free to check out his or her perceptions – whatever their source – with parents or other significant adults. A youngest child, however, is apt to check with siblings whose pronouncements about the nature of things are often precise, comprehensive, authoritative – and absolutely incorrect.

Sometimes a child's accurate perceptions are not validated by others or may be actually denied. 'What do you mean Aunt Ethel doesn't like you?' an adult will exclaim. 'Of *course* she likes you! Didn't she give you that beautiful book for your birthday?' And the child's very astute appraisal that Aunt Ethel is the nastiest old biddy in six counties is totally denied while he or she is brainwashed into viewing her as a paragon of sweetness and loving kindness. When accurate perceptions are denied often enough, a child may well begin to doubt his or her own ability to make valid judgments.

It is not only your perception of current events that may have been invalidated, but your memory of past events as well. Adults do not at all view the world in the same way that most children do – although our development from child to grown up is such that we ourselves don't realize how differently we saw life then from the way we see it now. For a child in the first form, a sixth former is up there with the adults – almost fully grown up; while for a college student a sixth former is scarcely distinguishable from a third former.

This being so, you may have remembered the dog next door – the one whose barking scared you so much – as being enormous. 'Tush, tush,' says your mother. 'Why that was a little cocker spaniel, and you and he were the greatest of friends. You used to pet him all the time.' Your older siblings almost invariably follow the parental example in denying the validity of your memories – not realizing that for you it may have been the first experience of getting to know a dog (or going to the circus, or going to the beach, or whatever).

Sad to relate, it is often the youngest child who is ridiculed and put down for not seeing things precisely as others do. You might recall how your continued belief in Santa Claus or the Tooth Fairy evoked the exchange of winks and knowing glances among your siblings. Or the giggles that started when you innocently expressed a truth of the second form that was considered old hat by the family fourth and fifth formers.

Parents, alas, often lose patience with their younger children. Mothers and fathers who have explained the workings of shoelaces, or the need for personal hygiene to three of their offspring may become impatient at having to explain these matters to a fourth or fifth child. And the youngest may be so often asked 'What's wrong with you?' or so often told 'You're crazy!' that he or she finally begins to worry about in fact being crazy.

Having been at the bottom of the totem pole, you are most apt to have this experience of doubting the validity of your perceptions because you never had the experience of seeing a younger sibling going through the same process of naiveté-clarification-understanding which helps make personal experience more acceptable and puts many things into perspective.

You may have been a youngest child who dared to ask aloud 'Am I crazy?' You can remember (we hope) the relief you felt when the answer came back 'Of course not! *Everybody* feels that way sometimes.' However, if you were not one of these lucky children, but went on wondering about your ability to see the world as others purported to see it, you had two opinions. You could keep on checking it out until you found a kindred spirit, or you could clam up and spend a lifetime bedeviled by private fears regarding your ability to separate illusion from reality. Last-borns as a group tend to suffer serious doubts about their ability to solve problems rationally.

Like so many things in life, this common fantasy about somehow being out of step in one's thinking assumes different forms and different degrees of intensity across cultures, personality types, and groups (in this case, ordinal positions). This being so, we have observed that when singletons worry about it they keep their fingers crossed and hope for the best (because their characteristic self-confidence allows them the benefit of the doubt), middle children seek refuge in obtaining affirmation and reassurance from peers outside the family circle, and last-borns are often subject to excruciating episodes of disorientation and self-doubt. When and if this happens to you, our suggestion is that you take a leaf from the middle child's book and ask as many people as you can, 'Have you ever had the kind of thoughts and feelings that I'm describing to you? Because right now I'm feeling very much alone in what I'm experiencing and I'm in a lot of pain about it.' This will help you feel much less isolated and we're confident that if you ask enough people, you'll soon find that you aren't so alone after all.

Another sad fact of the youngest child's life is that you may have received more than your share of blame for all sorts of mishaps. Older siblings often figure that if they blame something on you, they will escape the consequences and you will be spared, too, because you are just the baby who doesn't know any better. If too much of this goes uncorrected, your sense of truth and reality may become shaky or you may have grown up feeling exempt from serious criticism, and thus not well prepared to be held accountable for your conduct in the world. If this was the case you may have come across to others as a temperamental and touchy spoiled brat. You know, and we know, that you were more confused than anything else.

In some families, however, the baby does get blamed for the misdeeds of others. What is more, as youngest child you generally suffer from the lifelong belief that everyone else was born into this world with all the heavy ammunition while you had none at all. You always seemed to be the only one in the family to misunderstand instructions, misperceive events, and to never know the score. As a result, you tend to be very skilled at two characteristic techniques of defense. One is sheer denial. Having been told so often that you were in the wrong, you are more expert than you probably think when it comes to putting others in the wrong – denying the truth of any assertion they might make which you are in an unassailable position to contradict. For example, you might say, 'No, my friend, we definitely agreed to meet at your place, *not* mine,' and even if that turned out not to be the case, people might find it easier to pick up Mount Ararat and cast it into the sea than make you budge from your position.

You also learned how to sniff out the faulty logic in other family members' thinking and to become quite Jesuitical in your justifications of your own conduct. You probably became skilled at a very tender age in the use of examination and cross-examination in your quest for the rule of justice, law, and reasonableness. When you find yourself in a corner, however, a kind of desperation can take over, as though you *must* win the battle, just for once. For you, once you've thrown your hat into the ring, any admission about being in the wrong constitutes a confession of inadequacy which you find very hard to bear.

Of course, the reality of the matter is that you have as much right to make mistakes or be in the wrong as anybody else. If you can learn to accept this, you may well be able to extricate yourself from those narrow corners before you've pinned yourself into them.

When it comes to anything involving your personal privacy, *ambivalence* is the watchword as it is in so many other areas of your life. You are more accustomed than other birth orders to having your personal space invaded with impunity, so you are far more candid than most people – one of your most engaging qualities. At the same time you know almost as well as middle children how to keep a secret once you have determined to do so. Consequently you can be an extremely adroit liar when you put your mind to it. The only hitch is that your fibs tend to be somewhat on the colorful side, a bit over elaborate (unlike those of the only child who managed to acquire a much more glib tongue). And you fear ultimate exposure, so the price you pay for your prevarications is very stressful indeed. Small wonder that you most often opt for total and complete honesty in all of your dealings. There isn't the slightest doubt in our minds that the little child in the fable who loudly proclaimed the legendary emperor's nakedness was a last-born.

Children in your ordinal position often show a devilish propensity for hurling a well-aimed dart at the Achilles heel of their elders. We've done no research on the subject, but we would be willing to bet that the majority of redoubtable critics in literature, music, theatre, art, television, etc., are youngest children (unless, of course, these critics are singletons who, as we have previously noted, 'do not suffer fools gladly nor hardly anyone else at all'). Owing to the fact that, deep down, you never expect to have your opinions taken seriously by the world, your tongue is a lot more acerbic than you think, so that you are seldom aware of your very unusual capacity to hurt people's feelings profoundly and cuttingly. And that's something of which you need to be more aware.

A most engaging quality of yours – on the credit side of your ledger – is that you are often endowed with a rollicking sense of humor which may take the form of clowning. We have mentioned your propensity for twisting the lion's tail in a manner that doesn't always have the approval of others. The obverse side of the coin is your special talent for inventing devastatingly funny parodies aimed at the Council and any other establishment. Satire and parody are apt to be your forte which, when combined with your gift for mimicry, can have a roomful of people in stitches. Must we remind you that your apprenticeship began during early childhood in the form of outrageous public shenanigans aimed at embarrassing your more sober and dignified elder siblings? Probably not; such incidents constitute your most cherished and delicious childhood recollections, and you delight in replaying them in adult form whenever you get a chance (which is however often you wish).

You seesaw between high energy and paralysis; goal-directedness and procrastination; overconfidence and discouragement; honesty and prevarication; desire for acceptance and iconoclastic nose-thumbing; and so on. You deal with this by means of a pronounced 'all or nothing' approach to life. It is easy for you to conclude that life is cheating and depriving you – or else deliberately discriminating against you and treating your needs with cruelty and contempt. At such times it is easy for you to roll around in mountainous waves of self-pity or self-condemnation – a very depressing state of affairs which may even give rise to a 'what's the use of living?' attitude.

The important thing to realize if you find yourself with those feelings is that underneath your despondency is a considerable amount of rage. So if, at such times, you can possibly accept the 'furious child' in yourself and allow yourself to feel that anger, your depression will probably lift. (This is generally true of depression for anyone, by the way.) But when trying to get in touch with your submerged anger, there is a basic rule which must be observed in the struggle to obtain relief: don't search out a righteous, noble, or self-justifying reason for your anger. Look instead for a resentment which you are reluctant to acknowledge in yourself – because it seems to you petty, or evil, or unfair, or ungrateful, embarrassing, *or* (and this is particularly important for last-borns) because you are afraid that your anger won't have any clout in the world, and you are convinced that if you express it you'll wind up dying of humiliation. This is what Albert Ellis calls 'catastrophizing.' First-borns are often specialists in *weltschmerz* catastrophizing (a kind of abstract depression about the sad state of the world and one's personal 'responsibility' with regard to it), but you last-borns are given to a more personal kind of despair, usually with a greater inclination to blame others rather than yourselves for whatever is tormenting you.

While it may have been unpleasant to feel that you were under perpetual surveillance by the big people in your environment, you may have reaped a definite advantage from this particular state of affairs: that is, a certain sense of invisible protection. The same family members who took delight in revealing at the dining table something about you that you had thought was completely private were also quite likely to materialize (seemingly out of nowhere) at your moments of direst need – when you were about to toddle across a busy thoroughfare or taste a bottle of cleaning fluid or had got yourself trapped in a patch of brambles. This side of the 'goldfish bowl' equation imparts to you a certain curiosity and predilection for exploring – a trait generally shared by no other ordinal position except that of the many-faceted only child. Your brand of exploration tends to be physical and geographical – involving unfamiliar neighborhoods, countries, continents, bodily and spiritual experiences, and the like. You often rush in where more timid souls fear to tread, without the slightest fear of getting lost which plagues so many people.

At the same time you are more likely than other birth orders to have experienced what we call a 'Dump the baby' syndrome – repeated experiences in which older children put their bikes, roller skates, sneakers or whatever into high gear with the sole purpose of leaving you far behind; in short, abandoning you. The upshot of these two trends is that you're apt to be a combination of diametrically opposed postures: on the one hand you can be a trailblazer who is totally without fear of getting physically lost while on the other hand you are extremely vulnerable to anything which looks as though other people are intent upon ditching you – leaving you in limbo, in the lurch, and emotionally lost. To put it another way, you have a tendency to feel that yours is a charmed existence while at the same time living in constant dread that all those near and dear to you (especially lovers) may at any moment abandon you. We have no way of knowing his birth order, but Solon the Lawgiver has been quoted as saying that 'Life is never so good and never so bad that it cannot reverse itself with a single turn of Fortune's wheel, and at a moment's notice.' In other words, your existence is neither a charmed one nor is it doomed to the pain of ultimate abandonment and isolation and lostness.

A last word about a special breed of youngest child – one born eight or more years after your parents have come to believe that they had changed their last diaper and purchased their last jar of baby food. While everybody may have seen you as the youngest in your family, what with sibs so much older than yourself you were also to all intents and purposes an only child, with all of the advantages and disadvantages discussed in Chapter 1 – and a few more to boot. A question arises with regard to the circumstances which brought you into the world. There's probably no need to remind you that you're popularly known as a 'change-of-life baby' – i.e., a child born when your mother (and, yes – perhaps even your father) was entering that difficult period of midlife crisis. Although it's possible that some women may stand a greater chance of becoming pregnant at this time in their lives, others may experience a sudden wish to have one more child before their child-bearing years are over.

There is the possibility that your parents, believing (with the onset of menopause) that your mother had passed beyond any likelihood of pregnancy, had dispensed with whatever birth control method they had been using up until then. In which case you were indeed an 'accident,' and may well have been told as much throughout your childhood. However, you may have had the good fortune to stand as a living testimonial to a rekindling of your parents' love for one another – in which case your birth was probably greeted with enthusiasm and joy. Accidents of this sort, however, are rather more apt to be treated as disasters. If this was so in your case, you undoubtedly spent your childhood either playing the role of the unexpected stroke of misfortune, or leaning over backwards in a lifelong effort to avoid further displeasing or inconveniencing anyone.

If you were this kind of youngest child/singleton, you could be said to have had siblings – of a sort – but whatever their number, their role was more that of ancillary parents. Although they may have helped you with your homework, they also took it upon themselves to monitor your behavior and to see that you did as you were told, meting out reward or punishment with that sure knowledge of right and wrong which so often characterizes older brothers and sisters. One sibling (whether male or female) may have taken on the role of the parent who intervened between you and the playground bully, and another may have taught you how to bowl. But chances are that one or another of these 'grownups' (for a child under age six, that means anyone over age fourteen) considered you a pest or a burden. If one or more of your sibs was a teenager, it's almost a sure bet that your arrival was seen as a mortifying public advertisement of your parents' continuing sexual activity.

In sum, it is quite possible that you were welcomed, bossed around, coddled, adored, and disliked – all at once. Whether or not you responded with self-assertion or with self-effacement, one characteristic that typifies this particular birth order is an unusual amount of confusion as to what kind of person you really are. Such a state of puzzlement is also frequently encountered in the only child of divorced or separated parents, and for the same reason – contradictory feedback from various adults and near-adults in the environment. To be sure, children who grow up with brothers and sisters near their own age get plenty of feedback, but they learn to shrug it off; something much more difficult to do when the judgments come from adult figures in your life. You must bear in mind that when you were around age seven (the age when most youngsters begin the lifelong process of asking themselves 'What kind of person am I? – who is this Me?') your sibs were in their teens or older. Due to the fact that you perceived them as grownups, you were in no position to sift the perplexing array of opinions which came at you from all sides and threatened to overwhelm you. By 'opinions' we don't simply mean verbal material; some of the most striking things we learn about ourselves during childhood are gleaned from the ways in which other people respond (or fail to respond) to us. Remember what we have said previously – that singletons grow up in a kind of goldfish bowl. Never was this more true than in the case of the youngest/singleton child. Your bowl was lined, metaphorically speaking, with those distorted mirrors one occasionally sees at carnivals – each giving back a different (and sometimes grotesque) image of a Short You, a Tall You, a Fat You, a Skinny You, etc. Consequently you are in need of accurate feedback which will give you a more stable self-image. Well, if it's any comfort to you, all of us have this difficulty. Where you get into trouble is that you've grown accustomed to assuming that other people's perceptions of you are always valid. Once you give yourself the right to consider the source, you will learn to take other people's opinions with a grain (no, handful) of salt. Meanwhile, don't give up hope and don't stop looking – the real you is bound to emerge sooner or later.

CHAPTER NINE

Youngest Girl

Your ordinal position has a special distinction: people from large families are likely to hold opinions about it which are both firmly entrenched and emotionally biased. (The same is true for your male counterpart but to a somewhat lesser extent.) People who have never given a thought to the subject of birth order (and their number is legion, we can assure you) will often wax eloquent about yours. You win the Blue Ribbon when it comes to the sobriquets with which others refer to you – e.g., Baby-doll, Tiddler, Pip Squeak, Muffin, Little Brat, and so forth. You are rarely (if ever) the subject of dispassionate contemplation. You are very apt to have been either spoiled, or else teased, tormented, and otherwise made to feel inferior. Sometimes both occurred as one or both of your parents spoiled you, and your siblings got even by harassing you in secret but effective ways.

Neither alternative bodes well for your developing into the kind of adult woman who can confidently conquer her problems. Because it so happens that being 'spoiled' and being 'scapegoated' add up to precisely the same thing: *deprivation*. It is impossible for us, when a client comes for an initial consultation, to determine whether or not we are dealing with a case of outrageous childhood overindulgence or (equally outrageous) emotional starvation. The human outcomes in both situations are surprisingly similar. Both kinds of treatment produce a person who has low tolerance for frustration and a pretty unrealistic conception of their own and other people's rights, boundaries, limitations, and true capacities; a person who wants to possess the world with a little gold fence around it – the spoiled child because she has almost always got her own way, and the deprived child because in many respects she has almost never got her own way.

In the next chapter we speak of the youngest boy's extremism, and the words we use for the various opposing tendencies in his personality – the polarities – are largely words that describe behavior. The terms which one might use for describing your polarities – your extremes – are most apt to be emotion words that have to do with your way of perceiving and/or experiencing things. Self-doubt/grandiosity, subjectivity/objectivity, meekness/haughtiness, acceptance/demandingness, introspection/externalization, etc. You seem to fall at one end or the other of each spectrum with no nuances of shading in between. It goes without saying that you may have grown up under such fortunate circumstances that you are less prone to extremes than most of your co-ordinals, but we think that there are probably at least some areas in your life where the emotional extravagance of your birth order shows itself.

Before we say another word, however, we would like to reassure you that there is much to be said in favor of emotional extremism – its intensity, for one thing. Even if you are at the introversive, self-doubting end of the emotional spectrum you will have to admit that you are not wishy-washy about it. In short, you give everything your all. Deep down you are rarely neutral about anything. No need to tell you that your intensity is a double-edged sword: the painful side is the depth of your suffering when you are unhappy, but your capacity to experience joy and ecstasy is a rare gift, which you are all too prone to underrate. The delights which we accumulate in the course of life are what stand us in good stead when the going gets rough – if we can only stop agonizing long enough to realize it. Your tendency to dramatize setbacks while forgetting your triumphs is something you need to guard against.

Nowhere are your polarities more evident than in the social sphere – where you may be either the life and soul of the party or a wallflower; sex pot or prude; chatterbox or bump-on-a-log. Whichever way you jump, you generally don't do it by halves. Moreover, you are inclined to do your own thing, not trusting yourself to accurately evaluate the feedback of others and be guided by it. For this reason, you often remain single longer than other birth orders, either maintaining your own home or perhaps living with a married sib – usually a sister and her husband.

First let's talk about the 'spoiled' aspects of your upbringing and get them out of the way before going on to other matters. For one thing, older sibs of both sexes are more likely to parent a youngest girl than a youngest boy, and, as we have pointed out elsewhere, a child's idea of caretaking can often leave much to be desired. *Exhibit A:* pushing you in your baby carriage along the sidewalk at breakneck speed under the pretext of giving you a thrill, while you screamed in terror. *Exhibit B:* letting your temper tantrums carry the day because you were 'so cute' when your face turned blue with fury. *Exhibit C:* giving you everything you wanted or asked for because your sibs wished that your parents had indulged them in like fashion – i.e., they were acting out a youngster's notion of what it means to be a 'good' parent (always saying yes and never saying no).

Add to the above their tendency to button your clothes for you, carry you up and down stairs, bathe you, dress you, play doctor or nurse with you (as though you were one of those plastic dummies that first aid students practice on in their classrooms). That is, they were likely to do whatever they pleased with you when your parents' backs were turned – which in a large family can be pretty often.

Like your male counterpart, you often got things wrong and lost your belongings, but he was usually berated for his dawdling and ineptness on the assumption that such scolding would, in the long run, help him along the road to self-sufficient adult malehood. The road staked out for you, on the other hand, was pointed toward the land of dependent princesshood as your environment conditioned you to expect that others would be always eager to service your every whim.

Most damaging of all to your future welfare was the way in which your family may have permitted you to get away with various behaviors which they would never have tolerated in any of your older siblings – telling lies, for example, or tattling, or playing spiteful tricks. All very endearing in the bosom of your family, perhaps, but considered reprehensible in the larger world of adults. When a small child is allowed to practice deceit, the boundaries between truth and reality become seriously blurred. The child becomes conditioned to feel that she or he can manipulate those boundaries at will, and then comes to believe that 'truth' belongs to whoever wins the power struggle, that is, to whoever can shout the loudest or be the most intimidating. Once this belief is established, guiding principles become confused and chaotic so that your self-image (the ability to size yourself up and to take your own measurements in a number of life contexts) can get lost in the shuffle. During our early childhood years each of us is dependent upon those around us for the feedback necessary in order to form a fairly valid and coherent picture of who we are. From this feedback, as we grow older, we build up rules of conduct along with our self-concept, and some capacity for seeing ourselves as others see us. If we grow up manipulating the people in our environment, however, we automatically play high, wide and handsome with our self-concept. This means that our self-evaluation fluctuates from day to day and from situation to situation, depending upon whether or not we have 'won' a particular power struggle.

This business of your image is just as crucial and emotionally loaded for you as it is for those around you. It is also subject to the very same biases referred to in the opening paragraph of this chapter. You therefore tend to see yourself as being completely one thing or completely its opposite, with no modifying ifs, ands, or buts. Consequently your emotional extremism has its greatest impact upon the ways in which you experience both yourself and the world of other people. Thus, acting on these beliefs, you are either quite skilled at getting people to do things for you, or else you are a demon do-it-yourselfer. (We know a young lady who tried to simultaneously direct, film, and act in her own movie.) Because of the fact that you grew up in a family where you were 'too young' or 'too little' or 'too clumsy' to do things for yourself, you continued to feel a sense of personal ineptness long after the age when your older sibs had become accomplished shoppers, dish-washers, room-tidiers, and errand-runners. Nobody wanted the job of seriously instructing you in how to handle money, strike a bargain, or pick out your own clothes. As a result, you can now be subject to extreme mood swings – very up when things are going your way and very down when they aren't. Bear in mind that your view of the world fluctuates accordingly; friends may be seen as dear and loyal supporters when you feel good about yourself and as downright enemies and betrayers when you're feeling deflated. These moods can affect the way you see every element in your life, from the people next door to the political party you espouse.

Your older sibs, of course, probably got a lot of satisfaction in playing parent to you as a youngster, even if they sometimes resented having to drop whatever they were doing to baby-sit or otherwise administer to your needs. If you were loved, cuddled, and cared for, you no doubt developed into a spritely and easygoing person or even a kind of Pollyanna who looks at the world through rose-colored glasses.

If, on the other hand, your family made you feel more like a burden and a bore, you may have a tendency to be an irate and somewhat paranoid Cassandra. Cassandra, you will recall, was the youngest child of the Trojan king of legend, Priam. She was always making accurate prophecies about dire happenings to come, but nobody paid the least attention to her and she felt quite desperate about it. It's not easy to grow up outclassed, outmaneuvered, and out-talked by one's elders – especially at those times when you perceive they are wrong. It always seems to you that you have to talk louder or faster or otherwise try much harder to get your point across than others do. For this reason, you may occasionally strike some people as a bit shrill or abrasive. It isn't that they don't like you or are against you, but that you often put them on the defensive to such a degree that you don't give them a chance to demonstrate their liking for you.

Such people notwithstanding, you invest your energy in a wide circle of personal acquaintances and lively friendships, desiring little in the way of material possessions. Whether your reputation is one of saintliness or cussedness, you are apt to be more widely known than most people get to be unless they are outright celebrities.

Like most youngest children, you have a way with children – provided you don't have to be with them twenty-four hours a day. This, of course, raises problems if you are a biological mother and have children of your own. As a spiritual mother (teacher, nurse, tutor, etc.), you are on much more comfortable ground and give unstintingly of your empathy and compassion. You need regular time off from being a mother in order to restore yourself and regain your perspectives.

Owing to the aforementioned compassion, you can sometimes be a pushover for a soft touch – that is, you can over-identify with anyone who gives you a sob story about how deprived and put-upon they are (the parasitic professional orphans of this world). Before you know what has hit you, you're lending them your life savings, spending hours on the phone listening to their problems and trying to rescue them from whatever tragic plight they feel trapped by – the way you wish that somebody had rescued you in your time of need.

A word which often applies to you is gullibility – one end, again, of a polarity. Here we are talking about extreme naïveté versus extreme suspicion. You can be overly trusting and, on the other hand, overly suspicious. We think this is merely two sides of the same coin. In order to protect yourself against your own tendency to be a suc..er, you subconsciously lean over backwards and tell yourself, 'Beware! Play it safe and trust nobody.' Thus you may often puzzle other people by seeming very warmhearted one moment and highly cynical and suspicious the next. Our subconscious, sadly enough, always thinks in terms of dichotomies or opposites – big versus little, all good versus all bad, black versus white, and so on. Actually, there is no substitute for learning to size up each situation on its own terms. If you do this often enough, you will eventually be able to distill a number of more realistic guiding principles which will stand you in better stead when it comes to assessing future challenges.

In line with the foregoing, you may find that you will often feel anxious and/or downright guilty when things go well for you – as though some unseen force were about to suddenly step in and punish you for it by tarnishing your success or by making you look like a pipsqueak or a fool in the eyes of the world. Our subconscious can try to sabotage our successes in this way in order to gain mastery over a fall that it considers inevitable due to the presumed ill will of an uncaring world. In a scene in the film, *The Good Earth*, Wang the peasant and his wife are proudly discussing their infant son's future when, realizing that the spirits might be listening, they immediately begin bemoaning how ill-favored and untalented the child is lest the spirits be jealous and vindictively harm their offspring. Anthropologists tell us that in many cultures it is customary to recite tales of woe to the hostile gods when one is doing well, so that they will take pity on the suppliant and leave him alone. The point is that the subconscious is shared by all races, colors, and creeds the world over. It is, moreover, very superstitious and can believe that self-denial, self-punishment – even self-destruction – will save the day.

If you expect punishment in retribution for whatever 'goodies' you garner in life, your own subconscious can often provide this for you by arranging things in such a way that you will bring down upon your own head the anticipated martyrdom and anguish. It is important to realize that other options are realistically available to you. Pain is not necessarily the most direct route to survival and emancipation, and if you can wheedle or coerce your subconscious into taking a chance, you will most likely discover that there are more pleasant – even joyful – solutions to your difficulties.

Your woes rarely appeared to be taken as seriously as those of your sibs – even though they may have been exactly the same. When they were struggling over maths problems, it was a big deal; and when they had their first 'serious' romances, everybody responded with such interest and concern that one would have thought they were straight out of *Romeo and Juliet*. But when your turn came, your maths problems were looked down upon as kid stuff and your heartaches were patronizingly dismissed as puppy love. The most painful part of all this is that, deep down, you grew up with a part of your own self which to this very day disparages your problems and denigrates your pleasures. It is not surprising, therefore, that in a desperate effort to prove the importance of these matters to yourself and the world, you can sometimes be quite melodramatic. In *Little Women*, Amy, the youngest of the four March sisters, had a distinct flair for histrionics which Louisa May Alcott (Jo) describes in a literary tone that precisely parallels the dismissive attitude of an older sibling.

If by chance you were allowed (or permitted yourself) to take your theatrical penchant seriously, you may very well have learned early that you could be a great hit as a comedienne, especially when it comes to clowning. Clowning is, after all, a very resourceful way to poke fun at all sorts of people while simultaneously poking fun at the self – thereby avoiding any discomfort. As any clown will readily admit, an audience 'can't laugh *at* you if you're laughing at yourself; their only choice is to laugh *with* you!' Not only that, but they actually adore and admire you for it. After all, a sense of humor about oneself is not generally a characteristic of the older children in a family. So, when life gets you down, it may buck you up to remember your fine sense of humor and let it come to your rescue.

As we have observed elsewhere, young boys are inclined to make friends among themselves by sharing sports, games, and other task-oriented pursuits, whereas girls are more prone to form their same-sex friendship bonds on more emotionally intimate grounds, such as the mutual exchange of secrets, hopes, and fears. (We don't mean that either sex engages in one or the other activity exclusively; only that there is a different emphasis with one sex compared with the other.) Thus, you as a female child were more keenly attuned than your male counterpart to the fact that while all the Big People seemed able to ferret out your secrets whenever they wanted to, they also managed to keep you in the dark about anything they chose to conceal from you. Consequently (although you may not want or even be able to remember it), you may have indulged a strong subconscious temptation to get even either by becoming an inveterate tell-tale or by devising roundabout ways of leaking secrets that Big People may not have realized you even knew in the first place. At the same time, you may well have acquired an abiding respect for those secrets which other people let you in on so that hell itself could freeze over before you would ever betray a confidence.

Now, this business of family secrets is a thorn in the flesh of nearly all last-borns, but it is especially trying for youngest girls whose medium of relating to others is more verbal and social than that of youngest boys. And you certainly had to develop your antennae more highly than did the older children in the family if you were to make any sense of the many veiled and whispered events in what must have seemed a most baffling environment indeed. Not surprisingly, then, of all ordinal positions yours is the most inclined toward manifestations of ESP (extra-sensory perception), such as telepathy, location of lost objects, precognition, and the like.

Owing to your characteristic lack of self-confidence regarding the validity of your perceptions, however, you are usually anxious about and distrustful of your 'spooky' hunches. You either keep them to yourself and secretly worry whether you may be going bonkers, or else you seek the support of kindred souls by joining groups – which may range anywhere from mystical cults to scientifically respectable organizations – with whom you can freely share your experiences. By this we don't mean to imply that other people lack this psychic quality – merely that their environment did not make it necessary for them to develop this rarely used capacity, whereas your early childhood bewilderment made it almost imperative for you to strengthen this particular set of 'psychic muscles.'

You can go a long way toward building self-confidence by simply keeping a written record of your various hunches and checking out the 'results' as they unfold. This should help you gain a clearer sense of which situations bring out your greatest accuracy and which are more likely to provoke distortions arising out of your own inner hopes, fears, and perceptual habits.

In fact, making lists of your real character traits can be a great aid in battling that constant sense of being basically unimportant and in making peace with the critic, the put-down artist, who resides within your own psyche. Such lists can be of infinite variety, but we will mention the six of them that experience has proved most helpful:

List No 1:   Things I know about, can feel, or can do.

List No 2:   Which ones am I *better* at than most people?

List No 3:   Which ones am I *less* good at than most people?

List No 4:   Which ones can I *improve* myself on?

List No 5:   Which ones had I better not waste my time trying to master?

List No 6:   Which of these are things that most people also give up on?

If you review these lists on a regular basis, we can almost guarantee that you will gradually acquire a more realistic and self-accepting concept of your genuine assets and human limitations. There is an old German fable about two frogs that fell into a pot of cream. One screamed and sank to the bottom while the other paddled furiously – because she couldn't think of anything else to do. Then suddenly a huge lump of butter took shape under her feet, providing a launch pad from which she was able to make a successful hop to freedom. So just keep on paddling – butter and freedom will be your ultimate reward.

CHAPTER TEN

Youngest Boy

In Ruth Draper's monologue 'The Italian Lesson,' she sends her youngest child, Billy, to fetch a newly arrived driver club and put it in Daddy's golf bag, admonishing him, 'Keep your mind on that *one thing* until you've got it done. There's a good boy; run along now.' And when Dad, on the phone a few minutes later, inquires about the driver, his wife informs him that 'I sent Billy after it. I *hope* he understood – probably broken by now.' You get the message: don't trust the Baby Boy; he's too little, too scatterbrained, too weak, too undeveloped, etc. Like your female counterpart, your first and major role in life was that of a chronic dependant who stood in need of perpetual instruction and constant caretaking. Such a state of affairs would hardly be considered conducive to the building of a self-confident adult.

And yet, strange to say, this very type of conditioning (or 'shaping' as it is called nowadays) may have greatly strengthened your capacity to eventually become a lot more independent than most people. For, unlike the youngest girl, you grew up in a world which pushes male children to stake out their lifetime occupations at an increasingly (and absurdly) early age. While girls are encouraged to seek their ultimate fulfillment in a dependent marital setup, boys in all walks of life are expected to be breadwinners and go-getters, and can become doubly self-assertive when they feel that their own initiative is being blocked by others. In addition, dependency on the part of men is universally frowned upon in Western cultures. Your choice, then, was

either to surrender and be dependent or to fight back and
be your own man.

It is important to bear in mind that much of the
conditioning and shaping of our childhood is done with
the best intentions in the world. At the same time we all
know that 'the road to Hell is paved with good intentions.'
Your older siblings meant well even when they were filling
you with false information and faulty directions for living.
As for how these things affected your formative years, we
might ask you how many times during the course of your
childhood you were earnestly entreated to pursue some
goal or other – only to have a sibling (or any older person)
suddenly appear out of nowhere exclaiming 'Oh, no, do it
this way! Isn't that easier? No, like this! Isn't that more
fun?' If that person also happened to be a slightly older
sibling, he or she may have made a rude remark or two
about your ineptness, stupidity or unteachability. Whether
rude or merely thoughtless, chances are that he or she then
took over and completed your project with what seemed
like lightning speed and breathtaking dexterity. Sometimes
your helper may, in fact, have been a very gifted teacher
from whom you acquired considerable knowledge that you
still find useful. More often, however, the frequent derailment of your goals produced in you a combination of
confusion, anger, discouragement, and what the late
Robert Benchley so aptly termed 'a voluptuous sense of
futility.' You have become known as the one who 'never
finishes anything.' Lest we appear overly simplistic, we
make haste to add that shaping has to be repeated very
frequently and consistently over a very long period of time
for it to take root and influence the developing personality
in any permanent way.

Zoologists tell us that the actual struggle to emerge from
its cocoon is itself an essential stage of a butterfly's
emancipation, and that any outside 'help' invariably proves
fatal. Youngest children – of either sex – often get the

feeling that they are not being allowed to do their own growing up but exist in a confusing world where they are being admonished to 'grow up and stop being a baby' one minute, and reminded that they're 'not old enough yet' the next. Knowing when to help and when not to help is a very delicate business which draws upon the parenting skills of adults and siblings alike. Nowhere are the stakes so high and so precarious as they are in the case of the youngest boy, whose helpers are so often only neophytes themselves; only one chapter ahead of him in what they are trying to teach. Small wonder that it's very difficult for you or others to gauge precisely when you need help and when you need to be left at liberty to hash things out on your own.

Is it any wonder, then, that you are prone to dawdle and procrastinate in the face of important undertakings? Because in the background of your awareness there is the constant fear that somebody might suddenly interrupt your private activities and, in the process of 'helping' you, somehow manage to make you feel awkward and foolish. 'Help' is a difficult issue for you for another reason as well: you may have perceived the well-meaning and truly helpful older sibs and adults of either sex as casting aspersions on your masculinity; while those who were *not* helpful seemed like betrayers or put-down artists. Chances are that you still react negatively when others try to offer you assistance.

As a result of the foregoing, you are likely to display strong contrasts between dependency and independence in your relations with the world. On the one hand you may be subject to wild panic attacks during which you rush around like Chicken Little shouting 'Help me, somebody! My sky is falling'; while on the other hand you are often able to take on gargantuan projects and carry them through to completion. Your most characteristic lifestyle oscillates between a limp kind of helplessness and astonishing demonstrations of true grit. In this respect yours is the most paradoxical of the male ordinal positions – perhaps of all birth orders. More than any other personality discussed in this book, yours is characterized by a penchant for extremes: extreme aggressiveness/extreme passivity; extreme integrity/extreme deviousness; extreme forbearance/extreme intolerance; extreme stoicism/extreme bellyaching; extreme punctuality/extreme procrastination, etc. Your relationship to the working world runs a similar course. You tend either to choose your life's work at an unusually tender age or else hop from one job to another in a pattern which may persist throughout your lifetime.

A major component of the extremism which typifies your birth order derives from the important figures of your childhood often having been divided into two opposed camps – those who overindulged you, and those who made you toe the mark with a vengeance. To be sure, each of us has known at least one youngest boy who was allowed to get away with murder because he was so endearing in his manner of going about it (or of lying about it afterwards), but our society is far more likely to tolerate overindulgence of a youngest girl than of a youngest boy. With you, the lines were probably clearly drawn between those who were overly harsh and those who were overly protective. With the first you are presented with a picture of yourself as the fly in everybody's soup – a pest and a failure. In the second instance your latent Sun King may get activated into a state of such grandiosity that it seems to you that everything you do is touched with genius. In either case it is very difficult for you to evolve a stable and usable picture of yourself as a person who is neither completely a pauper nor entirely a prince, but the inhabitant of a vast plateau (where the majority of people live) which can include some aspects of both.

You are now prone to feel dashed (the pauper) when people criticize you rightly or wrongly, and you can also become an inflated balloon of conceit (the prince) in response to a well-meant pat on the back. It therefore comes as no surprise that recognition scenes in drama and story (you know the kind – the beggar boy is suddenly revealed as the lost prince) are very dear to your heart. You long for public recognition: for the biggest reward at the lowest cost, although sometimes you are (paradoxically enough!) willing to work long and hard in order to achieve your goals.

Whatever else the world may have appeared to require of you, it did not usually expect you to be especially foresighted or responsible in the usual sense of the word. You therefore took your clues from those nearest and dearest (and most influential) to you. But, as always, your extremism shows itself; you are apt to be either extremely penurious in the management of your finances or else you may be a compulsive gambler or borrower. In like manner, you can be chronically late for appointments or else known for your strict punctuality. When your lifestyle veers to the casual side of the ledger you are prone to berate yourself for falling short of your own and other people's high standards. Conversely, when your pattern tends to strive for excellence you often have the unhappy (and untrue) conviction that you are the only person in this whole wide world who makes it his job to meet deadlines when they come due.

You are particularly prone to dawdle and dilly-dally when you have sincerely committed yourself to meet *somebody else's deadline.* You will often find yourself saying 'I promise to have it done by the end of next week' because you have an almost irresistible impulse to prove your own intrinsic worth to the world by saying '*I* can do it!' whenever volunteers are called for. We suggest that when you find yourself dragging your feet as the eleventh hour approaches, it might be helpful for you to deliberately schedule a chunk of time to indulge yourself in whatever distracts you from what you 'should' be concentrating on. We further suggest that you alternate your 'shoulds' with scheduled leisure time – as a reward for work accomplished. Most of your procrastinations boil down to one central issue – presenting the results of your endeavors to others for their evaluation. Again, your biggest fear is that you will be diminished – 'they' will criticize, sneer at, condemn, or just plain ignore your accomplishments, the way you felt your family did. Your reluctance to face such unpleasantness is quite understandable, but trying to protect yourself by dawdling is not going to solve the problem.

What you are really struggling with in all of this is your extreme vulnerability to anything less than loud praise and what the psychotherapist Carl Rogers has dubbed 'unconditional positive regard.' It is one of the sadder facts of life that the painful things which happen to us are generally easier to take than the conclusions we come to about ourselves as a result of those events. You are no exception to this rule. Behind your fear of rejection is the fear of the loud-mouthed critic deep inside yourself who will start calling you a 'failure' or worse. The best antidote to this self-denigrating tendency of yours is to try letting yourself hear the positive side of the world's response to your achievements. You may want *complete* acceptance – with no strings attached – but if you stop to think about it, you will realize that acceptance by anybody is rarely unqualified, and when it is, you can be pretty sure there is something fishy going on; that's probably the time to look for the 'strings.'

There is another element which has contributed to the formation of your tendency to procrastinate: interruption (or derailment). This has had a different effect on you than on a youngest girl, who is encouraged to engage in socially process-oriented and nurturant activities which are far more amenable to interruption than the more end-result-oriented pursuits of boys. Not only that, but girls have ample opportunity for observing the ways in which adult females must eventually learn to cope with all of the countless interruptions which take place each and every day of their lives. Boys, however, are presented with quite a different role model – that of the adult male – who is generally allowed (at least in the home) to complete his tasks with relative freedom from disruption. Given such a model (accompanied by pressures to emulate it) boys are more vulnerable than girls to the harmful effects of derailment, and few ordinals are more subject to it than you are. Needless to say, no child – whether male or female, whether first- or last-born – likes to be told to drop whatever he or she is reading (or watching on TV, or playing with in the backyard) in order to wash up for dinner, or empty the rubbish, or perform some chore 'right this minute!'

Let us interrupt *ourselves* for a moment to explain an important psychological mechanism that Alfred Adler has referred to as 'compensation' (whereby we try to make up to ourselves for our own feelings of inferiority). For example, when toddlers are learning to walk, they quite naturally fall down a lot. Most children during that stage of development enjoy building a tower of blocks and then deliberately knocking it over with great delight – as though to say, 'I fall down by accident, but this time I made it happen on purpose (and so I am now in control of the Falling Experience; I am the Boss). Hurray for me!' In like manner, a much-disrupted and frequently interrupted youngest boy may acquire a compensatory habit pattern of unconsciously interrupting himself. And that constitutes a major part of what procrastination is all about. The main point here is that in our society each boy is expected to grow into a man whose entire status and security rests upon his capacity to formulate and pursue with relentless singlemindedness a long-range goal, so you can see how important this aspect is. At the other extreme, by the way, is a capacity for dogged concentration unequaled by other ordinal positions.

Meanwhile the effects of either your self-doubt or your unusual self-assertion can show up in many areas of life, from the way you take care of your wardrobe to the degree of intensity with which you relate to a love partner. The most difficult thing for you to achieve is a *balanced appreciation* of your own solid achievements; a certain objectivity which neither inflates nor derogates them. Just because you aren't a genius or superstar doesn't mean that you're the insignificant tiddler your sibs may have treated you as. Once you succeed in working this problem through, however, you tend to be a real self-starter whose tenacity is rivaled only by that which is customarily attributed to first-borns.

An outright bid for power in the world of wheeling and dealing is not apt to be your style in life because (although you may secretly wish to take over and run the entire show according to your own lights) there is another part of you which fears being shown up as inept. Consequently you are most apt to outwardly thumb your nose at vested authority while inwardly knocking yourself out to render service beyond the call of duty. Your secret hope in this case is that your considerable contribution will eventually be publicly recognized and receive the full credit which you believe to be its due. When the recognition you seek is not forth-coming in the manner which you have envisioned, your nose can get very out of joint.

You are not always as forthright as you think you are when it comes to saying what you really want, so you can often come across to other people as querulous and tiresomely repetitive. You have, unfortunately, been con-ditioned to believe that *nobody* listens to you or hears a single thing you have to say – especially if it's in the nature of a complaint. 'Crybaby!' is a frequent jibe aimed at last-borns by their elder sibs. As a result it requires a great effort of will for you to state your case in the calm and well-modulated tones which the world of your elders (and your own better judgment) seems to call for. And rest assured that in any group situation you tend to regard all those present as your 'elders' – even persons much younger than yourself.

As the youngest in your family you no doubt believed that everybody around you was born knowing how to swim; only you had to go through the laborious business of learning how to do things. You may even have found the process humiliating because it's one thing to fall down on your face in private and quite another to do it when, as the youngest child, you feel that the entire world is looking on. And, alas, even when the entire world is kind enough not to snigger at your ineptness, you will suffer from your own unflattering comparison between Clumsy Me and all those Competent Others who never seem to fall down at all. You could not see, from your perspective, that your older sibling had as tough a time learning as *you* did. Your older brother might have been in despair at his inability to learn algebra, but the very fact that he was studying a branch of mathematics which you could not understand even when it was explained in the simplest terms made him seem light-years ahead of you. Because of all the suffering that went along with acquiring skills, you are apt to be a very patient and understanding teacher who has a special compassion for 'slow learners,' and you help them along in very creative and supportive ways.

You did, however, find some ways to learn without having to ask or entreat your 'elders' for help. For you above all other birth orders tend to be a self-teacher who prefers to learn skills almost secretly – through books, experimentation, private instruction, etc. – rather than taking formal courses in classrooms which you imagine to be teeming with all those 'elders.' Again, in a spirit of table-turning, you now imply to a startled world that your newly acquired expertise was 'always there' – almost as though you were born with it.

Generally speaking, your social relations are marked by a characteristically ambivalent combination of sunny gregariousness and an almost truculent aloofness. As in most areas of living, you grew up with more than your share of instructions when it came to what might be called 'public relations' – i.e., 'say hello to so-and-so, dear.' 'Keep your hands to yourself at Aunt Jane's – don't meddle, or handle things' (the implication is that you will surely smash them – a fate to which your sibs appeared to have been immune). And so on. As a consequence, you may enjoy very large and festive public occasions, but when it comes to people whom you know personally, you prefer to be in small cozy groups – especially when you are the host, or otherwise pretty much the center of attention.

In the romantic and sexual sphere there doesn't seem to be any discernible pattern – except the usual extremes. By which we mean that you are either dedicatedly monogamous or else a free-wheeling swinger; a passionate satyr or a shy violet who is plagued by real or imagined concerns about impotence. Whatever the case may be, you are inclined to react to it with a great deal of intensity – whether private or shared (another one of your dichotomies). There are, however, no ifs, ands, or buts when it comes to your penchant for becoming passionately involved; with you it's all or nothing. You are either a giver or a taker; a supporter or a supportee; a lover or a beloved, etc. For you there is almost never a genuinely reciprocal relationship. All of your eggs are in one basket, or all of your partner's are in yours. Your love life is, therefore, apt

to be quite stormy and filled with heartbreak longer than
that of most other birth orders – perhaps until you reach
middle age – at which time you will probably discover to
your surprise that just *being* with your beloved is all you
need.

Another area in which your extremism is likely to show
itself is in the handling of anger and aggression. Like most
societies, ours has traditional strictures against physically
attacking anyone smaller than oneself. Aside from cases
wherein the smaller party poses an outright threat to life
and limb the most common exception to this rule is apt to
occur when your sense of helplessness takes a form of
behavior which your older sibs (and even some adults in
your environment) consider to be obnoxious beyond
endurance. Sometimes they simply hold you at arm's length
until the angry tempest blows itself out – as it usually does
quite quickly, for you are not inclined to hold grudges. Or,
you may have grown up in a family where there were no
qualms about administering corporal punishment whenever you got out of line. In either case you are conditioned
to feel that anger and aggression on your part have no valid
place in the scheme of things. Consequently you tend to
either sit on these feelings (whining, complaining, or feeling
depressed instead) or else to give way to violent and often
ill-timed or inappropriate bursts of indignant fury. Chances
are that at the same time you have developed a rare
capacity for sarcasm or else the youngest child's famous
talent for mimicry.

Any way that you take it, you were not, in all likelihood,
given as much freedom as your female counterpart to voice
hostility or resentment openly within the bosom of the
family. (Our culture seems to permit more volatile emotional expression to girls than to boys.) Consequently the
chances are that you had recourse more than any other
ordinal position to what is known as 'passive–aggressive'

outlets for your pent-up feelings of annoyance. Passive-aggressive behavior can be described (simplistically, we admit) as behavior which on its face is not hostile (nor even under one's conscious control), but which in fact packs a wallop that can only be interpreted as aggressive. A common such outlet for youngest boys during childhood is bed-wetting. It may appear at irregular intervals for several years into adolescence, but ultimately disappears for good.

Forgetfulness is another passive-aggressive outlet which originates at an early age and which may persist throughout your life. Like bed-wetting, it is not something one can control consciously, and no matter how upsetting it may be to oneself and to others, the plain truth of the matter is that one genuinely cannot help it. Of course, not all forgetting is passive–aggressive in nature; only some of it – e.g., instances which involve your fulfilling promises and commitments made (often unwillingly) to other people, which they are counting on. The more you can learn to deal frankly with your exasperations (rather than sweeping them under the rug and quietly saving them up for a big explosion), the less you will feel a need to subconsciously take refuge in this kind of behavior.

Tied in with forgetfulness is another coping device – denial. As a child, confrontations in your family often made you feel that the cards were stacked against you – so that you denied everything, to the point where you really believed that it was not you who ate the extra piece of cake, or left the bicycle where Dad would trip over it. The only problem is that denial can become automatic, so that healthy confrontations and working-through of problems become difficult at best. And so you often go through life with a certain kind of chip on your shoulder which announces to the world at large that you may be 'small' but you're prepared to fight in one way or another for what you consider your fair share of recognition. If you can learn to

'walk softly but carry a big stick,' your presence will make a
far keener impression than you have ever dreamed was
possible. Meanwhile, you have a strong tendency to talk
when you should be listening. By not listening you often
miss out on the genuine respect which is being accorded
you. If you could only allow this fact to register you would
not have to be so touchy.

Let's go back to the business of your lifelong yen to be
Boss and Director of Traffic. The main stumbling block to
this endeavor arises from the fact that so many of your
childhood projects got support from your elders – whether
or not you asked for their help. As a result you look for
(and subconsciously expect) the cooperation of others in
the fulfillment of your plans. You, in fact, get upset if they
don't do the 'job' you have secretly assigned to them.
Unlike the redoubtably independent singletons (described
in Chapters 1–3 and Chapter 8), you are prone to resent
deeply any reluctance you perceive on the part of others to
rally round your dedicated endeavors. To you it often
seems that there is no end of supervisors to interfere when
you want to be on your own, and nobody – but nobody – to
lighten the load when you really need it. If you can lengthen
your 'fuse' and cultivate a little more tact about such
matters, you may be able to bring about a more productive
balance in your 'task-oriented' interactions with your peers.
And, believe it or not, most people regard themselves as your
peers rather than as your elder siblings – a role which they
do not appreciate having imposed upon them.

The rebellious maverick part of your nature combines
with your 'Emperor's Clothes' brand of honesty (both
touched upon briefly in Chapter 8) in such a way as to
produce an innovative streak which is a very important – in
fact, essential – ingredient of that mysterious whatever-it-is
called 'creativity.' We mentioned earlier your propensity
for do-it-yourselfism. You also have a knack for finding

short cuts – which has often saved the day when (other people's) deadlines had to be met. These all combine to make the chances very great that you have it in you to invent new and useful objects or ways of doing things. Next to first-born males, youngest males (especially the youngest of three or four boys) constitute the birth order voted 'Most Likely to Succeed.' This doesn't seem to hold true for your female counterpart – probably because in our culture, even now, most girls are raised under enormous pressure to follow a lifescript which is comparatively limited, conventional, and which makes relatively little room for innovation. (Only girls and some oldest daughters are often exceptions to this rule.)

You may find that writing, painting, and all the other 'arts' are also areas where you can give free rein to your unconventional explorations. Except for the comic theater, the performing arts are not apt to be your bag. They require you to spend too many hours in repetitive and concentrated rehearsal with no immediate payoff to lure you onward. And in your childhood experience, the role of star performer was apt to be pre-empted by an older sib.

To summarize what we have been saying: your energy, keen powers of observation, and basic integrity (your fibs are usually self-protective or else harmless 'tall tales' aimed at enhancing your image in the eyes of others) are all assets which you can learn to utilize to offset your sense of helplessness and bafflement in a confusing world. Above all, remember that – believe it or not – everybody finds the modern world confusing, even your 'elders' who so often appear to have all the answers.

PART TWO

Two-Sibling Combinations

It is a sad fact of life that parents, try as they may to play fair and to love each of their children equally, are not capable of it: Such a feat is not humanly possible: people are simply not made that way. None of us can possibly legislate the amount of love we feel toward another person any more than we can control the amount of love that others feel toward us. For people to pretend otherwise constitutes a foolish and unrealistic exercise in self-deception.

Fair-minded parents can, of course, be even-handed in the way they treat their children. But while it is possible to love all of them abundantly, each child is unique, and expecting oneself to overlook this fact is both unfair and disrespectful. Inevitably, therefore, parents the world over usually display a perfectly natural tendency to harbor a sort of special feeling toward at least one of their children. Since tiny tots are famous for never missing a trick, they (unfortunately) always seem to sense exactly where their parents' affections lie. And there isn't much that a well-meaning parent can do about this state of affairs except to be aware of it and to avoid cruel and thoughtless acts of favoritism or discrimination.

When a parent has a soft spot in his or her heart for Tom, say, rather than for his brothers, that parent most often 'adopts' Tom as his or her own special protégé. This does not necessarily mean, however, that Tom is invariably showered with special privileges or favors. It can sometimes happen that far more is expected and required of the favorite. Excessive demands for achievement, excellence, loving kindness, or even rational thinking may be heaped upon his or her little head. This matter of parental choice is – obviously – a crucial factor in personality development. Much of its clout can be attributed to parental birth order, by the way, and we believe a discussion of this topic has particular relevance in dealing with the subject matter of this section.

At the present state of our knowledge it is impossible to predict which child will get 'adopted' by whom. Generally speaking, a person is inclined to favor others born in his or her own birth order, and this is usually a purely subconscious process. It will therefore come as no surprise that singletons tend to choose other singletons to be their best friends, while a woman with one younger sister will often befriend a man who has one younger brother. Other ordinal positions display a similar trend, with the notable exception of oldest and youngest *boys*, who often team together as though seeking to re-establish a childhood relationship that was mutually rewarding.

Mothers and fathers are no exception in this regard. Parents who were first-borns in their own family of origin will often feel a close bond with their own oldest child; last-borns may feel closer to their youngest, and so forth. By the same token, parents may sometimes reject the child who now occupies the same ordinal position that a problematic (or even disliked) sibling once did. If you know an oldest child whose mother or father seems to bear down hard on him or her, ask yourself whether the parent in question was a younger child who felt put upon by the oldest child in his or her own family of origin. The answer you get may lead you to a clearer understanding of much behavior which would otherwise appear quite puzzling.

In large families the children work out various alliances among themselves and so, to a certain degree, buffer and compensate for the element of 'specialness.' When there are only two children in a family, however, the going gets rougher, and that process which we have just referred to as 'adoption' has a much more powerful impact upon each child. And it seems to be the rule rather than the exception in two-sib families. If the two sibs are of opposite sex, which one gets taken under the wing of which parent may rest heavily upon each parent's relationship to his or her own family of origin. A man who only had sisters may welcome the opportunity of relating to a son – or he may welcome a daughter as being someone he already understands and can comfortably relate to. The same principle also applies, of course, to mothers.

Parents, however, don't necessarily adopt one of the children (even in a two-sib situation) with equal enthusiasm. For example, both parents may adopt the same child – to the relative neglect of the other. Both parents who were themselves *youngest* children and grew up worshipping an older sib may latch onto their first-born in such a way that their other child gets relatively ignored. On the other hand, one parent may subconsciously adopt one of the children (for whatever reason) so exclusively that the other parent will 'favor' the other child to compensate for the obvious inequality. This pairing off of parents and children can often lead to a distorted family lifestyle, whereby a sort of 'my team against your team' tradition becomes firmly entrenched. While such behavior often takes the form of playful mock-rivalry with healthy consequences for all concerned, it can sometimes be destructive and divisive. When parents and children pair off, it doesn't require any sophisticated training in developmental psychology to realize that embattled same-sex (mother and daughter versus father and son) or opposite-sex (mother and son versus father and daughter) teams could adversely affect the emotional expectations and coping styles of any adult whose childhood was significantly influenced by such an environment.

As psychologists we do not feel that birth order is necessarily the most important factor in shaping personality. It is, however, one of the most interesting determinants of certain aspects of behavior. In the two-sib family, it can always be relied on to point out the origins of significant lifelong attitudes and to deepen and enrich our knowledge of what makes us tick.

CHAPTER ELEVEN

Older Brother of Younger Sister

Regardless of the age gap between you and your younger sister, yours is the male ordinal position most likely to be the Good Guy. This is true especially in the world of older men. (Women find you somewhat less compatible.) You have a certain easygoing, low-key manner which doesn't make heavy demands or go around stirring up trouble. This outward show of good nature practically guarantees you the comradeship and good will of the men with whom you come into daily contact. Lest we seem to be describing a 'hail fellow well met' kind of extrovert with a joke for every occasion, let us join with you in stating that such flippancy would not sit well with the more serious side of your nature. You are in reality far more prone to be on the shy side. You may have tried your hand at being the life of the party once or twice, but were too bashful to carry it off with flair, and so abandoned further efforts in that direction. (You could be considered a 'closet' extrovert however, because you so often take quiet and vicarious pleasure in the shenanigans of less reticent people who delight in saying or doing outrageous things before a shocked – but titillated – public.)

You are far more complicated than anyone would guess. People who have known you for many years are apt to startle themselves with a sudden realization: 'It's funny – we've been working together in the same place for all this time and yet, actually, I don't really know the guy at all.' You probably aren't aware of it, but your protective coloration is very successful! It isn't a matter of hiding your feelings behind a poker face; if that's all it amounted to, your peers would consider you a creep or a zombie and wouldn't like you as well as they do. It's more a matter of your skill in filtering your emotions so that the only ones you reveal are those which you're convinced will be acceptable to other people. Any feelings that don't fit this criterion usually get repressed – with the result that even you are not aware of their existence. At this point we would like to draw a crucial distinction between those two words – *re*pression and *sup*pression. The latter refers to the process whereby we consciously feel an emotion but voluntarily push it down or squelch it for some reason (to keep peace with our employer, for example). The former refers to an involuntary turning off of an emotion at its source, before it ever comes to conscious awareness. It is repression more than anything else which accounts for the complexity of your character.

Although it may be difficult for most of your family, loved ones, and associates to picture you as complicated, you yourself are often aware that there is more going on deep inside you than meets the public eye – not to mention your own. Still waters can run deep, but they can also go underground and flow in hidden channels of unknown depth. It's as if you long ago made up your mind not to be an 'emotional type' in your outward behavior toward the world. Then, in order to be convincing in that role, you had to carefully arrange your inner life so as to make sure that there were no chinks in your armor for untoward feelings to leak through.

Our hunch is that this all-important decision had something to do with your sister. If she came into the picture when you were aged four or thereabouts, your parents may have conveyed the impression – deliberately or otherwise – that boys (or older brothers, anyway) are supposed to be dignified, princely, and controlled. In our culture 'masculinity' for little boys is too often defined as 'that which is not feminine.' So you may have added your own formulation to the effect that only little girls of this world act in a messy, noisy, uncontrolled, emotionally volatile manner – and you certainly weren't about to be mistaken for a girl. It isn't at all unusual, incidentally, for boys in your birth order to scour the neighborhood soon after their sister's birth, ringing doorbells and asking if anyone wants a 'brand-new baby girl.' Even when the two of you are close in age and very fond of each other, she is likely to be typecast as the 'emotional' one while you are given praise for being always calm, cool, and collected. By and large, then, you saw your childhood environment as permitting her to be more expressive while encouraging you to repress your emotional reactions.

A second aspect of repression has to do with amnesia – the burying of painful experiences almost as soon as they occur. All children do this, and the subconscious of each of us is a veritable storehouse of such 'forgotten' material. Each individual develops a personal style of defending against the various emotional threats which arise from inside or outside the self during childhood. Some of us find solace in routines and rituals like counting things and making up lists; others blame the weather or Lady Luck for their misfortunes; and so on. Your chief defense is most often repression, and an accompanying amnesia for most things that happened before you reached age six (or even later). We have noticed that youngsters seem to use this particular defense when an ongoing problem puts them at a perpetual disadvantage. In your case, your sister's birth probably started it all. Female infants generally respond better to soothing and are easier to handle than male infants. You may have been going through the notoriously obstreperous and talking-back behavior which characterizes boys at age two, four, and six while she was usurping your throne, your place as center of the family's universe, and your mother was telling her friends how much more docile girls are than boys. Undoubtedly such a degrading state of affairs did not sit well with you. There was probably a seemingly endless period in your very young life when nothing you did seemed to earn the parental praise and approval to which you were accustomed as the first-born. Because you were still too young to put your sense of outrage into words, you acquired skill at repressing it, feigning docility in an effort to upstage your diminutive rival. If you were like most boys in your ordinal position, this maneuver was highly successful. You became the quiet, cooperative (but aloof) Crown Prince and soon 'forgot' your previous torment because you had buried it so deeply that from then on even *you* could not call it to mind. Consequently you get along in the world of other people and are liked by almost everybody you meet.

A motto for you, then, has been 'Don't stir it up.' At an early age, you learned to hide your feelings when you were aware of them, and to repress them otherwise. But repressed feelings don't fade away; they come to the surface altered or disguised, often in the form of rather amorphous feelings of anxiety and malaise – frequently along with physical sensations of dizziness, stomach upsets, attacks of panic, etc. Another escape hatch lies in the realm of dreams and fantasies, although you are not apt to recall your dreams upon awakening. Most people dream about six times a night, and people who 'never dream' simply do not recall them. Researchers in this highly complex field characterize people as 'dream recallers' or 'non-recallers.' Men in your birth order are usually located at the non-recaller end of the scale.

When it comes to the fantasy department, however, that's a horse of a different color. Often – when you least expect it – a daydream comes winging at you from out of the blue; and usually with obviously sexual or hostile connotations which might cause you a lot of needless alarm. Why 'alarm'? Because basically you have learned to be a very conforming guy and you are very rough on yourself whenever you experience any impulse or desire which you think the world considers bizarre or in any way abnormal. So you button your lip, share them with nobody, and suffer in silence.

Let us offer you some reassurance. The capacity to satisfy our wishes in the form of imaginative fantasies is a very useful one. The ability to do shocking or unapproved things in our minds – and with imagined activities there are no holds barred – is a healthy escape valve (underutilized, unfortunately, by many people). Philosophical teachings to the contrary, thoughts are not equivalent to deeds. If they were, any one of us could 'think' our way into winning a sweepstake or 'think' a loved one into being cured of a terminal illness. Thoughts may lead to events and help make them happen, but that doesn't make them equivalent. Many people fear that if they indulge in fantasies of an aggressive or sexual nature, one thing will lead to another and things will get out of hand. While this is not outside the realm of possibility, there is a great deal more evidence that says that people with fantasy outlets are less likely to build up the kind of tension which erupts into antisocial behavior.

All of which brings us to the nitty-gritty: your close personal relations. There is probably nobody in the whole world – friend, relative, lover, or psychotherapist – whom you are willing to trust with your deepest yearnings. This is not simply a matter of reticence, however, but a fear that your feelings will be rejected by the listener, and an anxiety that you may open the floodgates too far and let loose more worrisome dynamics than you bargained for. Going all out is, for you, too risky in terms of your need for public acceptance. So, when in doubt, you're prone to say nothing of your inner self.

It may seem surprising in view of your pent-up desires, but you are the least likely of all birth orders to pursue a hobby for more than a few months. While your daydreams are often packed with action, your daily life is apt to be given over to reading, film-watching, spectator sports, and other passive pursuits. Once in a while you may take up motorcycling or golf or tennis, but before too long the cycle gets sold, the golf clubs or tennis rackets begin to gather dust in a cupboard somewhere.

Part of this has to do with a genuine gregariousness on your part. You like to do things as part of a small team with lots of companionship and mutual endeavor. For this reason you are to be found working in sales more than any other ordinal position. How, one might ask, could anyone who is so secretive about revealing himself be outgoing enough to function as a salesperson? Well, it so happens that you have probably acquired consummate skill in deflecting people's inquisitiveness about you and getting them to talk about (and reveal) themselves. You come across as an excellent listener. If that isn't salesmanship, we don't know what is! Moreover, it's axiomatic that good listeners almost always acquire a reputation for being brilliant conversationalists, mostly because they are usually adept at asking questions which draw people out and encourage them to talk about themselves. Small wonder, then, that you wind up knowing a great deal about them while they end up knowing next to nothing about you – except that you are 'such an intelligent guy – he sees eye to eye with me about everything!'

In other situations, though, you pay a price for your self-protection – for while others may feel that they don't really know you or understand you, it's a debit on your ledger that you don't feel known or understood by others. The sense of personal isolation arising from this can sometimes lead you into moods of discouragement and feelings of futility. May we respectfully suggest that your humanity is far more acceptable to others than you might think. So don't be afraid to make modest experiments in self-revelation.

Despite everything we've said so far, there is a distinctly paradoxical side to your nature when it comes to your outward behavior. Generally speaking, you are a person who is subject to instantaneous likes and dislikes, and although your instinct is to play your cards close to your chest in your overt dealings with the world, this isn't meant to imply that you're not capable of occasional impulsive behavior. Either you jump into the swimming pool wearing your best suit, as it were – or else you hold back and watch while somebody *else* does it. You are apt to be more comfortable in settings where the 'rules' are most clear-cut; you become even more cautious than usual when other people's expectations are either indistinct or else downright baffling.

Your relationship with your father is apt to be an unrewarding one, tinged sometimes with bitterness. More often than not you tend to regard him as ineffectual, even though you find it difficult to pin down the origin of this feeling. We don't know either – but our *guess* is that it's another hangover from the early days when the advent of your sister overturned your world and you felt betrayed by Dad. Either he appeared to switch his loyalty from you to her, or perhaps he was insensitive to your needs at that time. Consequently you *might* be described as 'father hungry'; always seeking a substitute Dad who could be all the things to you that your own father wasn't.

You may, for example, idealize a superior at your place of work and become his loyal defender. In actual fact this man may be a curmudgeon whom nobody else can put up with, but *you* somehow think he can do no wrong – and he loves you for it. In this context your habitual role of Good Guy really does hold you in good stead – because (with rare exceptions) you are able to carry it off without offending your coworkers who might otherwise accuse you of 'boot licking.' For their part, they just think you're blind where he is concerned, and they forgive you for your blindness since you never seem to be using it to their disadvantage. If one were to believe the much advertised opinions of a few psychiatric experts, one would expect that you would be inclined to satisfy your 'father hunger' by seeking out homosexual relationships with older men. And yet such does not seem to be the case. You may have experimented with varying your sexual outlets, but they usually remain isolated experiments. Your psychic economy is much too concerned with getting perspective and mastery of male–female relationships, i.e., finding a woman who will 'forsake all others' and cling only to you.

Although your mother came in for her share of the blame in producing your younger sister, it appears that you and she were able to keep something going over the years. Your mother could appeal to you to be her 'little man,' which was a lot more flattering than your father's bafflement and refusal to play referee or second. Besides which, after the first year, your mother did not seem as taken in by the baby's charms as your father. For this reason you resent Mum a lot less.

As for your relationship to your sister, it is probably the most complicated of all sib-ships, surpassed only by the complexity of hers to *you*. You may have experienced her as a brat or a pest or a pain in the neck during your early growing-up years, but your propensity for repression again came to your rescue. To put it simply, you withdrew the hem of your royal garment and, without realizing it, 'disenrolled' her from the human race. As we've pointed out, you simultaneously disenrolled yourself by putting your own emotions at arm's length. The point is that once we refuse to deal with another person or group (racial, religious, or ethnic) we begin to treat them like *things*, and thus deprive ourselves of an opportunity for learning how to interact with them in mutually enriching ways.

Although, as we have noted, this is your general style of dealing with emotional transactions, it becomes particularly troublesome in your relations with women. You learned as a boy how to tune out your little sister whenever you found her presence or conduct burdensome – a trick you still utilize with females who inconvenience or displease you. Nobody likes to be tuned out, but women – more sensitive than men to the nuances of interpersonal communication – are apt to find such behavior quite maddening. Since you shy away from expressing your own feelings openly, it is possible that the furor which you thus cause provides you with a vicarious outlet for your own pent-up tensions. (If we are afraid to do something ourselves, we can often subconsciously manipulate others into doing it for us.) Small wonder that women sometimes purse their lips – but keep their own counsel – when somebody starts talking about what a Good Guy you are!

When you are very close in age to your sister, the result can be an overly protective attitude toward the female sex and a tendency to be overly tolerant of their transgressions. 'She didn't mean any harm' can be a kind of slogan for you. Yet, unlike the younger brother of an older sister, you are more apt to be competitive with women – even though you go about it in roundabout ways – while remaining blithely unaware. In the role of husband or father you may often do things like bringing the youngsters a glass of water or taking them to the john in the middle of the night while their mother is fast asleep. No doubt you feel convinced that you are doing such things out of sheer helpfulness, but the children and their mother may subconsciously see it otherwise – i.e., that you are competing for the title of 'Best *Mother*' in the household. It's not *what* you do so much as the *way* you do it. Oddly enough, however (and we can offer no explanation for this), you are most apt to marry a woman who happens to be an older sister with one younger brother (see Chapter 12). If that's the case, you may rest assured that she will find ways of making herself one up on you. Should you succeed in proving yourself the better cook, interior decorator, nursemaid, housekeeper, or whatever, you will soon discover that she has in the meantime landed on part of your turf and firmly planted her flag there!

Of all first-born male birth orders yours is the one least likely to join the rat race in pursuit of worldly success. As we noted above, at a very early age you became acquainted with the joys of daydreaming and fantasy as a way of dealing with life's frustrations. And you continue to use your imagination that way rather than using it for so-called 'useful' (hard cash) everyday activities. Consequently your career ambitions tend not to be highly pressured; you sort of drift into things and then stay in a good spot – sometimes for many years. When your name comes up for promotion, your boss may be puzzled: first, because you don't seem particularly eager for change and secondly, because he is often astonished to realize that he has scant first-hand knowledge of your capabilities.

It's another example of the price tag attached to your hesitancy about putting your cards on the table. It may, we think, also be part of your childhood role as Crown Prince: it offends your innate sense of dignity to get out among the masses where you would be covered with mud and/or risk falling flat on your face. Another cause may be the fact that having been dubbed the 'Future Prime Minister,' you prefer to rest on your laurels. In any event, you have learned to excel at maintaining the status quo, and you enjoy creating

an atmosphere of timeless ease in which you and those close
to you can bask. As one researcher observed, you like peace
and fun above all else, and people enjoy and appreciate you
for that. The more you dare to risk opening up to other
people, the less like a loner you will feel and the more
fulfilling your life will become.

CHAPTER TWELVE

Older Sister of Younger Brother

For very few first-born children is the arrival of a younger sibling the cause for unalloyed rejoicing – whatever the family and the child may anticipate. You are no exception. Like your male counterpart (the older brother of a younger sister) you probably experienced a number of unexpected and ambivalent emotions when the new baby brother came home from the hospital. Perhaps you had fancied that a younger sister would be more to your liking. If you were four or over, you may have had last-minute second thoughts, and secretly decided (or perhaps even declared quite openly) that you would prefer to continue being the family's one-and-only child. In any case, here he was – receiving a great deal of attention and concern which, up to now, had been yours alone. Although you may not remember it now (due to the mechanisms of repression which we described in Chapter 11), your reaction was probably one of consternation – a characteristic response of children in our society when they discover the physical differences between the males and females of our species. (We say 'in our society' because anthropologists, such as Margaret Mead, assert that in cultures where everybody runs around naked from infancy through adulthood this problem doesn't occur.) To state it briefly, when confronted with each other's nakedness, young children find it hard to make sense of the fact that little boys have a 'thing' while little girls do not. Each goes through his or her own moment of truth and tries valiantly to come up with an answer which will satisfy the need for self-worth and self-acceptance as a member of the male or female 'club.' Little boys ask themselves 'How come she doesn't have a Thing? Did she have one and it was taken away? Will this happen to me? If so, can I avoid such a calamity? Will she grow one later on? Will she steal mine?' etc. Little girls ask themselves a lot of similar questions: 'Did I have a Thing once? What became of it, and why? Or will I grow one later on? Or will somebody give me one? Or will I have to earn it? How come he seems to have been born with one? Or will I have to steal one?' Of course these ideas are seldom that fully articulated, so it's a rare child who can formulate his or her doubts and fears in such a way as to present them to Mum and/or Dad and thereby obtain some clarification – especially when Mum and Dad are themselves up tight about it all and may even pretend that such differences are nonexistent. And so it is that these questions of major importance to our future lives go unasked and largely unanswered. Many children come to their own conclusions which may be marvels of logic for a three-or four-year-old. Bits and pieces of data are added to these conclusions throughout our growing-up years so that our subconscious minds are, to a considerable extent, the repository for a vast collection of early childhood puzzlements, theories, hopes, fears, and undigested facts. We must also point out that having or lacking a penis is also symbolic of all the prerogatives that go with being male or female and that even very little children catch on to what these prerogatives are and how to exploit them.

Getting back to you, though. Chances are that the first hurdle you had to leap was when you concluded that this new rival for the limelight was born into the world equipped with a Thing – a discomfiting realization shared by your male counterpart. His conclusion, however, was that his little sister was getting all the goodies because she didn't have a Thing – which, quite logically, caused him to wonder whether his own Thing had been responsible for his dethronement. You had two factors going for you if you were aged four or over, however. In the first place, your environment was busily encouraging you to rehearse for a future role in the world as wife and mother via doll play, tea-party games, helping mother, etc. Thus you had been sufficiently conditioned to 'play mummy,' and the advent of a real live baby to fuss over could have appealed to that aspect of your social conditioning. Secondly, this little newcomer with his all-important Thing was, after all, a mere blob of babyhood. You, on the other hand, felt, in all likelihood, well entrenched in your father's affections. In addition, your mother may have welcomed your earnest assistance, however childlike, in helping out with traditionally female tasks of household management and infant care. Your gender role conditioning gave you a face-saving and viable solution to the demeaning and outrageous dilemma in which you had found yourself when the stranger first arrived. Your brother's Thing, after all, would be much less of a threat if he (and It) were to be placed firmly and permanently under your sisterly supervision, so you took advantage of a female prerogative – the supervision of children. He could be allowed to live, and you would be his auxiliary mother and trainer – while he would *always* be your baby brother. As such, he has undoubtedly been the lifelong recipient of a kind of relentless loyalty on your part – a feeling that you are somehow responsible for his welfare – which is more typical of your birth order than any other. You may see him very seldom. You may feel that you have absolutely no interests in common. You may have – after a childhood filled with conflict or apparent indifference – come to be fairly good friends. But whatever your relationship, he usually knows that he can depend on you, and that you will come to his aid whenever he is in need.

Thus, your characteristic willingness to shoulder responsibility began early on in life – first as an only child, and subsequently as an assistant mother to your younger sibling. Our impression is that you saw yourself – subconsciously – as faced with a double challenge. On the one hand you wanted to maintain your status as Dad's pride and joy, while on the other you went on carving out a place for yourself as Mum's reliable helper. This provided an early training ground in dealing with others where you acquired considerable experience in diplomacy and 'political' compromise. You view your parents nowadays with a loving tolerance of their flaws and you do not understand why your brother is so emotionally involved with them. We do not know for certain why this should be so, but our hunch is that this is a defense against getting caught up in the concerns of one or the other parent. You early learned not to take sides.

More than any other ordinal position, your role is likely to be that of Organizer and Peacemaker, and the slogan which accompanies this role is 'It's all up to me.' You were cast in your lifelong role of Problem Solver at a very tender age, with a tendency to ask 'Why all the fuss?' when others get upset. But along with this has developed a simultaneous reluctance on your part to let anyone guess that you have problems of your own to wrestle with. It's almost as though you secretly believe that you don't have a right to feel helpless or at loose ends – like other people. For even when it comes to your own biggest upsets you ask 'Why all the fuss?' and feel that it would be an unbearable humiliation for you to openly admit your hurt or puzzlement, let alone seek help from anyone.

And yet it is here that your basic sense of practicality comes to the rescue – not to mention your gift for diplomatic face-saving (your own face in this instance). Because you almost always find a way whereby you can pocket your pride without losing your self-respect and go after the guidance you need – but always in the spirit of one expert meeting in consultation with another. For you never take anything on faith. Your second slogan is 'Show me! Prove it to me! Then I'll test it out for myself.' You are usually very polite in your way of going about this, but you like to deal with facts rather than hypotheses – unless they hold up in the world of hard data. Dictionaries and encyclopedias pose no threats to you, and your capacity for memorizing and retaining factual material is often quite remarkable. When you apply it in combination with your tendency to be conscientious and thorough about everything you undertake, it is not surprising that many women in your birth order become teachers, lawyers, doctors, librarians, scholars, and supervisors of large and efficient undertakings. You are particularly adept at taking note of details and following through on them; little escapes your notice or your highly developed sense of accountability.

By the time you got to secondary school you were probably more competent than your age would suggest. The chances are that you adjusted to school with little difficulty – although leaving your brother back home may not have been entirely to your liking. No doubt you hurried straight home after school as fast as your young legs could carry you – no loitering about the schoolyard for you – until your sibling was old enough to attend school on his own. Then it became your duty (most likely) to accompany him to school and shepherd him back home afterwards and to be his 'big sister' in all that this term implies in the way of watchful protection and childish guidance.

As a small girl your relations with classmates of both sexes was what might be called a mixed bag. Boys had a certain grudging respect for your straightforward assertiveness and self-confidence. Generally you appeared self-contained, and if you favored a tomboyish lifestyle, the boys may even have accepted you into their games and other pursuits, although your competitiveness might have tended to get out of hand from time to time. You would do well to curb a strong temptation – often subconscious, we grant you – to treat men in a fashion which is patronizing and sometimes downright contemptuous, albeit unintentional. Such tendencies generally simmer down with the onset of adolescence when you gradually modified a long-held tendency to regard all male contemporaries as bumblers and fumblers who stood in need of your firm supervision.

As for female age mates, your stance has always tended to be one of reserved circumspection and wariness. Your feeling of competition with males doesn't extend to members of your own sex. You're not at your best when you have to compete with other women, and you are well aware of this fact. You had to work out a *modus vivendi* with your mother – and the subtle 'politics of detente' that this involved left you with the hard-won conclusion that 'least said, soonest mended' is a wise policy to follow in your dealings with other women. Although you usually have one or two close (and mutually loyal) women friends, you are more likely than women in any other ordinal position to feel most comfortable in the company of men – either singly or in groups. By this we mean that you prefer the less intimate issues which make up the bulk of male conversations, and you feel more at ease with the less nuance-laden male idiom. Again we confess that we have no hard data to go on, but our educated guess is that even within the present-day feminist movement, you and women like you find yourselves having difficulty dealing with those interpersonal complexities which appear to characterize the 'female temperament' as it is viewed by our society.

In coming to a clearer understanding of your own psychological make-up, it is important to bear in mind that you were an only child for the first few years of your life. As we observed in Chapter 2, the female singleton generally has a close relationship to her father, so that more often than not she absorbs a lot of the intellectual approaches and accompanying rhetoric which are associated with 'maleness' in our society. If this was part of your conditioning, then you learned a lot – perhaps without realizing it – about how to simplify and present a relatively pragmatic point of view, how to defend a position, and how to translate your ideas into a program for their practical application. Consequently you often display a gift for solving knotty problems with forthrightness and dispatch. But while your habitual sense of diplomacy usually serves you well, you can get so carried away by your own sense of certainty that you sometimes come across to others – men and women alike – as bossy or manipulative. Generally speaking, however, you are very adept at smoothing ruffled feathers and making the necessary conciliatory gestures – provided you can do so with that unusual combination of dignity and poise which is your trademark. Otherwise you are prone to withdraw into a chilly, 'no comment' kind of aloofness.

At the same time you are reluctant to become involved in the purely personal aspects of a group enterprise, even though you're a good team player, and this can create a certain distance between you and your female associates. While they have genuine respect for your abilities, they often can't help wondering what makes you tick. They seldom dislike you; they merely find you puzzling, and occasionally resent your characteristic insistence on down-to-earth logic. When the emotional chips are down in your dealings with other women, your way of withdrawing into aloofness can baffle and upset them. You don't cotton on to frivolity in either men or women, and while your grooming is most often impeccable, you don't take to every passing fad – a cause for wonder among your friends when you were a teenager and perhaps even now.

Independent person and self-starter that you are, many of you are very sensitive to other people's assertions (overt or covert) that you may be deficient in what our culture considers 'feminine' behavior. Consequently you either decided early on that they could go fly a kite (your birth order invented feminism long before it became a movement) or else you made up your mind to rectify the situation. So with that thoroughness which characterizes your approach to any project, you can sometimes lean over backwards in demonstrating your willingness to have doors opened for you, chairs pulled back for you, taxis hailed for you, and to let yourself be 'dominated', etc. – *ad nauseam*. Sometimes your insistence on such things (especially etiquette between the sexes) can become a bit overdone.

Another aspect of your executive ability is your penchant for creating and maintaining organizational systems in your personal and vocational life. You seem able to be methodical without even having to think about it. The mothers of little girls in your ordinal position have often been heard to offer comments like 'You should see how neatly she arranges and puts away her things! Lord knows, she never learned that from me – I'm totally disorganized by comparison!' This element of thoroughness makes it possible for you to undertake ambitious projects and see them through from start to finish. Less disciplined souls may regard you as some kind of workhorse, but you bring so much enthusiasm to your undertakings that to you they hardly seem like work at all. So complete is your dedication that it frequently rubs off on other people who in turn get swept along by your excitement as well as your unusual – believe it or not! – singleness of purpose. This in fact is the reason you work so well in team endeavors; your eye is always on the ball, and you inspire others with your quality of total commitment to the mutual goal. Unlike the youngest child in a position of leadership or expertise you are able to sense and to accept the respect of others, and seldom go around feeling insufficiently appreciated. You can indeed be as competitive, jealous, and quarrelsome as anybody else, but your general demeanor is apt to be one of firm self-assurance – in fact, some people consider you smug. You rarely make rash moves, and almost always check the situation first; you only become involved when you feel sure that you know what you're stepping into. Some people may be envious of your obvious capabilities, but that – sadly – is part of human nature. You would do well, however, to avoid your tendency to be abrasive in situations when the ill-informed quarrel and you experience yourself as the only one who really knows the score.

Your tendency to map your moves in advance probably earned the respect of your girlhood teachers. However, your basic independence of spirit was such that we'd be surprised if you ever ingratiated yourself into the awkward role of Teacher's Pet, although your teachers liked you – and you (in your quiet, 'let's stick to business' way) liked them.

Part of this derives from your task-oriented approach to things. Lessons and study come naturally to you; you regard them as challenges to be mastered. You rarely give up on an undertaking, and often push doggedly onward when everybody else has fallen by the wayside. School for you, therefore, has always been a 'task' which you set out to fulfill – more for your own satisfaction than for any praise you might reap. While you certainly are not shy about speaking up when you have to make a point, you don't grab the limelight and your classmates are often surprised when they find out that yours was the highest grade in the class. We think part of the reason for this comes from the fact that when your little brother was a toddler and his conversational abilities were strictly limited, your ability to put your ideas into words and to understand what was said to you were the major means whereby you maintained your lead (your three- or four-year head start), especially in the eyes of Dad. Although your brother may have caught on and have generated his own brand of linguistic ability somewhere along the line, chances are that it took the form of writing – the written word being a mode of expression which does not invite interruption. You were perfectly willing when you were children to do his talking for him. And you tend nowadays to enjoy thinking on your feet, debating issues with all comers, so that you are not always the most patient of listeners. That is, you sometimes have your mouth instead of your ears open. You like to express your opinions and, while you are well informed in many areas, you derive much pleasure from letting people know where you stand, well informed or not. 'Wishy-washy' does not apply to *you*!

In light of the above, it comes as no surprise to find that the teaching profession is almost second nature to you. Even if you don't teach in a formal setting (from preschool to college) we'll bet that you have given paid instruction in some form or other, either privately or in your line of work. You are a born teacher. You have a way of combining patience, persistence, and singleness of purpose in such a manner that students regard you with that warm affection and respect which is the reward of gifted teachers the world over. Not to be in a position where you can teach and instruct is a real loss for you more than for any other ordinal position. We therefore suggest that a great deal of fulfillment would be added to your life if you could think of something – anything – that you'd like to teach people. With your penchant for learning all about a subject (whether you take a course in it, or else simply read every book on the matter that you can lay hands on) there is almost sure to be something which you know more about than most people – and which they would be happy to learn from you. Think about it. We realize that you don't like to take advice unless you have asked for it (fat chance of that!) but we would like to count on that very practical streak in you which we imagine would ultimately respond to the above by one day asking yourself, 'Well – *why not?*' Having talked about what a gifted teacher and instructor and advisor you are, it's now time to do an about-face and say flat out that in our opinion you aren't particularly fond of children, as such. By this we don't mean to call you a bad mother or imply that you don't or would not enjoy motherhood. It's just that your freewheeling nature is apt to feel rather trapped by the kind of housewife/mother role which our society likes to outline for its female members. Perhaps as a result of childhood baby-sitting with your brother, you prefer situations wherein your custodial chores are clearly defined in terms of a kind of contract that can be stated in terms of specific duties and hours and minutes – an arrangement best suited for a teaching position of one sort or another. Put another way, you have learned to treasure having a regular chunk of your own time to do with as you please, and it is very upsetting for you to find yourself in any situation where you are not provided with periods for rest, recreation, and independent activity. Children, students, and other 'needy' persons are all very well and good in their place, but you feel most productive when you can firmly count on time for 'cultivating your own garden.' Anyone (adult or child) who expects you to make a full-time career out of parenting – whether children, nieces and nephews, your own sib, students, or whoever – has another guess coming!

As for love partners, you feel much the same way; you want your partners to be the kind of people who have their own 'garden' to cultivate. You expect (and require) that, at the very least, they respect your need of private space and not infringe on it. In like manner you expect your partners to be in charge of their own boundaries, and if they can't manage to be so, you consider it their problem and not yours. You thus gravitate toward people who are accustomed to having their own enterprises – totally separate and independent from yours. These psychological requirements are best fulfilled by men who have one sister – older or younger. You and your partner are quite familiar with this kind of battlefield so that while this very fact may give rise to interpersonal frictions, you also have a major advantage; the experience which both of you have acquired in your respective roles over the years. You are, in fact, most apt to team up with a man who was the younger brother of an older sister. And for some reason which is beyond our present understanding, this particular combination is the one and only interaction in the love/romance department which we find occurring with noticeable frequency. Your next most prevalent choice is the man with a younger sister. This, needless to say, can be fraught with problems: you are accustomed to having males listen to you with a certain amount of respect (albeit somewhat grudging at times). He, on the other hand, is used to being the Crown Prince who listens to women when he damned well feels like it. You get the picture.

In line with the assumptions on which this book is written (see Introduction), it goes without saying that the closer in age that each of you was to your sibling, the more harmonious you are likely to be as love partners. Most remarkable of all is your willingness to live with someone (husband, lover, or roommate) whose interests and proclivities are quite different from your own; it doesn't bother you that he follows pursuits which are of no interest to you – or shares none of yours. On the other hand, you do not like your partner to enter too deeply into an arena which you have staked out as your bailiwick. 'You do your thing

and I'll do mine' is your watchword. Again, this is a further
reflection of your intense need to have and maintain your
own space.

Birth order aside, the man you marry or team up with is
apt to be a loner socially and preoccupied with his work.
He does not have your almost instinctive liking for people
nor your social know-how, and his job is often one where he
is left alone to pursue his occupational goals. He may
indeed be 'married to his work' – sometimes to your
chagrin, despite your aforementioned respect for people's
right to do their own thing.

In the emotional sphere you are not inclined to wear your
heart on your sleeve. You are far more comfortable telling
people what you think rather than how you feel. Strong
emotion is apt to be experienced by you as an abject
surrender to the irrational side of life – like your brother
with his temper tantrums, bed-wetting, and erratic outbursts. This need to keep your cool is something you share
with the only girl, but with one important difference – you
had a younger sib who was 'allowed' more freedom of
emotional expression than was accorded you. To be sure,
your elders probably clucked and shook their heads in
dismay, but the fact is that he got away with it. And so you,
unlike the only girl, have always harbored a secret (or
perhaps a subconscious) yen to kick over the traces and
indulge in an emotional scene or two of your own. The big
hitch is that this rare occurrence only takes place when you
feel pushed beyond the breaking point, and your subsequent disapproval of your own behavior – not to mention
humiliation at having lost your composure – is very severe
indeed. You are most proud of your ability to put mind
over matter, but you often shortchange yourself when it
comes to your human right to give vent to your emotions.

Another price which you may unwittingly pay is in the
area of interpersonal (social) relations. You often tacitly

deny others the right to express their feelings in sponta-
neous ways as you rush in to make peace, give advice, and
otherwise bring order out of chaos. Consequently your
mind-over-matter approach is often interpreted by other
people as meaning that *you* don't *mind* and *they* don't
matter. Once again – with all due regard for your dislike of
unsolicited advice – we make bold to suggest that you
would enlarge your life considerably if you could practice
putting yourself 'in the other person's skin,' as the French
say. That is, to practice empathizing with their feelings –
however 'irrational' they may seem – and thus develop the
same skill which you so often display when it comes to
picking up their thought patterns.

Meanwhile, therapists, counselors and other advisors
enjoy having you as a client. You are always prompt, you
always pay your fees on schedule, and your no-nonsense
integrity is a truly refreshing phenomenon. You listen
attentively to everything which transpires during the
session, and rarely forget anything. You make it almost a
point of honor, let it be said, never to acknowledge that any
contribution has made any significant difference in your
life. Nevertheless you do your 'homework,' act promptly on
insights and realizations mutually arrived at, and steadily
climb the ladder of self-realization in your own determined
and most private way.

Speaking of privacy, you are almost as good as your
younger brother when it comes to keeping from the world
what you don't want it to know. (Perhaps you learned from
each other.) For what it's worth, we have noticed that other
women are most apt to find this quality offensive, whereas
men are likely to consider it as another part of your
admirable discretion. We believe the reason for this
difference may stem from the fact that females are inclined
to rate personal intimacy in terms of one's willingness to
exchange secrets and confidences. Males, on the other

hand, are more prone to gauge closeness in terms of shared activities (e.g., a renowned author had a close male friend who often paid him visits during which the two of them would sit smoking their pipes together in silence for an entire evening). In any event, your sense of reserve about personal matters can be taken by others as a sign that you don't trust them – and perhaps you don't. However, protecting your privacy can sometimes be overdone to the point where it creates needless distance between yourself and others. Again, if you can try to empathize with *their* perspective, this may help you to be a little less guarded. Small risks can often produce large gains.

Your diplomacy, ability to organize, and sense of responsibility make you shine in the working world. And if you learn to deal well with advice – both taking it more enthusiastically and giving it more circumspectly, you'll probably find your circle of friends widening in a way you thought was reserved for others only.

CHAPTER THIRTEEN

Younger Brother of Older Sister

The most important thing to keep in mind about your growing-up years is the fact that they were strongly influenced by females. Chances are that you felt literally swamped by women. Even if your sister was a mere two years older than yourself, at age five she was being conditioned to be 'motherly,' and a three-year-old younger brother was a fine subject upon whom she could practice. In addition, your household may also have included a widowed or unmarried aunt or other single female (somehow unmarried *uncles* aren't usually part of a nuclear household). Of course, the female side of your family didn't do anything as obvious as putting their heads together and deciding upon your comings and goings; their collaborations were far more subtle.

First of all, your mother was busy enough so that she was probably grateful whenever she could justifiably delegate any of the responsibilities of raising you to your sister. In so doing she could also congratulate herself on giving her daughter a head start along the road to motherhood. What your mother didn't realize (and your sister has by this time no doubt forgotten) is what went on behind the scenes as your sister clumsily rehearsed her future role at your expense: 'Do this.' 'Don't do that.' 'Here, let me show you.' 'I'll do it for you.' Even in households where parents can afford nursemaids and other help, little girls almost insist on helping with the baby and where they are not allowed to help, they supervise.

However kind or solicitous your sister may have tried to be, a small child does not have a true grasp of what parenting (or teaching) is all about. More often than not, your sister's 'helpful' behavior reflected about the same level of empathy one might expect from any little girl busily manipulating a favorite doll. The only drawback is that you happened to be a real live human being and not a doll. A doll is impervious to mistreatment – well-intentioned or otherwise. You were not. At the same time there were probably many occasions in your childhood – especially as a toddler – when your sister was able to play a genuinely protective and supportive role where you were concerned. So that when you contrast that kind of behavior with various other sisterly activities which seemed to you to be blatantly obtrusive, you are apt to be overcome by a bewildering sense of ambivalence. Children under age three do not have precise memories of events or of their time sequence, so that things which happen to them are frequently remembered in a confused and dreamlike way.

The younger of two children often grows up with very mixed feelings about the older child, not knowing whether to look upon the sib as loving friend or mortal enemy; kindly helper or obstinate drag. The older of the two, on the other hand, often regards the younger as a pal in some ways and a burden and a pest in others. It is our strong impression, however, that the ambivalence which younger sibs experience is far more dramatic, so that the elder sib can look like an invincible oppressor at one moment and a magical rescuer/protector the next.

This particular type of ambivalence is liable to be reflected in adult life as a seesaw tendency to be overly suspicious on the one hand while being overly trusting on the other. In other words, you're inclined to divide the world into two camps – those who can be trusted completely and those who can't be trusted at all. This holds particularly true when it comes to your relations with women, where you are generally more on guard than you

might think. You are, into the bargain, more prone than
most males to fret and fume about whether a particular
female – old or young, woman or child, employer or
employee, friend or lover – is taking you for a ride or not.

But getting back to you and your sister. As we have said,
a small girl's concept of how to be a mother is no more
accurate or appropriate in many of its manifestations than
one could expect it to be. Her way of doing the job
consisted largely of giving orders and telling others (even
adults) how to conduct themselves in her effort to display
and maintain her superior status as the one who got there
first. In fact, a lot of her mothering behavior was an
attempt to identify herself with the grownups – at least so
far as you are concerned.

When the age gap between sister and brother is greater
than two years, each additional year enhances the sister's
fantasies of know-how, superior wisdom and superior
status – so that her 'management' of you may have been
quite relentless. (Younger sisters appear to be more
resourceful in dealing with this kind of situation – but that's
in Chapter 18.) Of course, she didn't regard herself as being
bossy or manipulative – and still doesn't. More often than
not she perceives it as her duty to guide her little brother,
and guide him she does – everlastingly.

Naturally, it is quite likely that your mother counter-
manded the little girl's 'orders' with her own. As a result,
you soon had two diligent maternal females focusing
considerable attention upon you when you were trying very
valiantly to find your own way in a world which seemed to
you intent on pushing and pulling you this way and that.

Now, if, in addition, there was also a grandmother or an
aunt in your household, then you really had a three-ring
circus. This third woman may have been highly vocal about
her own deeply held convictions about how a little boy
should be brought up. Or, she may have kept her opinions

to herself and intervened on the sly – exerting her influence upon you when nobody else was looking. She may even have disagreed so strongly with the other female members of your family that she became a secret ally, as together you conspired to thwart the influence of the other two. However, we find this to be more the exception than the rule. From your perspective it most often looked like all women were in cahoots with one another, while you weren't in cahoots with anybody. Since – with some exceptions, of course – the kind of conspiracy referred to here is basically a loving one, aimed at doing what will be best for you, it does not ordinarily give rise to nightmarish paranoid feelings that 'everybody is out to get me.' What it does produce will be discussed later on in this chapter.

At this point the question arises: 'Where was your father all this time?' The answer is usually 'Out.' The next question: 'What did your father do about it?' Again, the sad answer, more often than not, is 'Nothing' – or 'Next to nothing.' Not that he didn't care; he, like most fathers in an industrialized society, was away from the family all day – during which time he usually had quite enough interpersonal choreography to deal with so that he was loath to handle any more of it when he returned home at night. And in any case, most Western men take a benign but hands-off attitude toward infants and toddlers.

Feeling pushed around – however gently and lovingly – by your mother and sister cannot but have produced feelings of resentment, however deeply you might have buried them. Even to this day it may be difficult for you to get a handle on what your elusive feelings of resentment are all about, and to what extent you also have trouble figuring out how best to cope with them. By the time your father got home at night, you may have given vent to your pent-up tensions by being restless, rebellious, or even complaining. Attempts to win Dad's attention were likely to be pre-

empted by the 'more important' concerns and demands
made upon him by your mother and sister. Even your need
for support and companionship from the other male in the
family was one more part of your life that seemed to get
pushed aside by females.

If you were fortunate, your father had a similar need to
'get away from the women' now and then – in which case
you both managed to stake out a territory in which you
could share some kind of private recreation together. Your
father – who may have been secretly concerned about the
fate of his young son's masculinity in such a female-
dominated household – in all probability selected conventional 'male' activities for you to engage in together
(shooting, fishing, carpentry, attending sports events, etc.).
However, while this kind of exclusive male companionship
is in many ways meaningful to both father and son, it rarely
involves much in the way of heart-to-heart talks (such as
can often take place between fathers and their only-child
sons). Quiet enjoyment of one another's company was most
likely the keynote of your times alone with your father.
'Let's not make waves' was its motto as well as its chief
restriction. While it is our observation that males – in our
society, at least – are not heavily into pouring out their
emotional concerns to each other, most growing boys do
manage now and then to communicate deeply with their
fathers about many things – not all topics by any means,
but a fair number. In your case the mutual wish to create an
oasis of emotion-free neutrality is apt to be a quite powerful
influence in your life. Thus your childhood relationship to
your father – nostalgic though you may feel about it in
retrospect – was characterized by that quality of good-
natured but emotionally distant rapport that has continued
to be the hallmark of your relationship to other males.

To you it must have seemed as though your sister had
been handed her authoritative status on a silver platter and

never had to struggle to learn anything, a misunderstanding that she was in no hurry to correct. Not only that, but her way with words was far more adroit than yours, and she always appeared to gain the upper hand in any verbal argument. She could always point out the 'illogic' of your thinking and make her exit while you were still trying to state your side of the case.

As a child you were probably more prone to fits of temper than any other ordinal position – such outbursts being almost exclusively directed toward inanimate objects. Pent-up resentment and psychological tensions have to go somewhere, after all, and while a favorite outlet of yours may be tennis (or squash, or hockey) another kind of release may be sought by kicking furniture and throwing things against walls. Our theory is that such behavior is the understandable result of your feelings of being stymied when it comes to putting your difficulties into words. When a boy has been unable to describe his experiences and frustrations with words, he uses a mode of expression from an earlier period of his life – which may involve the use of his muscles, or a deeper and more elemental form of self-expression via the 'body talk' of physical symptoms. These may include asthma, ulcers, headaches, and other ailments having strong psychological components. Although you are somewhat more vulnerable to alcoholism and other escapes than most birth orders, your lifestyle leans in the direction of vigorous and open protest.

Again, in your childhood you probably got along reasonably well with other youngsters in your age group, both inside and outside of school – but you tended to be reserved in your interactions with other boys. Even though you may have had one or two male pals, you generally kept other boys at arm's length; never completely trusting them – nor they you. Of course, your teachers found you 'cooperative' – a term which generally means 'obedient.'

In your career choice you tend to locate yourself in a field where women are not predominant – i.e., where their role is minor and ancillary. By which we mean that you're apt to interest yourself in such things as mechanics, carpentry, sports, mathematics, physics, or anything else which up to the present has been closed to females. While we can't back it up with statistics, we would make a guess that younger brothers with a single older sister are over-represented in the armed forces where women are scarcely to be seen and the nature of the job requires cordial but slightly distant relations with other men.

At the same time your occupational career may bear the signs of a hidden agenda of which you are probably not aware – namely, the secret impulse to expose your male boss's feet of clay. Depending on the type of job, this may take the form of openly picketing outside the premises or bringing charges against him (in court or elsewhere) or writing interoffice memos which playfully or otherwise are aimed at making him look incompetent. When you do this, it is, more often than not, your way of venting an old resentment at your father for failing to stand by you when you were a youngster. Deep down you regarded him as copping out and behaving in a weak manner where your needs for protection and support were involved. To the extent that you perceived him as giving in to the wishes, opinions, and demands of your mother and sister, you felt betrayed by him. So you may retain a subconscious urge to take your revenge on subsequent male authorities whenever you get the chance. To put it succinctly, you are forever in search of a strong ideal father while at the same time you have a lingering temptation to watch and wait for anything about him which can be interpreted as weakness. When you succeed, however, a certain bitterness may well accompany your 'exposures.' Sweet as the feeling of revenge may be, the sense of having been (once more) 'betrayed' is hard for you to live with. Because it means that you must begin your search for the ideal father all over again.

In our opinion the chief stumbling block resides in the word 'ideal.' When a small child is disappointed in an important adult in its environment, the invariable result is that the child envisions an ideal who will – someday – replace and make up for the disappointing reality. And this ideal lasts a long, long time. Once in a blue moon the wise and perfect teacher or steadfast and understanding friend may enter one's life, but the unfortunate part is that even when this happens, the child (once a boy, now a grown man) is usually not able to thrive on the relationship for very long. Why? Because his fear of reliving the early childhood disappointment prompts him to see betrayals where they don't really exist; and because an unconscious wish to even up old scores makes it difficult for him to refrain from seeking out the father figure's 'failures' and exposing them to the world. So if you've had a lot of trouble with male employers, foremen, supervisors, etc., this kind of pattern may be at the root of it. It is very easy for you to be a gadfly, an iconoclast, or a rebel without cause. Naturally enough, the person whom you are out to 'get' responds indignantly to your behavior, and he is in a position where he can slap you down and ultimately get rid of you – often with great reluctance and regret, believe it or not!

For reasons which escape our present understanding, you are less likely to adopt a gay lifestyle than any other male birth order with the possible exception of the older brother with a younger sister. Instead you are prone to form romantic relationships (marital or otherwise) with women who, if you stop to think about it, are very much like your mother or your sister in their appearance and/or behavior. Paradoxically, you are apt to gravitate toward women who are themselves older sisters with at least one younger brother. As for male friendships, while you may have had one or two close male playmates during boyhood, the quality of such friendships is usually a miniature version of your primary male-to-male relationship with your father. You tended to hold aloof from other boys (until at least adolescence or early adulthood) and to seek the attention and admiration of your mother's women friends.

Like your sister, you are most comfortable when your own and your love partner's roles are clearly demarcated – with special emphasis on which areas of life are each one's own bailiwick. Once these 'house rules' have been established, you are very touchy about any behavior which appears to intrude upon your prerogatives. At home you seek domestic peace and quiet (at any price – even at the risk of being henpecked). But you usually stake out a den, or some corner of the premises, into which nobody is permitted entry without a special (and rare) invitation from you. Once you have staked out a territory – grocery shopping, gardening, finances, or whatever – you will not brook any unsolicited interference from others.

Generally speaking, you are not inclined toward very close and warm friendships. At the same time you are probably the most gregarious of all ordinal positions; you enjoy gatherings where there are lots of people who know each other quite well and where the atmosphere is one of convivial and lighthearted camaraderie. Like the majority of last-borns, you are a keen and astute observer of the social scene and are quick to sense which way the wind is blowing. Unlike others, however, you know how to keep most of your appraisals to yourself. While you enjoy gossip as much as the rest of us, and can occasionally speak out of turn, you rarely do so when it involves a matter that impinges on your own sense of privacy. For there has never been a more private person than yourself once you have decided to keep your own counsel. Next to the middle child, you are the most secretive of all ordinal positions. We think this is because you *had* to develop evasive techniques and strategies in order to preserve a modicum of privacy so that some aspects of your life wouldn't get taken over by the adult (female) world. Your childhood struggle to protect your personal privacy has paid off in your considerable skill at masking your true feelings and sidestepping other people's curiosity. Because of it, you finally learned how to be diplomatic and tactful. In fact you may even come across as glib and conventional in the eyes of some observers.

Yours is the birth order most likely to kick over the traces during the teen years. During that period you often feel as though you cannot bear to deal with so much as one more suggestion or criticism or prying question from the women around you. At such times you yearn to break free and be on your own – to live on the street, join a commune, hitchhike across the country, become a ski or beach bum, join a cult, etc. Whatever forms this youthful rebellion may take, they all have one thing in common – a fierce determination to run your own life and to declare your independence from family ties; to see whether you can survive by your own wits, talents, and resources. It is not uncommon for your family to get very upset about your 'wild and ungovernable behavior' during this period, but the more they try to curb such behavior the more desperate and misunderstood you feel. The major portion of your despair comes from a lifelong feeling that the world simply will not listen to your needs, no matter how loudly you proclaim them. Your family, on the other hand, is convinced that when you are kicking and thrashing nobody can reason with you. Both of you are correct – in a way. What usually gets lost in the shuffle is your right to make your own mistakes and their right to express opinions about what you are doing. Failure to sort these factors out can result in considerable anguish for all concerned, and can goad you into perpetuating this behavior far into your early thirties. At this point. however, you generally decide that you've successfully made your case and sorted out what you want to do with your life. So you make peace with your family and go serenely about your own pursuits.

Like the older brother with one younger sister, you are not prone to confide in others, and deep introspection is almost never your forte. Instead, you much prefer to reason things out, and have little patience with such amorphous or abstract or 'zany' concepts as intuition or ESP. Consequently you are apt to be a person of firm and well-nigh unshakable opinions. Sometimes your reservoir of submerged resentment may erupt in vociferous public support of iconoclastic or unpopular causes. Failing this, you are the most likely of all birth orders to be an expert at behind-the-scenes wheeling and dealing. You are at your best as a big fish in a small pool, and you thrive in relatively small social clubs, organizations, task forces, and communities. In this kind of close-knit atmosphere you can be downright charming in the light-hearted and often amusing way which makes you sought after for parties and other festive occasions. Your girlfriend may tell you that you 'made a fool of yourself' but you know better; you haven't been checking out audience response all your life for nothing!

You are also more prone than other birth orders to develop drinking and other substance-abuse problems. In the light of this, we don't find it at all surprising that many of you lean over backward in the opposite direction – often being strict vegetarians, health food buffs, and totally abstemious when it comes to alcohol, stimulants, drugs, and sometimes even traditional pharmaceuticals.

The best way for parents to forestall the pitfalls of this ordinal position is to strike up a clear-cut agreement between themselves regarding those areas in which their boy can (nay, *must*) be allowed to have his own space – with a firm guarantee that in such areas the mother and sister will respect his boundaries and refrain from interfering. A special (but unsmothering) effort on the part of the father to establish a personal level of rigorously private confidentiality between the two males can also prove highly beneficial. Extreme care needs to be taken, however, to ensure that under no circumstances should such confidences between father and son be shared with the mother or sister without first obtaining the boy's permission; because in his view there is no greater crime than for one fellow to betray another's confidence. We regret to add, however, that if *you* should wind up the father of a first-born daughter and younger son, you will probably not pay much attention to anything we have said in this chapter. Insight and self-exploration are not your strong suit, and psychological concepts are regarded by you with considerable suspicion. But you can take heart in the wise saying (by Rochefoucauld?) which goes 'There is more faith in honest doubt than in half our creeds.'

Your rebellious period, painful though it might have been at the time, no doubt brought you many unusual adventures and tested your limits, thereby giving you a wealth of both stories and wisdom that delight your friends and strengthen your considerable abilities in your chosen career. Meanwhile, you can take justifiable pride in your unusual capacity to learn something new every day of your life.

CHAPTER FOURTEEN

Younger Sister of Older Brother

A number of years ago we asked thirty-five prominent psychotherapists in the Greater New York area to list the birth orders of their current caseload. We discovered that while first-born oldest children with three or more younger siblings rarely seek help of any sort, a close runner-up is you – the one and only younger sister of an all-wise older brother who – during your childhood at least – was probably touted by your parents as the Future Prime Minister. This is particularly noteworthy in view of the fact that your brother is by no means a stranger to the consulting room – where he seldom refers to you at all and often conveys the prolonged impression that he grew up as an only child. This is apt to hold true even when you are close in age and your life-long relationship has been as cozy as Hansel and Gretel. We have a pretty good idea why this is so, and believe that it will become clear as we proceed through this chapter.

If any child in this world has the right to cry out 'I didn't ask to be born!' it is you. Girls in your ordinal position, more than any other, feel that they grew up with the important cards in the deck stacked against them in their brother's favor. As astrologers are fond of pointing out when Saturn transits one of our signs, it 'builds character': we either sink or we learn to swim. And you did, in fact, learn to be much more of a swimmer than you have ever given yourself credit for. The kind of situation that confronted you – a dilemma not of your own making – must often have seemed quite hopeless to you.

Again, more than for any other birth order, your sibling

loomed over you like a colossus throughout your growing-up years, casting his powerful shadow into what must have seemed like every nook and cranny of your life – both public and private. Whichever way you turned, he was there – held up to you as an example of what a person 'should' be, either deliberately or else by inference. Inasmuch as he was first-born and male, it seldom occurred to him that his presence could be causing you such frequent anguish. After all, he was merely doing his thing – i.e., basking in the role of Prince when the opportunity afforded, and otherwise trying not to feel hurt or offended because *you* came along to (seemingly) monopolize for a time the family limelight. He didn't ask for you to be born, either, don't forget. After he recovered from his initial sense of outrage (as much as anyone recovers from such early blows to self-esteem), he may have decided to turn around and welcome you as the promised playmate and precious little sister – until some unpleasant things began to happen which he has swept under the rug and is probably not able to recall any more. Gift-wrapped packages which came into the house might have been his to *open*, but their contents were for the new girl-baby. Relatives and other visitors to the household may have given him 'equal time,' but it was you that they had really come to ooh and aah over. From being the 'one and only' he became the 'first among equals' – quite a comedown. Out of sheer self-defense he hit upon the device of taking refuge in daydreams, pretending (whenever he could) that you were a nonperson – a small female humanoid of no real consequence. Your wish to be acknowledged, protected, and loved by him was probably very central to your life, and any acceptance of you on his part brought sunshine into it. The extent to which you failed in your efforts caused you enough torment that you seldom admit to yourself just how important his regard was for you – let alone tell anyone else about it.

The most difficult thing for you was the element of confusion involved. Your brother's presumed place in the world (Heaven help *him*!) was already clearly and dramatically outlined. Who or what you were supposed to become was by no means as clear – and worse, nobody appeared to consider it important. You were, more often than not, permitted (and sometimes even encouraged) to grow untended, like a weed. Once you had settled into the family, everybody appeared to focus on your brother while it seemed that your feelings, fears, and aspirations were being patronized or passed over altogether. As is still customary with girl children in our society, it was taken for granted that your destiny was to eventually wed a reasonably acceptable man and bring up a family. We have carefully chosen the words 'reasonably acceptable' because in your family the chances are that, even within the conventional female role reserved for you, excellence was still and all being subtly discouraged. The family, deep down, did not seem to want you to attain even the distinction of marrying a man worthwhile or prestigious enough to outshine the Prince, your brother. So your perception of the world and your eventual role in it was that you were to keep a low profile and not even marry anyone of consequence.

We have mentioned that our casework experience with your brother gives us very little information about you unless we dig for it. But when it comes to your husband – forget it; he never gets mentioned at all!

What must have been particularly puzzling for you was the undercover quality of so many interpersonal issues during your growing-up years. Your brother probably wasn't openly hostile toward you; he had learned early on to hide his true feelings, even from himself. Your parents may have seemed to give you special status as the girl of the family; but their affirmative gestures were baffling, and never paid off in any way that you could really define for yourself. There were, in sum, very few areas in life which seemed to belong to you exclusively – while so many of the truly 'worthwhile' enterprises appeared to have been entrusted to your brother. Meanwhile, you were convinced that he knew where he was going, and that only you were destined to wander forever in a wilderness of ill-defined and unattainable goals. Even when you did manage to stake out territories of your own, you were not sure that they were truly worth taking seriously. You felt torn between trying to court the world's approval on the one hand or simply finding your own direction on the other.

Children need a great deal of support before they can shape goals of their own, and your world seemed far more interested in your brother's destiny than in yours. Again, a child's positive self-regard depends upon favorable feedback from the members of the family circle. When the child gets little or no such affirmation, confidence and optimism are diminished accordingly. In your case the 'youngest child' anxiety about never catching up may have verged on absolute despair. No matter what projects you undertook, the results never seemed to merit the kind of excitement which your brother's every tiny endeavor appeared to generate. In short, you have always found it very difficult to believe in or trust your own worthwhileness or the value of any contribution you make (large or small) to the world you inhabit. Even with redoubtable accomplishments you are prone to feel like a fake. Which brings us to another topic of great importance to you.

In your struggle to ward off puzzlement and to create areas of certainty in a baffling world you acquired some very useful qualities – persistence, determination, organization, and a capacity for hard work. You are also far more resourceful than you give yourself credit for, and are often able to create a field of endeavor which is all your own and of which you are the sole proprietor. Rather than function as one of many in someone else's bailiwick, you prefer, if possible, to set up shop for yourself and work on a free-lance basis. You might go into graphic design of some sort or teach an instrument (you often take a keen interest in music and art) but you are more likely to establish a service of some sort – with a staff of subordinates to keep the traffic moving. It's not that you have a need to be in charge; it's just that when you are the boss you are less likely to have to endure criticism (and criticism is something which you find painful to deal with more than any other birth order). Your continuing fear is that somebody may expose you as ignorant or incompetent.

Out of the raw material of this fear – which arises from your feeling that no matter how praiseworthy your accomplishments, any crown you wear is a stolen one – you have distilled a rare capacity for turning the tables on your adversaries. Let people try accusing you of anything and they will soon find themselves on the witness stand – explaining, justifying, and apologizing to you for their outrageous 'unfairness.' Having thus won the battle, you are then free to forgive them for their lack of humanity, whereupon they withdraw in bewilderment. In short, you have taught yourself how to confound other people (as you once felt confounded) and to pull the rug out from under their well-prepared attacks. It is one of your greatest strengths. However, it's more intimidating than you realize, and it can put a distance between you and others. It is precisely this combination of defensiveness on the one hand and fear of discovery on the other which makes you such a rare candidate for counseling.

You are apt to have a fairly wide circle of friends who enjoy your company and admire your pluckiness and hard-earned individuality. In social situations which aren't loaded down with heavy emotional vibes you are inclined to be gregarious. You meet people easily and have a gift for making them comfortable in your presence, which is every bit as noteworthy as your penchant for making them uncomfortable when you so desire.

When it comes to friendships, your most lasting and viable ones are apt to be with members of your own sex. We think this is because your relations with females are somehow simpler and more open; less entangled in hidden agendas on both sides of the fence. If a woman decides that she likes you despite your faults, the matter is settled for all time; if she doesn't like you, then you both go your separate ways and that's the end of that. For your part, you permit yourself to be more honest and less on guard with women, and other women can either take it or leave it. There is one single exception. Unlike most other birth orders, you rarely (if ever) form close relationships with females in your own ordinal position.

When it comes to men, the picture becomes more complex. Owing to the ambivalence which characterized your early relationship with your brother (admiration mixed with envy; a desire for his acceptance mixed with a wish to compete) you are apt to approach any man in a spirit of ambivalence that may now be subconscious on your part. By this we mean that you often carry in your hands a custard pie which you are capable of feeding to him at one moment or throwing in his face the next. Part of you seeks a man who is worthy of your respect – like your brother when you were very small – while at the same time you wish to avoid any possibility that he might embroil you in a battle of wits or wills. The two cancel each other out, however, if you stop to think about it. You are saying, 'I want an assertive man who will do exactly what I tell him to do' – a contradiction in terms! We are reminded of a teenage girl who, having just seen *Gone With the Wind*, couldn't make up her mind which kind of woman she wanted to be like in adult life – Scarlett O'Hara or Melanie

Wilkes. After giving the matter much thought, she decided that she could have the best of both worlds by being 'a *tempestuous* Melanie.' There *ain't* no such animal – nor is there a genuinely assertive man who will permit you to run his life, any more than you would allow anyone to manage yours. The difficulty you have in coming to terms with this particular aspect of reality accounts more than anything else, in our opinion, for the impression we have that of all ordinal positions yours has the roughest time in the romance department. It doesn't have to be this way, really. The more you can understand about your own personal history, the less you will be doomed to repeat it. Recognizing the likely source of your ambivalence will enable you to decide how to handle it in happy relationships with men.

Now let us do an about-face and state that the other pitfall can be a naive over-trustingness on your part. The reason for this is quite simple: overly suspicious persons are usually bending over backwards to protect themselves from a strong impulse to trust others – as an infant trusts the parents' arms. When you expose this side of your nature, you can be a patsy for the kind of man whose lifestyle is dedicated to the exploitation of other people. Such people are called 'con men,' and their specialty is an uncanny sense of knowing precisely what song your heart desires to hear – whereupon they commence to sing it as you never heard it sung before. In no time flat you can be convinced that your mutual 'chemistry' began three thousand years ago in a previous life and that you were made for each other. And so you make beautiful music together until suddenly he disappears (literally or figuratively) and you berate yourself for having been so gullible. 'How,' you ask yourself, 'could I have let myself be duped this way?!' We think we've got an answer; try it on for size.

All of us are born totally dependent upon our adult caretakers for nourishment, warmth, safety, and so forth.

Because our ability, as infants, to express our needs is very limited, our parents have to sense these needs and take care of them, and if for one reason or another they don't do this well enough, we suffer a degree of deprivation (great or small) which we seek to compensate for later on in life. The more deprived we are, the more exaggerated and unrealistic is the dream which we create for ourselves – a pot of gold at the rainbow's end, pie in the sky, knight on a white charger, Santa Claus; you name it.

This brings us to the subject of your mother. She may have been given to extolling your brother's virtues – real or imaginary – and this did little to enhance any feelings of warmth, trust, or closeness to her which you were seeking. On the other hand, she may have let your father (or other men in the family) do the extolling, and shared your lot as a kind of second-class citizen. But you were (understandably) not grateful for that state of affairs, either. Any way you take it, Mum is not likely to have given you as much emotional support as you probably required at that early time. Consequently your mother may feel stronger affection for you than you are able to summon up for her, and you are highly vulnerable to what might be termed 'the song of the all-giving parent' – especially when it comes from a man.

Why a man? That brings us to the subject of your father. Chances are very great that at about the time you became the kind of little girl whom fathers are inclined to adore (between two and three and a half years old) your brother was pushing age seven or so. That is precisely the age when many fathers begin to stop cuddling their boys and start keeping a sharp eye out to insure that the Prince does not wander into 'feminine' pursuits. This holds particularly true of your father – who may well have guessed that his son would be his only male heir. While you thus received your father's open affection, you were less likely to have got his encouragement and respect, or as much concern as your brother did. Like most children who don't realize how fortunate they are, you regarded this 'neglect' on your father's part as a deep and wounding slight – an insult to your intelligence and a lack of confidence in your worth-whileness as a human being. Add this to what you experienced in relation to your brother, and men don't add up as being very ego-building, do they? Small wonder that your female-to-male interactions are so fraught with *Sturm und Drang*!

Generally speaking, you grew up in a world where it often seemed to you that your brother had all the praises and rewards of life heaped on his head without ever having to lift a finger in order to earn them, whereas you felt that life required that you turn somersaults, jump through flaming hoops, and perpetually sing for your supper (a supper composed of leftovers from his princely feast). Deep down you have always had a secret desire to pull off a similar coup – to reap vast rewards with minimal effort. For this reason you chafe at credentials – certificates, licenses, diplomas, formal degrees, etc. Sometimes you will even imply (without actually lying about it) that you have studied a skill or a subject when in fact you attended a few introductory lectures or demonstrations. Your thinking here is 'why should I have to earn all of these so-called credentials when he was born with them? It's unfair and I refuse to give in, and anyone who thinks I don't know my business can go fly a kite!' This, of course, does nothing to lessen your sense of being a fraud. The fact of the matter is that you are probably a highly capable person who is loved and appreciated more than you are willing to let yourself know about. If you could just relax and risk trusting people a little more, your life could be a lot happier. You may get hurt once in a while – as all of us do – but getting hurt nowadays is not the disaster it was when you were little.

CHAPTER FIFTEEN

Older Brother of Younger Brother

In *1984* George Orwell describes the ultimate police state where Big Brother is the highest authority and posters proclaim 'Big Brother is watching you!' In actual fact, however, when it comes to you, that motto might well read 'Big Brother, you are being watched.' It is a fact which has shaped your life that while you may have been looked up to, looked over, and overseen, you were seldom overlooked.

When a new baby comes into the family, an older child can sometimes withdraw into his or her own private world. If you had been succeeded by a younger sister, you would also probably have done so. But when a second *boy* is born, parents and other relatives almost hang a sign around the older boy's neck reading 'Big Brother; protector, guide, playmate, confidant, coach, teacher, and role model.' That last designation, 'role model,' perhaps needs a little explanation.

In our society a little girl's preparation for her role as an adult woman consists in large part of simply imitating the behavior of her mother and various other important women in her environment. In a kind of apprenticeship, she learns the ropes and, by dint of careful mimicry, is assured of gaining admittance to the 'club' of grown women to which she is destined for membership.

With boys in this day and age, however, role modeling is not at all that simple. Before the Industrial Revolution fathers usually pursued their occupation at home – cobbler, cooper, chandler, blacksmith, weaver, farmer, etc. – and a boy underwent an apprenticeship-by-imitation similar to that of girls. But after industrialization almost all male occupations – aside from farming – shifted to places outside the home. Dad goes off in the morning to his job in some strange place foreign to your experience, and does things which you can only hope to understand 'when you're older.'

Granted, there have always been occupations – banking or going to sea or fighting in foreign wars – that excluded a man's sons, but nowadays unless Dad works down the street or next door, his children (girls as well as boys) see him far less of the time than they see Mum, schoolteachers, peers and siblings. So it is understandable that boys find it very difficult to conceptualize, define and measure themselves against yardsticks of 'masculine' endeavor which they scarcely comprehend. When one asks a boy of seven or eight what he wants to be when he grows up he usually replies 'a policeman' or 'a fireman' – probably because these are highly visible occupations, and he knows what policemen and firemen *do*. 'Catch crooks and save people, of course.' Key-punch operator, shoe salesman, lawyer, or department store supervisor are very elusive occupations when a boy is trying to measure himself against 'what a man should be.'

To further complicate matters, it happens that most clear-cut formulations about the subject are usually handed down to him by *females* – and couched in terms of what 'maleness' is not. Growing boys in our society are informed that males do not cry, do not tattle, do not fight with girls, must not be timid nor vulnerable nor 'sissified,' nor interested in things which are 'feminine.'

As a first-born boy, you were expected to sort out all of these don'ts and translate them into socially appropriate behavior. At the same time you were trying with all your might to fulfill a host of paradoxical expectations thrust upon you by zealous but inexperienced parents. You may wonder what we mean by 'paradoxical.' Put simply, your parents unwittingly placed you in a Catch-22 situation; on the one hand they wanted you to assert yourself and reach out for new realms to conquer (the pioneer role of all oldest children – especially male; see Chapter 4). But at the same time they did not want you to behave in any manner which might set you apart from your age mates as being different or abnormal. To give a concrete example: They may have made you skip a form in school when you were at the top of your class and then been disappointed when you brought home Bs instead of As. Thus your claim to fame suddenly became an albatross around your neck. In other words, you grew up with two conflicting sets of imperatives or injunctions; to be a daringly explorative pioneer on the one hand, and to be a play-safe conservative on the other. More often than not, you opted for the latter, and thus became the Guardian of Tradition *par excellence*.

In addition, you were tacitly handed another function – that of role model for your younger brother. Your female counterpart (the older sister of a younger sister) did not have to assume this task, since her mother and other adult females had pretty much cornered the market when it came to setting the standards for her little sister's 'femininity.'

Your cohort – older brother of a younger sister – had no problem with role modeling. The fact that little sister often felt under pressure to try to live up to her older brother's image was her problem, not his. *You*, however, were expected to set the standards; you were saddled with the challenging task of trying to keep your own vessel from capsizing and at the same time you felt duty-bound to strike a pose in the prow of your storm-tossed boat – a pose worthy of emulation by a younger male sibling. Not an easy assignment, to put it mildly! Your parents probably told you outright to 'set a good example' for your little brother.

It is part of parents' human nature that they are reluctant to go through explanations all over again to their next-born if they can possibly induce the first-born to take over a big share of the necessary instructions. Usually their fond hope is that the older child will feel honored by such responsibilities and will also acquire supervisory techniques and abilities which will stand him or her in good stead later on in life. Thus it is a common belief that by these means older sisters acquire practice in 'mothering' while older brothers gain 'executive' skills. However, as we just explained, less pressure is exerted upon older sisters when it comes to the role-modeling function.

Your brother's unabashed willingness – as a toddler at least – to follow your lead wherever and whenever possible was a plus factor, however. Many of your private anxieties and insecurities were assuaged by the presence of a worshipful disciple who was often happy to sit at your feet and absorb whatever gems of wisdom you chose to favor him with. You probably remember all the times when he was a recalcitrant brat, but you may have scant recollection or awareness of just how central your 'wisdom' was to his life and to the formation of his character. Like as not, it was you – and not the adults in his environment – who clued him in on such matters as the existence (or nonexistence) of God, the facts of procreation, the differences – real or imaginary – between the sexes, the actuality of death, what makes the sky blue, how to tell time, the motivations of various family members, etc. No matter that he grew up believing that 'babies come out of Mum's bellybutton' or that 'you should never touch your wee-wee because it might fall off.' You did the best you could, and you did teach him a host of truly useful things, information which you had acquired by dint of long and attentive introspection and observation. Your counsel smoothed and paved his way in a manner which he has probably never ceased to be grateful for. First-born boys excel over all other ordinal positions when it comes to complex verbal expression at an early age (contrary to the general belief which favors girls for linguistic precocity and boys for large-muscle coordination). You no doubt delighted the adults in your environment with your articulateness and positively dazzled your younger brother.

The fact that you and the adults in your childhood environment typecast you as a role model does not mean, of course, that he necessarily followed in your footsteps or assumed your attitudes – at least not in the way that you intended. He may have imbibed quite a lot of practical guidance from you, but his perception of your role in the world may well have sent him scurrying off in the exact opposite direction from everything you stood for – much to your discomfiture and envy. 'Discomfiture' because you took your commission very seriously (as you generally take all tasks assigned to you), and you probably felt that your brother's departure from your teachings was a personal failure for you; 'envy' because you have ended up with a strong sense that he had always appeared freer and less encumbered with responsibilities than you. He was probably allowed to go to bed at a later hour than you were at the same age; to gad about unattended at a far earlier age; to get away with various behaviors which you weren't allowed. It is quite natural that you should consider it patently unfair for him to be brought up according to more lenient rules than the ones you grew up with – at least in your early years. If you were like most boys caught in that predicament, you may have 'taken your case to court,' demanding redress of grievances and equal justice. At that point you may have been solemnly reminded that 'you are the older one' and therefore have more serious business to take care of. Or you may have been told that 'times change' and that rules catch up with the spirit of the times. The fact is that your parents did learn from their experiences with you – but it was your brother who benefited from it. This situation is enough to make anybody a stickler for rules (the letter of the law, not its spirit) and a loyal defender of time-honored traditions.

Small wonder, then, that of all ordinal positions yours tends to be the most conservative – that is, the most resistant to change (familial, cultural, philosophical, etc.) of any sort. This does not mean that you aren't capable of innovation and reform, merely that you're prone to evaluate life in terms of what is preservable rather than what is expendable.

Anything 'newfangled' tends to offend and alarm you. When you do shed all your inhibitions and jump on the merry-go-round, your 'free' behavior carries with it a sort of hysterical recklessness every bit as extreme as the conservatism which it displaced. Barring uncharacteristic extravagances, however, your most comfortable posture is likely to be that of the sober citizen. 'We are not put in this world to enjoy ourselves but to do our damned duty,' to quote Bismarck. This particular stance, however, carried the disadvantage of setting you up as the fall guy for your little brother and his young friends, who could on occasion drive you into frenzies of embarrassment, frustration, and rage. Folklore traditionally holds that childhood teasing and tormenting is the fate of younger children at the hands of their older sibs. While there is a great deal of truth in this, there are two dramatic reversals of this rule. You and your female counterpart, the elder sister of a younger sister, are often on the receiving end. In both cases your younger sib is able to devise diabolical techniques aimed at making you lose your cool, abandon your cherished sense of personal dignity, and otherwise behave like an elephant being tyrannized by a mouse. One reason why this particular state of affairs is so rarely recognized is because you were understandably reluctant to submit yourself to the added indignity of complaining to the adults that a younger child was picking on you.

Like so many children, you handled your fury as best you could, bided your time, and plotted revenge. As we observed in Chapter 7, 'getting even' is a basic human motivation – almost chemical in its inevitability. If some-body forgets to honor our birthday, for example, the chances are ninety-nine out of a hundred that when their birthday rolls around we will genuinely forget to make the accustomed contact. And so it was, like as not, with you. You managed to redress your grievances so far as your younger brother was concerned, but you almost always wound up with the feeling that whatever you accomplished in the way of just revenge was too little and too late. It's as if nothing can ever make up for the indignities you suffered at his hands, close pals though you may have been in various other times and contexts. You probably don't realize it, of course, but as the youngest child he had little awareness that he was exerting so much impact upon you. For this reason he may have experienced your vengeance as unnecessarily cruel and uncalled for. Never having fully comprehended the fact that you had areas of genuine vulnerability, he never could (and still cannot) understand the depth of your lingering resentment.

As so often happens with two-sib combinations, it is possible that you and your younger brother were boon companions and inseparably close to one another. Much depends on what was going on between each of you and your parents. There are a number of parent–child situations in which neither parent favors either of their offspring and neither Mum nor Dad may, in fact, have a true vocation for parenthood – so that the children team up with *each other* for mutual consolation and emotional support. In this kind of setup it becomes almost a case of the children versus the parents. But this is the exception rather than the rule. When it does happen – as with the Wright brothers – the closeness between the two reaches an emotional intensity which is legendary – and rarely matched by your female counterparts, the older and younger sister.

The circumstances of prehistoric life were such that the sheer physical survival of our species has been largely dependent upon the capacity of its males to form intense bonds of empathy and cooperation with one another. That groups of 'bonded' males can also launch warfare against one another is, unfortunately, the dark side of this particular coin.

Your adult relationship with your brother may or may not be cordial, but if the age gap is four years or less, chances are that a strong bond continues to influence both of your lives. This is especially true if you allied yourselves in any important way against the common 'foe,' your parents and/or other significant adults in your childhood environment. Since yours was the protective role in the relationship, you probably have had the heavier emotional investment in whatever bonds developed between you. Moreover, your involvement with your brother, defensive or otherwise, was at the expense of your relationship with females your own age. When, at adolescence, you started to show interest in them, it was as though you were seeing them for the first time. You are therefore apt to view women with a mixture of idolatry on the one hand (putting them up on a pedestal) and anxious distrust on the other. It doesn't seem to matter whether your childhood relationship to your mother was a close, warm, and healthy one; she was, after all, Mum. Females of your own generation tend to be regarded by you as exotic and strangely alien creatures who always hold all of the trump cards. In their presence you are likely to be all thumbs, as you secretly debate whether, or if, or when, to ask for a date, put your hand on her shoulder, steal a kiss, or whatever. Having become accustomed to a deeply empathic relationship with your same-sex younger sibling, you seek to establish the same kind of wordless awareness with members of the opposite sex – usually with perplexing results.

It becomes particularly difficult if you and your brother have grown away from one another in your adult years. You are apt to keenly miss his support. If such is the case, you would do well to find a 'replacement' for him; a close male friend in whom you can confide and to whom you can turn for that wordless emotional support in time of need which you got from your brother. (We would also add that all such problems are compounded in the case of males who are the oldest of three or more brothers; they grew up with a whole gang of male cronies. And you think you have troubles in the romantic/sexual area!)

You will recall that in our introduction to this section of the book we mentioned the tendency of parents to 'adopt' their own offspring – especially when only two sibs are involved. We also noted that it may be a 'transference phenomenon,' even though we didn't use that specific phrase. 'Transference' is a psychoanalytic term coined by Freud which refers specifically to the way in which a client in psychotherapy 'transfers' intense feelings – positive or negative – onto the therapist. The result is that the client perceives the therapist as embodying various emotionally loaded characteristics of one or more important people in the client's childhood environment. Stated more simply, the therapist – regardless of age and sex – may be variously seen as a replica of Mum, Dad, sibling(s), grandparents, teachers, etc., or as combining the best or worst features of all or any of these. From this realization it is but a short step to the recognition that transference is not confined merely to doctor–patient relationships. All of us experience it constantly in our everyday comings and goings. We often treat our boss like our father and fellow employees, teachers, pupils, friends, enemies, lovers, can be seen as modern-day versions of our beloved sister, brother/play-mate or wicked stepmother to a greater or lesser degree.

We said earlier that part of the adoption process may have to do with the role which either or both of the parents can assign to a particular child. Thus one youngster may be given the role of Big Brother or Sister or Little Sister or Brother, while another may be commandeered to play the part of the Dad's Right Hand or Mama's Angel or the Hell Raiser, etc. We also touched on the fact that parents can subconsciously influence the second of two same-sex children to 'stand in' for the son or daughter that one or both of them yearned for. Actually, this is more apt to happen when two *female* children are involved, when either of the two girls is in effect asked to be the 'boy' of the family. It is rare – but not impossible – for one or both parents to encourage one of their sons to take the place of a longed-for daughter. Oddly enough, it is far more common for both parents to regard their two boys as a kind of 'team.' A situation can also arise whereby each parent adopts one of the sons. Thus one youngster is Dad's boy and the other is Mum's boy. So far we have not been able to discern any pattern governing this particular choice. What does attract our attention, however, is the apparent fact that of all parental adoptions this last-mentioned one seems least damaging to the siblings. (This is in sharp contrast to the frequent situation between two sisters – where one is apt to be dubbed the Princess and the other the Princeling; so that strong rivalries can develop between them which may sometimes have lifelong repercussions.)

Despite the foregoing, however, one thing seems fairly certain: you were the 'big' brother while he was the 'little' brother. Or was it that certain? Small children take terms like 'big' and 'little' quite literally. So, if your younger sib grew taller than you – or larger-boned, or stronger, or more energetic, or just plain bigger at any time during your first eight years together, your roles may have got reversed in a number of ways. His physical advantages may have made him more of a pioneer, explorer, daredevil, risk-taker than your own endowments allowed you to be. Or maybe his temperament was aggressive, so that he learned how to beat you up or otherwise coerce you into playing the part of his younger brother. But even so, we have observed that a kind of protective concern about your little brother's welfare can still persist from those first few years when you were indeed the big brother and he was your protégé. In this case you are likely to have strong mixed feelings where he is concerned. On the one hand you long for the good old days of brotherly togetherness while on the other hand you chafe and rankle at the memory of countless outrages which you suffered at his hands. This helps to explain why your closest male friend is apt to be a younger brother in his own family, growing up with at least one older brother. Boys who are raised exclusively with one or more sisters are likely to be more female-oriented, and extremely skittish (in the 'fish out of water' sense) when it comes to creating a viable bond with other males.

By far the most prevalent pattern for your ordinal position is that of the older brother who grew up in the role of baby sitter, counselor, protector, mentor, and guide. A girl in your position (see Chapters 12 and 16) is allowed by most societies to assume that she has a certain right to be protected and nurtured and comforted by one or both of her parents occasionally. Two things may keep her from cashing in on this prerogative – a sense of responsibility, and her pride in being 'second in command' to her parents *vis-à-vis* the rearing of her sib. But the fact remains that this option – to cry when she's hurt – usually stays open to her, whether or not she chooses to avail herself of it. Such is not usually the case for first-born males. Tradition dictates that part of 'maleness' consists of being able to go it alone – 'Big boys don't cry,' and all that. Big boys also are not expected to disobey, or to be frightened, or to be baffled, or to be in need of protection, or to require consolation or to complain or to reach for emotional support (*moral* support? – yes; *emotional*? – well, seldom). For this reason you carry around more of a hunger to have an older brother of your own than most ordinal positions (with the possible exception of the older brother of more than one younger sister).

For some reason, the fathers of men in your birth order often end up acting more like another younger brother than like a father or the big brother you always wanted. This is especially true in your adult years, possibly because by that time you have acquired the reputation for being the family counselor and guide. This helps to explain the fact that you tend to gravitate toward men who will play an older brother role in your life (rather than the stereotypic father figure). As we said earlier, such men were usually younger brothers in their own families, by the way. We would add, however, that if you did have a strongly supportive Dad, it is quite likely that your choice of a pal will still veer in the direction of somebody who is himself the younger brother of a brother (see Chapter 17).

The 'let's tease brother' syndrome was by no means a one-way street coming in your direction. A talent for 'getting even' is likely to be the special province of last-born children – especially in larger families – but you are definitely a close runner-up in this department. To be sure, along with this goes the ability to get in your kicks in a compassionate and kidding but sympathetic way. At the same time there are doubtless any number of occasions available to your memory where you derived a definite sadistic pleasure in mimicking and otherwise tormenting your brother. In addition, next to the younger brother of a sister (see Chapter 13), you have the most easily triggered temper in the whole birth order zodiac. Like him, you are likely to express your anger in explosions of rage that take the form of chair-kicking or dashing things to smithereens on the floor. You are, however, more free with your hands than he is – so that when you get angry you can let go and swat, hit, and punch. This is understandable, since most cultures permit some rough-and-tumble among siblings of the same sex – especially boys. We all know that most parents won't permit such behavior in their presence ('You're bigger than he is; *shame* on you!'), but there's not much they can do about it when their backs are turned – as you well know. (Of course, little brother also knew the various ways by which you would get even with him – sooner or later – if he ever had the poor judgment to 'tell' on you.)

Much of your anger and frustration arises from any situation in which you perceive the reins of control slipping from your hands. For you are generally a most conscientious person, and you regard being on top of things as essential. You like to fulfill your commitments to the letter, and anyone or anything that gets in the way of your doing so can evoke your resentment. For when duty calls, you respond with all of the earnest endeavor and hard work you can possibly muster. You run a tight ship, and woe betide the dullard or sluggard who is placed under your command! Of course there are many situations where it is neither politic nor wise nor expedient at the purely practical level for you to give vent to your anger. This renders you a ready candidate for frequent bouts of depression. The reason for this is that a lot of what we call 'depression' is nothing more than rage which gets turned back upon the self.

Let us, at this point, put in a good word for anger. Anger is, after all, one of many emotions – one of the many colors to be found on our emotional artist's palette. It serves very useful purposes and is to our emotional life what various organs are to our physical existence – part of the life-sustaining equipment each of us is born with. There *is* no 'bad' anger any more than there is an intrinsically 'bad' shade of green, orange, blue, etc. There are only 'bad' ways of handling it – as well as stupid or enlightened or creative ways. Angry and aggressive feelings might also be likened to a bullet shot out of a gun. If you are surrounded by a stainless steel wall of prohibitions, there is no place for them to go and they will ricochet back onto their source – i.e., you. And this is what depression is usually about (except in certain cases involving advanced age and several other psychophysiological states). If at the onset of depression you can begin asking yourself 'what am I really sore about?' you may get the kind of honest answers which will cause the depression to lift. The important thing to remember, however, is that you would do best to look for the source of your anger in areas where you are apt to be least accepting of it. In other words, don't expect to find the answer in righteous indignation. If you are truly interested in locating the object of your fury, look instead for anger of an embarrassing, humiliating, or petty nature. Because that's why you repressed it in the first place – because, probably, you didn't think it was worthy of you (see Chapter 11 in which we discuss the difference between *re*pression and *sup*pression).

In the occupational sphere you come about as close as anyone can to being what might be termed the 'ideal employee.' You are punctual, rarely absent, cooperative, conscientious, and hard-working. You have little stomach for office politics or wheeling and dealing in general, and you seem to get along well with your coworkers – being cordial (though somewhat distant) in most of your contacts while trying your best to simply avoid anyone whom you regard as a possible source of interpersonal friction. In a word, you do your job, and keep any emotional involvement with colleagues to a bare minimum. What is particularly 'ideal' about you is your tendency to stay with the same employer for a longer stretch of time than any other ordinal position with the possible exception of male singletons. Part of this derives from your conservative nature, and part from the fact that while you generally like your job well enough, your home life and nonvocational interests are more apt to be where your heart is. All of these same qualities also contribute to your being a good pupil at school or in special training courses.

Where is the 'success' at which first-borns are said to lead the pack? Well, it depends on what one means by that word. If it consists in paying your bills promptly, balancing your accounts, conserving your resources, saving money on a regular basis, investing wisely, doing your job well and picking up your annual raise, then you are indeed a success. You almost never get yourself fired, and it is rare for you to mess things up except in the romantic/sexual sphere where – as we noted earlier – you are subject to considerable insecurity and confusion. The more dramatic connotations associated with the word 'success' are most apt to be found in first-borns with two or more younger siblings.

In conclusion, you are usually the man to whom people turn when they want somebody reliable. You learned your lessons diligently and well, have carried them out to the hilt, and haven't tried to change the rules. While you could perhaps do more to enliven your sense of humor (you need to be more *playful*), you have certainly earned the accolade, 'Well done!'

CHAPTER SIXTEEN

Older Sister of Younger Sister

As the big sister in a two-girl family you had a problem: no matter how diligently or conscientiously you strove to shine forth as a model of mature and responsible behavior in a feckless world, you always felt upstaged by your little sister. Her more extroverted and careless approach to life almost invariably appeared to earn more rewards for her than your high standards were ever able to gain for you. When you were both children it must have often seemed to you that she was permitted to get away with murder – to flout many of the rules which you had so carefully learned and built into the very fabric of your personality. While it is a sad fact of life that parents do indeed take a more relaxed attitude in their treatment of later-borns than they did when they were the nervous and inexperienced parents of an only child, it is also true that first-borns generally have no other children in the vicinity with whom they can compare (and thus modify) their perceptions of what the parents do or do not consider to be acceptable behavior.

In this regard it is important to bear in mind that perhaps the major part of parental training or conditioning is accomplished by nonverbal means. 'Brainwashing' would probably be a more accurate term for what child rearing and education are all about, regardless of the society in question. A smile, a frown, a sudden tensing of the body, a chuckle, an airy wave of the hand – all convey volumes of information to a small child (as they do – sometimes unconsciously – to us as adults). The child believes that survival itself in this bewildering world depends upon his or her capacity to accurately read the signals regarding each matter, great or small, which appears to either please or displease the all-important grownups. We must emphasize 'appears' because an inexperienced toddler is prone to catch onto a single instance and build out of it a universal rule by which he or she may be governed henceforth and throughout an entire lifetime.

Thus it was that you, like the majority of other first-borns, built into yourself a lot of imperatives that were undoubtedly more sweeping, more uncompromising, and more all-inclusive than your parents ever meant. Your sister, on the other hand, appeared to deliberately thumb her nose at all you stood for, and what's more, was allowed to get away with it. Her greater freedom of expression (both verbal and behavioral) seemed to be forever putting you at one disadvantage after another and repeatedly casting you in the unpleasant role of the Heavy, Old Stick in the Mud, or Wet Blanket. It is no surprise, therefore, that women in your ordinal position have felt so outmaneuvered and eclipsed by their younger sisters that they have often been heard to say, 'In actuality *I* was more like a younger sister and she was more like the older one.' In such cases it would seem that your sister – the family extrovert – pre-empted the role of leader, and let you be the shy follower.

Another important matter to take into account is the fact that in most cultures the world over, parents almost always hope that their first child will be male. While this state of affairs is rooted in the patriarchal nature of most societies, there also seems to be a psychological pull on a woman pregnant for the first time to present her beloved with a healthy eight-pound replica of himself. New parents will have undoubtedly discussed the possibility that their first-born might turn out to be a girl, but at the same time they have held in reserve the fantasy that their next child – or the one after that – could be a boy. Despite such self-reassurances, however, there is a very powerful temptation to unconsciously raise the first-born girl according to many of the values our society customarily assigns to the rearing of a male child.

It's more than likely that this kind of behavior was augmented by the arrival of your younger sister – especially if your parents had decided to limit the number of their offspring. The effect of a 'last' female child upon your father's conduct was apt to have been particularly pronounced as he felt tempted to treat you more than ever like a companion and colleague-in-the-making. It seems that when there are more than two girls in a family and no sons at all, the youngest girl is most often singled out by Dad (with the tacit collaboration of the other family members) to be 'the son he always wanted,' but when there are only two, the older is more often chosen to fill this role.

However, another outcome is also quite frequent: *both* parents may shift gears when a second girl enters the home, so that you feel suddenly demoted from your role as Dad's Right-hand Man and suddenly subjected to all manner of 'feminizing' tactics while your sister is permitted – and sometimes even encouraged – to be tomboyish. Whether you were reared as a Lieutenant to Dad's General or as the Young Lady of the Family – either way, you probably wound up feeling that the role assigned to you was far less enviable than your sister's. In the first instance you get saddled with many of the same responsibilities as an older brother would have to carry (but with few of his prerogatives) while your sister flounces around in the role of dainty Tinkerbell or the Pretty One; while in the second instance you get relegated to the status of Princess in the Tower – waiting for someone to rescue you while your sister is allowed to bat around in the marketplace with the common folk (who always seem to have more fun than royalty).

Like your male counterpart (the oldest boy with one younger brother) you often found yourself walking a very shaky tightrope whereon you tried valiantly to preserve a balance between your tendency to think about serious philosophical matters and your commonsense, practical approach to life. When you tried to find larger meanings in life, other people (especially your sister and her cronies) were apt to poke fun at your 'impracticality,' but when you addressed yourself to mundane chores and getting them done, you often found yourself being stereotyped as an unimaginative plodder. Sometimes it must have seemed that no matter what posture you assumed, the response of other people was either patronizing or else downright derisive. The feelings of vulnerability which arose from this have persisted into adulthood, and no matter how poised or skilled or thick-skinned your laboriously created public front may be, there is always the lingering dread that some smart aleck will try to make you look like a clumsy fool. When in doubt, therefore, your most comforting maneuver is simply to put your shoulder to the wheel and redouble your efforts to excel. Otherwise you tend to demobilize – scattering your considerable energy and know-how over too wide an area for you to comfortably cope with.

You probably enjoyed a rather close and collaborative relationship with your father – at least during the early years before your sister got vocal and ambulatory enough to offer much competition where he was concerned. For this reason you are often taken aback if you are ever treated with disrespect by a male employer or supervisor. Unlike the only girl (who had to develop more tact and diplomacy), you approach collaborations with men in a naive spirit of equality and, more often than not, feel shocked, wounded, disappointed, and outraged when they do not respond in kind. It is very difficult for you to understand the fact that a male supervisor is likely to experience your forthrightness as a *threat*. It would be easier for you in the work world if you could determine beforehand the birth order of any males (or females) whom you might consider working with or for.

You would find the most harmonious accommodations with a man who was either an only child or the oldest brother of brothers only. Such a man usually has high regard for anyone (male or female) who likes to 'get a job done right,' and – never having had female siblings – has no reason to imagine that his own prestige and ways of doing things will be anything but enhanced and facilitated by your sincere and earnest efforts. Of course, if he'd been raised by an authoritarian, or domineering and manipulative mother (grandmother, aunt, etc.) and you remind him of *her*, that's a different story, but that's a chance we all take. The next best bet is the younger brother of an older sister. While this man might worry that you'll take over his department (and as we have noted elsewhere, he usually locates himself in a field wherein the only female help is likely to be strictly limited to stenographic or Girl Friday status), he will be quite happy to give you your own bailiwick to manage as you see fit, and matters of rank *per se* will not be important to him – so long as you stay out of his way. Otherwise you are likely to have a rough passage. Another birth order you would work well with is the oldest brother who had more than one younger sister and no brothers. In all likelihood he has long ago accustomed himself to sharing some of his responsibilities and prerogatives with at least one of his younger sisters. Surprisingly, you don't usually get along too well with other oldest sisters in collaborative situations, although you form close and lasting friendships with them at a purely social level.

You are generally known for your high standards, your capacity to come straight to the point, and for your steadfast loyalty to persons, beliefs, and causes which have earned your critical respect. You do not hand out bouquets, nor do you accept them, unless they are well deserved. Your steadfast integrity is your greatest asset and at the same time can be your own most costly liability. You are apt to be a 'take charge' person who knows what she is doing and deeply resents it when bumblers are elevated to positions of authority and command – especially when you suffer as a result, either financially or because they frustrate your efforts to fulfill your commitments conscientiously. This was probably true even during childhood; yours is the ordinal position most likely to be chosen by teachers to oversee routine chores like blackboard-wiping, pencil-sharpening, paintbrush-cleaning, etc. – all of which you viewed as privileges rather than drudgery.

Everybody has always respected the fact that when *you* do a job it rarely, if ever, needs further work, revision or redoing. You aren't the most tactful person in the world when it comes to making your assistants aware of their deficiencies, but you also give credit where it is due, and you have too much pride in your own abilities to ever be a boot licker. Come to think of it, though, you might do well to be more aware of other people's human need for reassurance, praise, acknowledgement, etc. After all, you aren't the only one who has earned the right to receive praise now and then. A few kind words from you – directed in the right quarters, but with honesty and sincerity, of course – can go a long way toward smoothing out many of the bumps in your life.

Our impression is that you favor romantic partnerships with quiet, easygoing persons who prefer to take a back seat in domestic affairs. You enjoy being the Director of Traffic – a skill at which you generally excel – but there are times when you need the support of your loved one. At such moments you can feel profoundly – even bitterly – betrayed when he does not rise to the occasion. Experience has taught you that to give open expression to your angers and resentments is more often than not apt to be an exercise in futility and humiliation. You are more likely, therefore, than other women to swallow such emotions – and thus become a candidate for ulcers, periodic bouts of depression, and a feeling that you are getting nowhere in life.

The closer your younger sister is to you in age, the more ambivalent your feelings about her are apt to be. Put another way, when you are separated by about two years or less your relationship is likely to be more that of twins (see Chapter 19), whereas a wider age gap, especially four years or more, is apt to produce clashes, power struggles, animosity, rivalry, and other kinds of problems between you.

Female children in our culture grow up to be more clothes conscious than male children. So the distinction between your clothes, jewelry, and other accouterments and those of your sister may well have taken on special importance for you. They became a symbol of everything you experienced as unfair and galling in your childhood relationship to one another. Consequently it could have been extremely painful for you to see her wearing your favorite, but now outgrown, dresses, jeans, blouses, boots, sweaters, etc. This would be especially painful if any of these things just happened to be more becoming to *her* than they were in the days when they were yours exclusively. For her part, the wearing of clothes that were once yours probably makes it second nature for her to borrow or otherwise appropriate items out of your present wardrobe. Again, in our society females are more apt than males to feel 'raped' by anyone who invades their wardrobe without asking permission. As is usually the case for first-borns, the chances are that insult was further added to injury by your parents who so frequently exhorted you to be a good sport about these various and sundry outrages: 'You're the oldest, after all; you should be more tolerant of your sister. And besides – you can't wear two scarves at once, can you?

So why not let your sister wear your other one if she wants to? Don't be selfish and spiteful! You're old enough to know better. It won't kill you to share things with your sister, will it?' Had you been able to give a candid answer (and perhaps you did), it would have been a simple, unrehearsed 'YES! It *will* kill me to have my identity usurped without my voluntary invitation or permission!'

A probable consequence of the foregoing is that you learned how to be an expert bargainer with all the younger sisters of this world, and most of your relationships with younger women are, by and large, harmonious and easygoing. Otherwise your interactions with any female who even remotely reminds you of your sister will probably be characterized by anything from total avoidance to the fiercest kind of vindictiveness and scapegoating. There is a powerful force in human psychodynamics which is known as 'transference.' In psychotherapy this refers to the tendency on the part of the client to attribute to the therapist all sorts of personality traits, attitudes, and values which characterized persons who were important during the client's growing-up years. However, this phenomenon is not limited simply to the *therapeutic* situation – it goes on all the time in our daily lives. We 'transfer' onto friends, coworkers, subordinates, bosses, and even perfect strangers, some of the emotional reactions and expectations first elicited by parents, siblings, and other main actors in our childhood dramas. Sometimes we may be consciously aware that so-and-so reminds us of so-and-so, but more often than not the whole thing takes place at a totally unconscious level, so that we may react to one person as though she were an enemy from the past – when in fact she has only the most benign feelings with regard to us; or toward another person as though he were a beloved figure from our childhood when in actuality this person regards us as the incarnation of somebody from their own past who was 'bad news' during their own childhood. The point we wish to make here is that whether or not your sister was your 'twin' pal, or a fly in your ointment, you would do well to become particularly aware of the transference relationships which arise between you and other females – especially those younger or smaller in physical size (to the unconscious mind 'smaller' means 'younger'). We say 'females' rather than 'women' because it is very easy for a full-grown adult to get caught up in a transference involving a child of any age. Thus a ten-year-old niece or grandchild could easily come to represent your younger sibling.

There may well have been a *positive* side to the picture. Your parents might, for example, have been very supportive in allowing you both to choose an identical outfit which you both liked – much to your mutual delight. Likewise, you and your sister may have had to comfort each other with regard to a particularly distasteful outfit either of you had to wear. We are reminded of two sisters who often went to school in tears with arms wrapped around each other in mutual consolation about the 'ghastly zinc-yellow organdie dresses with huge bows at the back which we had to wear to school – where all the other girls giggled behind our backs and we couldn't wait to get home to change into our play clothes.'

In adulthood, you and your sister usually develop into fairly good friends with genuine good will and mutual respect for one another. However, from the point of view of the older one, there is almost always a lingering sense of distrust and, for lack of a better word, '*un*safety.' Mary (Bloody Mary) Tudor's distrust of her younger half sister (Elizabeth I) was in all likelihood not a mere matter of Renaissance politics.

More likely than not, it became your job – as for so many first-borns – to monitor the chores (and other activities) of your younger sibling. Naturally, being only human, you no doubt enjoyed the role of authority and trust which the adult world had assigned to you. But let's face it – the price that most oldest children pay for such 'straw boss' status is an inward sense of never-ending responsibility. You forever feel accountable for events in a way which goes far beyond what was embodied in the original childhood 'contract.'

First-born girls have more to contend with when it comes to caretaking duties than do first-born boys. They are more likely to be given the task of minding the younger siblings at an extremely early age. We live in a culture where little girls are encouraged to play at being grown women, imitating their mother's cooking, entertaining, concerning themselves with clothes, and 'looking nice,' as well as everything else which is (rightly or wrongly) considered 'female.' Little girls get toy tea sets, doll carriages, and simple needlework for special occasions or birthdays. So the transition from 'playing Mummy' with a doll to that of parenting a younger sibling is usually an easy step for a little girl to make.

Without being aware of the pitfalls inherent in such a role, parents may unwittingly place an extraordinary burden of responsibility on the older of two daughters. No matter how enthusiastically you may have taken to this role at first, your parents may well have lost sight of the fact that you were yourself a child, and therefore entitled to all the rights and privileges of genuine childhood. If your parents encouraged you to give up your prerogatives as a child, they played into your premature wish to be accepted as an adult woman – like your mother – while at the same time making it very difficult for you to come to terms with the anger and resentment which such a heavy sacrifice engenders.

If your sister's turn to do the dishes resulted in a slap-dash job, chances are that you were reprimanded for not checking up on her, and if she 'forgot' to perform certain errands (see Chapter 10, where this issue is discussed in detail), you were scolded for neglecting to remind her. Understandably, you were prone to regard this kind of situation as patently unfair: after all, if you had to make it your job to chivvy your sister until she fulfilled her obligations, you must often have felt a strong temptation to simply do it yourself and get it out of the way, once and for all. If indeed you yielded to this impulse, your sister may have been (understandably) quick to take advantage of your 'helpfulness' – which only added to your rankling sense of being a patsy for her inveterate 'irresponsibility.' In which case your sister may well have grown up regarding you as a kind of benign protector – while you, on the other hand, may harbor a lifelong resentment of her as an outrageous pain in the neck. Like your counterpart, the older of two boys, you may now feel baffled (and a little bit shamed) by the carefree and unabashed affection and esteem with which your younger sibling seems to regard you – in contrast to the lingering sense of resentment and hostility which you so often feel toward her. Try to forgive her, if you can, and to realize that much of what she did at your expense was really not intended to hurt you in any way. Believe it or not, she probably picked up on your secret enjoyment of your own authority, and simply went along with it. That it may have caused you a lot of suffering was not entirely her fault, after all. Your parents and the society they were brought up in has a lot to answer for when it comes to the excessive caretaker functions which it assigns to first-born children.

What could well be by far the most painful part of being the older sister in a two-girl family is the way in which it so often alters the first-born girl's relationship to her father. In many ways the close (and often extremely subtle) camaraderie which had existed between the two of you prior to your sister's birth seemed, in your eyes, to get suddenly derailed when she entered the picture; without warning your father appeared to saddle you with all the burdens of the first-born status and to withdraw most of the 'goodies' – handing them over to the newcomer in a manner which must have seemed a most painful kind of betrayal. Your indignation was most likely directed at your younger sister instead of at Dad, who you felt had abandoned you. (This is called 'displacement,' by the way.)

At this point in time you may have turned to your mother for empathy and support – with varying degrees of success or failure. She may have offered you a great deal of comfort in your time of need, *or* she may have been too occupied with the new baby to realize the unhappy state you were in. This would hold true especially if her view of the female gender role was not a very positive one. Within this kind of setting, your father may often have appeared to favor your sister at your expense: always apologizing for her infringements on your prerogatives and appearing to take her side in any dispute. On the other side of the ledger, you may have felt that your mother was the 'betrayer' who for some reason had a special affinity for your sister – again at your expense. If your father showed a similar inclination, you must indeed have felt shut out in the cold – and your previous loyalty to him could have prompted you to secretly blame your mother for 'brainwashing' your father on the baby's behalf. Any way you take it, unless you were reassured by both parents as to your own worthwhileness and value to them, you are probably still dealing with the ramifications of your suffering during those early years.

In some families the father does not encourage a close relationship with his oldest daughter because of problems of his own. He may, for instance, have had a bossy older sister. Or you may represent the younger sister who spoiled his 'only child' paradise. Whatever his reasons, if your father was not capable of closeness with you, you may have developed a genuine companionship with your mother – in which case it often happens that the father will then appoint his younger daughter to be the son he had always wanted. The family then lives as two teams under a single roof.

Researchers in the field of birth order find that girls in your ordinal position appear to be responsible, competent, and conscientious – but at the same time may be bossy, highly competitive with other females, and more than a little inclined to self-righteousness. Both boys and girls can feel somewhat intimidated by you – a fact which you don't seem to mind at all. One researcher tells us that as a little girl you preferred to play with other little girls for the most part, and that in the family you thought of yourself as 'Daddy's girl' and considered your sister as 'Mamma's girl' – but felt nevertheless that it was your duty to look after her. Another writer has taken these observations a step further; he sees you not only as being strongly attached to your father, but in active competition with your mother for the role of Daddy's Little Helper, or Second-in-Command. Other writers consider you to be 'the most independent of all girls at all ages.' And you excel more than any other birth order when it comes to card games, real estate, stock market speculations, and the like. You have what it takes to succeed in the working world, and your high standards make people value your approval. If you can curb a tendency toward bossiness, you have all the makings of a competent leader and a stimulating, loyal friend.

CHAPTER SEVENTEEN

Younger Brother of Older Brother

If your older sib was less than four years old when you were born, it is more likely that your relationship to one another has been generally close and rewarding throughout both of your lives. If he was around three at the time, you were probably the answer to his prayers for a playmate. That prayer, of course, was not as altruistic and innocent as it may sound at first. He was not aware of it, but one reason why he subconsciously wanted another child in the family was to be able to get away from the relentless parental spotlight. Once you arrived, he undoubtedly went through a period of wishing you'd go back to wherever you came from because you were receiving what seemed like more than your share of parental attention and concern. But when you were two years old (and he was five or so), he may very well have derived considerable pleasure and fulfillment from taking you under his wing – to instruct you, enlighten you, and otherwise offer all sorts of invitations to your adventurous and explorative spirit.

When dealing with family problems, it is often difficult to understand why the term 'brotherly love' has come to be synonymous with a special kind of close and affectionate bond, since the attitude of brothers toward one another can range anywhere from mutual coolness to distaste to outright hostility. The kind of sharing and support that one is more likely to observe usually arises from a sense of family duty – a kind of team spirit, if you will – rather than from any real feelings of high personal regard. Genuine brotherly love, when it does appear, shows up most often when two boys are the only children in a family and, most important, are close in age. Then the two often form close ties of inseparable companionship and reciprocal concern which only death can sever.

If you had this kind of relationship to your older brother you were fortunate indeed because you grew up with a playmate, friend, and helper; someone who could think up exciting projects and help bring them to fulfillment – or, if they failed, could make the failure seem less of a blow by the sharing of it. While it is true that your brother often initiated your mutual endeavors and often had the final say in how they should be carried out, there was never any doubt in either of your minds that the projects belonged equally to both of you – along with the fun, the pride in accomplishment, and the fulfillment. The result of this kind of sibling relationship, of course, is that you generally enjoy partnerships with other men, and are often bewildered when a business associate or chum wants to hog the lion's share of whatever glory, profits, or good will accrue from your joint collaboration.

If, on the other hand, your older sib was held up as an example for you to emulate – which is usually the case when you are more than four years apart in age – your experience of 'big brothers' and the attitudes which it has left you with will be quite different.

In families with several siblings a boy may have more than one example to follow. He might hero-worship one of them, fight with a second, totally ignore a third, make a special comrade of a fourth, etc. But when you have only one brother (and no sisters) – that brother is more apt to function as friend, enemy, good example and closest male relative all rolled into one.

With so much riding on your relationship to your brother, he can certainly be a source of the deepest frustration as well as the greatest fun. If he came into the

family four or five years ahead of you, you are likely to
have found yourself in the position of a Johnny-come-
lately. Not only had he fulfilled all the roles mentioned
above, but he was also encouraged to look upon himself as
Lord High Everything Else, and wasn't about to let you
forget it. You could never slay this dragon; you couldn't
fight him, and he rarely permitted you to join him. By
virtue of his head start over you, he was more articulate in
stating his point of view when you quarreled as children.
Being your parent's first-born, he also tended to have their
respective ears and to be considered a sober, honest, serious
lad, every bit as concerned with your welfare as they were.
You could (and did) learn to be the happy-go-lucky one in
the family. But, knowing that you could not win in an open
contest with this firmly entrenched Beloved of the Gods,
you discovered early on how to use humor as a weapon.
You could make fun of your brother's shortcomings, but
you usually managed to do it on the sly, appearing to laugh
with him rather than at him. Poking fun at his friends was
another way of getting even, but again, in such a spirit of
good humor that if he complained about it he was told by
others not to be an old sobersides and to learn to laugh at
himself.

If you happen to have been Mum's special lad, however,
there is one major fact of your life which can make a lot of
difference – i.e., you grew up as the youngest of *three* males.
If for any reason your brother felt burdened by either Dad's
partiality to him or Dad's envy of you on account of your
closeness to Mum, both you and your brother may still
carry around a considerable amount of ambivalence (or
downright resentment) toward one another, each of you
thinking he got a raw deal.

A very large percentage of youngest boys are prone to be
procrastinators. Of all last-born males the one most apt to

find himself becalmed is yourself, the younger of two brothers. We think it is more likely to be the case when your brother and Dad form an achievement alliance from which you are excluded or which otherwise causes you to feel inadequate. If they are both musical, for instance, or given to carpentry, and you are not able to keep up with them, you may lapse into discouragement, wool-gathering, day-dreaming, or what other people regard as laziness.

What the world does not realize is that you are subconsciously furious at them for leaving you behind, and when one can't find a suitable (or acceptable) way of dealing with anger, there's no place left for it to go except inward upon the self. The result is a strong tendency to become depressed for days (and sometimes weeks) at a time or else to drift along with feelings of helplessness and unrealistically lowered self-esteem. On such occasions nothing you do seems to add up to anything in your own eyes or the world's. During such periods it is useful to have a stable circle of friends who can lend you their support – by reminding you of your genuine assets and capabilities. For this reason it is essential – repeat 'essential' – that you make a close friendship circle for yourself and maintain it through thick and thin. Keep in touch with these pals on a regular basis – through phone calls, lunches, outings, after-work drinks or coffee, etc. *Don't* keep score on who last phoned whom, whose turn it is to get in touch with whom, etc. Otherwise you will end up feeling friendless and forlorn when you most need comfort and bolstering. No need to feel ashamed of such needs – we all have them, and our obligation to ourselves is to see that they are taken care of.

Whatever the age gap between you and your brother, you are apt to be far more daring than your more conservative sibling. Again, regardless of the difference between your ages, he is more inclined to be Guardian of Tradition while you are more prone to be an iconoclast; a twister of the lion's tail; a bucker of the mores. Although such behavior may have been to his despair the chances are that he secretly envied your spirit – (subconsciously, at least) – even though he may have delivered countless lectures and harangues to the effect that 'you'd best mend your ways unless you want to wind up behind bars.'

The fact is that of all ordinal positions yours is the most openly antiauthoritarian. Anything which represents the darker side of any 'establishment' coin is like the proverbial red flag to your bull. More group-oriented than your brother, you prefer to join revolutionary or protest organizations even though you will sometimes accept a benign, paternalistic mentor. You may not realize it, but a fair amount of this rebelliousness represents a certain thirst for attention on your part, and this may have been reflected in behavior problems during your school and growing-up years. In those days you would go out of your way, more often than not, to prove to one and all that you were not content to spend your life in your brother's shadow – nor to bask in his reflected glory, either.

As a rule you have a basically sunny disposition and, despite the seriousness with which you take your antiestablishment stands, you have made it a point to steer clear of your older brother's more somber view of things. Aside from your cherished campaigns against the Council, you are inclined to be easygoing and to believe that most things work themselves out eventually – so let *others* do the worrying, at which they seem so proficient. For this reason you are the least likely of all ordinals to find yourself in deep water, psychologically speaking, except for the tendency to become depressed or discouraged which we spoke of earlier. You are apt to cherish a deep-down conviction that a basically supportive world stands ready to

offer you advice and help whenever you need it. You
therefore have a strong capacity for shelving problems
indefinitely. Running to counselors and other therapists is
not your style! Sometimes, however, it would be a good
idea to seek out a little help when the going gets rough. In
our opinion the Little Red Hen ('I'll do it *myself*') was in all
likelihood a youngest child – and probably not a hen at all,
but the younger of two roosters!

Oddly enough, the two of you are less likely to be 'adopted'
by either parent than your female counterparts (or any
other two-sib combination, come to think of it). Of course
it is possible that one or both of your parents happened to
subconsciously regard (and treat) you as the daughter they
never had, but such a state of affairs is very rare indeed. It's
far more common for both Mum and Dad to regard you as
'the boys' – a pair; almost like twins, discussed in Chapter
16. This is probably due to the fact that in our own and
most other societies boys are considered an asset in that
they are usually self-supporting and can be relied upon to
leave the nest in early adulthood – as opposed to girls, who
may hang around home base for an indefinitely prolonged
period, especially if they remain unmarried.

So far as intra-family adoption is concerned, you are
more likely than your brother to be Mum's kid. Why this
should be so is anybody's guess. In some families, the
amount of rivalry produced by this factor is minimal. In
other families it can set off a never-ending game wherein
one team tries to get the jump on the other. The form it
generally takes is rank-pulling by Dad and the older boy
versus gossiping by Mum and you. If you happen to fall
into this particular pattern, some of the less likeable habits
you picked up en route may persist to this very day – a
tendency to run to a mother figure with tales about the

awful things people are doing to you, etc: a not-very-pleasant trait which other people don't appreciate – especially in school or your place of work or other settings where such crybaby tactics are particularly inappropriate. When you work for a woman, you tend to form a close relationship with her, and try to make herself and yourself a team that excludes all the other workers. Men are particularly resentful at being dealt with in such an indirect manner, so if you're having difficulty and friction with male coworkers (subordinates, peers or superiors) this may constitute the major reason. We suggest that you make a strong effort to be more upfront in your dealings; you'll find that things begin to go a lot more smoothly.

Another variant of your birth order occurs when your brother is four or more years older than you. Such a brother may mightily resent your advent upon the scene, and if he is around the angry age of eight or nine he can be almost murderous in his rejection of you. By this we mean that he may have a) bossed you around and tyrannized you most unmercifully; b) refused to acknowledge your presence and thus treated you as though you were virtually invisible; a nonperson; c) regarded you as a pest and had ways of making his own accomplishments look positively gargantuan in comparison to yours; and d) had ways of teasing or tormenting you – as though to pass along his own personal frustrations. Naturally, you could not have appreciated any of these behaviors; and (also naturally) you devised ways whereby you could even the score. This brings us to a concept which you will probably not find in any standard textbook on psychodynamics because it is our own formulation, which we are happy to share. To wit.

There are only three major emotional *motivations* of the human psyche, both conscious and/or subconscious, and these are: 1) to obtain rewards or 'goodies'; 2) to avoid pain or danger; and 3) to get even.* Of all ordinal positions yours is the one most dedicated to getting even if it's the last thing you do. We have noticed elsewhere that the middle child also excels in tit-for-tat score-keeping (see Chapter 7) but your style is often less personal. By this we mean that instead of avenging yourself upon the specific person or persons who were the cause of your discomfort you are more inclined to abstract and generalize your grudge – aiming it at a whole class of people, such as 'capitalists' or 'bureaucrats' or 'polluters' or any other group of whom you disapprove. During childhood, however, your book-balancing tactics may have been more specific – like waiting for your brother to turn his back and bend over just long enough for you to let fly a rotten tomato. We've already mentioned your resort to humor as a weapon in this warfare.

Then there is the size factor. Somewhere between the ages of six and twelve you may have grown physically larger than your older sib. We have no medical statistics behind us at this point, but it is our distinct impression that during childhood you often get to be taller, stronger, better coordinated, and more energetic than your brother. In the primitive language of the subconscious mind, you often (rather suddenly) become the 'big' brother while he (equally suddenly) finds himself the smaller and weaker one. It is during this period that you may start paying him back in kind for whatever pain he may have hitherto inflicted upon you. The truly sad result is that when such is the case, the older brother's feelings of outrage and humiliation produce

---

* The first of these are part of Freud's 'pleasure-pain principle.' Our feeling is that 'evening the score' is almost a physical need and may indeed be physically based.

deep wounds which rarely if ever heal. In all probability he will offer any number of reasons to explain his hostility toward you when confiding to a close friend or love partner, for example. But none of them will be the real reasons – namely, that you unleashed your pent-up resentments in ways that surprised and baffled him, and Mum and Dad somehow permitted you to get away with it. For this he has never forgiven you and may even hold a grudge against one or both of your parents into the bargain. From your point of view his ill will may appear baffling and uncalled for. Like most youngest children, you find it almost impossible to think of yourself as wielding that much clout in the world (see Chapter 8). As for any lingering resentment on your brother's part, to your way of thinking this is merely one more manifestation of his penchant for playing the role of the heavy.

Which brings us once more to the subject of role modeling which we have touched upon in other chapters. On the one hand Mum and Dad wanted your brother to set an example for you – a responsibility which he neither wanted nor relished. On the other hand he was also entrusted with the job of showing you the ropes – a task which, more often than not, brought out a more protective and friendly side of his nature. You may have felt that he was often bossier than the job called for, but you were flattered at being let in on so many of his more 'grown up' secrets and skills. At the same time you undoubtedly experienced a certain impatience with his earnest pontificating approach to life. In order to offset what so often came across to you as pompous and lacking in humor, you may have often felt tempted to play Martha to his Mary – i.e., to be the carefree Family Clown in contrast to his Chief Cook and Bottle Washer. (In ancient times bottles were very costly and could only be entrusted to the hands of persons who took their duties very seriously.) Again, he may have been appalled by your lightheartedness, but at the same time he may have taken a secret and vicarious delight in your antics. Even so, your own tendency was to use whatever you could distill from his teachings and let the rest go by. In short, emulating the role that he was intently modeling for you was not your cup of tea, and you chose to be more frivolous – careless in areas where he was conscientious, full of sunshine when he was gloomy, and so on.

When it comes to personal goals you are likely to get caught up in a conflict between two extreme types of behavior. You either devote yourself to the fulfillment of your aims with a relentless concentration, or else you dawdle, procrastinate, and find yourself getting nowhere. During your active periods you rush around like a squirrel hoarding nuts for the rough winter ahead, and during your unpredictable bouts of nonactivity you feel like a sailing-boat in irons – becalmed, helpless, waiting for a rescuing wind to arise out of nowhere. This holds true especially in the case of onerous burdens and chores; being 'lazy' or 'dreamy' or 'scatterbrained' can be a subconscious way of inviting other, more supervisory types to step in and relieve you. For this reason you find it particularly difficult to follow pursuits which call for regularized routines – like practicing an instrument, preparing a lesson plan, doing pushups, or whatever. Your tendency is not to do today what can possibly be put off until tomorrow. Thus you live in the present moment more than most people do – a characteristic which is both an asset and a liability. On the plus side it adds a lot of spice to your life which would otherwise be missing, while on the debit side it inclines you to spend money (and energy) lavishly, without regard to that time in the near or distant future when the bills must eventually be paid. Just as in childhood – when your toys were likely to soon get lost, stolen, broken, or discarded – you frequently lose track of your objectives or else allow them to wither on the vine. 'Tomorrow is another day' comes close to being your slogan in life.

In line with your aforementioned yen for participating in protest groups you are more of a joiner than a leader; more a follower than a trailblazer; more likely to respond to an opportunity than to create one. The directions you take in life depend to a considerable extent upon the ebb and flow of your moods – which in turn are strongly influenced by the amount of encouragement and affirmation you can evoke from those around you. For, like most youngest children, you set great store by the ways in which other people respond to you, and you harbor the unshakable notion that nobody in the world gives one hoot in hell what you think or feel about them. To you life is a one-way street in which you are the only one who has to struggle again and again merely to pass muster – let alone distinguish yourself in any lasting way. The one thing you feel most sure of is that when you offer your sympathy or compassion somebody will be there to lap it up. Chances are that you have developed a fine gift for empathy for those who are suffering; an ability to listen and to bind up other people's wounds.

The source of this ability for many boys in your ordinal position is that they often find themselves functioning as confidant and general ego-booster to their older brothers, odd though it may at first seem. Particularly when the relationship between you has been a warm and loving one, your brother may get the idea that your life is a lot jollier than his, and so he turns to you for guidance and comfort. This does not, of course, make you envious of his position or desirous of emulating him. The difference between the two of you in this respect is that while you feel fairly certain that you could play out his role (if you wanted to take life all that seriously), he despairs of ever being as devil-may-care as you so often appear to his eyes. Aware of his never-ending sense of entrapment, you may have often found yourself trying to pull him out of his doldrums. To this day it is not usually difficult for others to evoke your empathy and understanding. So far as your relationship with your brother is concerned, it gave you a chance to repay him for whatever comfort and protection he extended to you when you were very small.

You learned a great deal from observing your older brother's myriad stresses and strains. Not wishing to make his mistakes, you almost instinctively learned to be more of an extrovert, more gregarious, more buoyant, and better able than your sib to bounce back from emotional upsets. Put another way, you learned how not to be somber, apprehensive, a recluse, a shy wallflower, a pessimist, or a carrier of the world's burdens. What you probably have yet to learn is how to avoid going to extremes. It isn't really necessary to be either all one thing or else its exact opposite; there is a wide and verdant middle ground, and it is not to be confused with 'middle of the road.' Nor is compromise the same as cop-out. Inhabiting the plateau and making it your base of operations can be every bit as adventurous as the peaks and the pits – and a lot more rewarding in the long run. Try it – you'll like it!

CHAPTER EIGHTEEN

Younger Sister of Older Sister

Of course it is possible that you enjoy rolling out your own pastry dough, shepherding your children back and forth from school, opening the door with a smile for your husband and conscientiously observing your family's religious traditions – while your older sister is involved in open marriage arrangements with several people and cherishes a droll childhood snapshot of herself in which she lifts her leg to a fire hydrant in mock urination. But we think it quite unlikely. It's usually the other way around. Older sister (see Chapter 16) is usually the upholder of tradition. You are more apt to be the bohemian iconoclast. As a matter of fact, we know of only one case where these two roles were reversed.

To understand the younger of two sisters, one must bear in mind that in most societies the world over, both parents usually have a strong investment in producing at least one *male* child before they write 'finis' to childbearing. Your Mum and Dad wound up with two daughters and no sons. We can't say that they were actually *unhappy* with the situation, but chances are that one or both of them had a lingering sense of discomfort about it. For both parents to prefer girl children – at the deep-down emotional level – is not uncommon; but the point is that most parents believe they should want at least one male child. This is particularly true of men in patriarchal societies like our own, where carrying on the family name – that is, the father's family identity – depends upon producing a male child and then doing all in one's power to ensure that the son in turn marries and produces at least one male child.

Before we elaborate on this theme, let's note that, unlike the older of two *boys*, your sister was probably not required to set herself up as a role model for the development of your 'femininity.' To be sure, your big sister was expected to blaze trails for you in some ways, but we have the strong impression that two-sib sisters are generally permitted to be different from one another to a greater degree than are two-sib brothers. To put it another way, parents are more inclined to treat their two *daughters* as distinct individuals, but somehow expect two sons to be more like fraternal twins.

As we noted in Chapter 16 on your sister, when there are only two girls in the family, the father most often seems to expect the oldest to fulfill the role of 'son.' But when there are more than two girls, or if for any reason the bond between your father and your sister was not very close, you may have become his son substitute or at any rate his favorite. In this way Mum and your sister constituted one alliance while you and Dad were on the other team. For many families this kind of setup works out fairly smoothly, but in families where Dad has the unpleasant responsibility for being the sole disciplinarian, rivalry between the two teams can get very rough indeed.

Under such circumstances Dad is often prone to decide any issues between you and your sister in your favor, while Mum usually takes a back seat in the struggle, unable to exert much clout on your sister's behalf. If this happened in your family, then we have no need to tell you how mightily your sister sometimes wished that you had never been born. Hell hath no fury like a first-born dethroned and made to face the downfall by her father's preference for her rival. The more devastating the dethronement the more severe and unforgiving the fury. If you lived through that kind of situation, you must have often found your sister's hostility quite puzzling; you saw your father's partiality as simple justice. And yet somehow you knew that your sister's anger had to do with your own closeness to Dad. Tough luck for her, then; it wasn't your fault.

Altogether, her towering resentment of you must have been pretty hard to take sometimes. This kind of big sister has ways of reducing her younger sibling to a state of impotent rage when they are alone together. If this happened to you, you probably often wanted to strangle her on the spot. We know, in fact, of instances where younger sisters have actually tried to do so. But you also had your own technique for evening the score – by pushing your advantageous relationship with Dad into her face whenever the opportunity presented itself. Naturally she did not appreciate this gesture, nor can you blame her.

The problem is (or was) that you and she were engaged in a steady state of undeclared war. And when a state of chronic friction exists between two such sisters, chances are that you wind up feeling 'I'm damned if I do, and damned if I don't'; either she is hostile to you for being pretty and/or popular and/or spoiled, or else she envies you your freedom to be a tomboy and hoyden. She can make it quite clear that she is Second in Command, and that in the family female pecking order you come in a dismal third (*last*)! Under such conditions you, like the middle child (see Chapter 7), learn to fall back on a support system outside the family circle – in which case you do all in your power to steer clear of your sister's various grudges and hidden agendas – which are silently countenanced by your mother.

The complexity we referred to does not end there. You may have done all in your power to be worthy of Dad's compliment in forming a sort of 'father-to-son' bond with you, and basked in the bright sunshine of his favor, regardless of any hassles it may have created between you and your Mom or your sister. Perhaps he encouraged you to be a fighter in the playground, or an athlete, or a sober companion on long philosophical walks or other outings alone together, or to join him in his favorite masculine pursuits. So far, so good – up to a point. Then, when you entered puberty and began to notice boys and to generally pay attention to your attractiveness as a female, your Dad, quite without realizing it on a conscious level, may well have felt betrayed by this transformation from imaginary son to flesh-and-blood, honest-to-goodness *daughter.* At that point he may very well have turned his favor back in the direction of your sister. Suddenly you found yourself in a kind of bewildering and mysterious 'dog house' while your sister reclaimed her long-lost throne as the Princess. More likely than not, your Mum was now willing to welcome you back into the 'society of women' despite the fact that you had spent so many of your growing-up years as the disobedient hoyden, tomboy, and general raiser of hell about the premises. While your sister may not have exactly welcomed you into that 'club,' she nevertheless had the consolation of knowing that she was again Mum's and Dad's Crown Princess. Therefore she could afford a certain amount of *noblesse oblige* and allow you to play the role of Duchess to her Princess. If perchance you happened to be obviously more attractive than she, that's a different matter; in that case you have probably been at odds with each other for as long as either of you can remember. And that's how it is likely to remain. However, there's no telling what kind of event or circumstance may one day bring you into warm, loving sisterhood with one another.

If neither of you was blessed with a disproportionate share of talent, beauty, or brains, old wounds got healed and you and your sister were able to establish bonds of genuine love and mutual support. This may appear surprising at first, but remember that from the day you were born, she was probably able and willing (with plenty of encouragement from family, relatives, and neighbors) to function as your Little Mother. Thus you had a loving bond between you for the first years of your life. And if neither of your parents had any inclination to make you into the 'son we never had,' this bond may have evolved into a lifelong alliance which has remained firm and strong to this very day. This is what most women mean when they assert that another woman 'is like a sister to me.'

When you reflect upon all the complexities outlined above you can appreciate why it is more unusual for either of two sisters to make such a statement than it is for either of two brothers. Because when two boys are involved, it most often happens that one gets 'adopted' by Dad and the other by Mum, and there the matter rests for all time. Unless, of course, one or both parents treat one of their sons (usually the younger) as the 'daughter we never had' (in which case the advent of puberty and adolescence can place him squarely in the same predicament in which you may have found yourself at that stage of development).

In the sexual sphere males are – for reasons not completely understood – more turned on by visual stimuli than are females. Put simply, this means that the proverbial pretty face (especially when accompanied by other physical attributes which are pleasing to the eye) is what first captures a male's attention and arouses his erotic/romantic interest. This is not to say that females are insensitive to such stimuli; it's just that females are more responsive to the personalities of other people – rather than what they look like. Now it is a fact of the human condition that in all societies throughout the human race there are strict taboos against what is known as 'incest,' but there is a great deal of variability in how this word is defined. For instance, some societies strictly forbid a female to even so much as *speak* to male members of her mother's clan. At the very same time, however, it's all right for her to have intercourse with her own father – which may in fact be *required* as part of her preparation for eventual marriage.

In our society the term applies to sexual activity between any close kin – i.e., immediate family (parents and siblings), and in some groups even to uncles, aunts, and cousins.* We know nowadays that incest occurs far more often than was once thought but that is beside the point. Our point here is that, since men are more easily aroused by visual beauty, fathers are more apt to become more embarrassingly aware of a daughter's physical attractiveness than a mother is of her son's. Along with Dad's arousal comes a great deal of subconscious guilt and confusion which can lead him to behave in uncharacteristic ways toward either you and/or your sister. He may suddenly become shy about kissing or touching you. Or he may make jeering or critical remarks in response to your faltering experiments with make-up, hair styling, clothes, etc. He may start admonishing you to 'cover up' in ways you consider prudish, old-fashioned, or downright silly. He might also become suddenly hyper-critical of your friends and associates, both male and female (males being seen as 'up to no good' or else unworthy of you; females as a potential 'bad influence' who might lead you into following their promiscuous example). Most common of all, he may start making a fuss about curfews and you may find him waiting up for you when you return from dates. During this troublesome period when

* Note that in *Hamlet* Shakespeare considers the Queen 'incestuous' for marrying her brother-in-law.

Dad is trying to deal with his subconscious turmoil, Mum can often act as a much needed buffer – staunchly defending your rights and helping you along the rocky road to full-grown womanhood.

On the other hand, some mothers go through a period when they envy their daughters' youthful freedom and popularity as they see their own heyday receding further and further into the past (complicated sometimes by the onset of menopause). In that case, Mum also may have behaved as oddly as Dad. Now you had two parents waiting up to cross-examine you upon your return from a date, asking all sorts of questions. Is it any wonder that adolescence is the tumultuous ordeal that most of us find it to be? Such turmoil almost invariably simmers down and gets straightened out within a couple of years. At age eighteen you generally leave the family to attend college, or enter the job market, or even to begin life with a love partner of your choice. In the meantime the chances are that you and your sister settled many of your differences and drew closer together in an alliance of mutual support and sympathy. As a lady of our acquaintance put it, 'I became friends with my sister when I realized that we had both grown up in the same concentration camp.'

More than any other female ordinal position (with the possible exception of middle child; see Chapter 7) you tend to be a joiner of organizations. Political parties, protest groups, labor unions, the Girl Scouts, the armed services – all are inducements for you to continue expressing the kind of team spirit, self-assertiveness and love of adventure which you learned back in your tomboy period. You especially like to be part of a well-defined, highly visible, and very mobile band of dedicated colleagues, and the more you move around the better you like it. For you know how to put down roots and how to pull them up with equal ease. It doesn't bother you in the least to be working in a particular city for a year or two and then be suddenly reassigned to another post hundreds of miles away – with the tasks of getting to know a whole new group of fellow employees, making new friends, and settling down in a new environment.

We can think of several reasons why you are able to do this. First, a lot of the outside activities in your pre-adolescent days involved play groups or gangs which were largely dominated by males (or, as sometimes happens, by 'male' values in an all-girl group of rebels). This meant that the group changed personnel faster and more frequently than happens in tradition-minded 'female' cliques – which tend to be more stable as well as being more cohesive (i.e., current members risk being accused of disloyalty if they drop out, and acceptance of newcomers is reluctant at best). Thus you acquired some very important social skills at a very early age. You learned to say hello and goodbye in a spirit of good-natured camaraderie. You came to regard group membership as involving larger, less personal, and more task-oriented values which transcend the emotional aspects of one's participation, unlike all-female cliques which lean heavily upon intimacy and subjective sharings. And, finally, you picked up the ability to indulge in that relatively 'safe' and surface mode of communication known as 'small talk.'

This last is a capability for which Americans of both sexes are known throughout the world; it is even claimed by some that they have raised small talk to the level of an art form! If you happen to be a taciturn soul, this is far from typical of your ordinal position. For, generally speaking, you are without a doubt the blue-ribbon, nonstop conversationalist of the entire birth order zodiac. Once you start rolling, you can pick up on any topic and move with lightning rapidity from one subject to the next – whatever the last thing you said reminded you of. If someone refers back to whatever theme it was that got the conversation rolling, you have in all likelihood forgotten what they are alluding to (that was a full half-hour ago, after all), and have to retrace your steps in order to make an appropriate response. Unlike the male singleton who is apt to drone on in a manner which loses sight of audience reaction (see Chapter 3), you are generally a more entertaining raconteur, and your only fault is that you often simply don't know when to stop. You rarely pause for breath and often don't let your listener(s) pause for theirs. In short, you lead the conversation rather than following it, and so you tend to overload your listeners' circuits – leaving them a very scant margin for collecting their wits, digesting all you have said, and offering a fully thought-out response. Added to this, more than most youngest children you are more apt to spill other people's deep dark secrets without meaning to. Wishing to prove that you are every bit as much in the know as your older sister, you can often accomplish this by revealing certain matters which other people wish you would keep quiet about. Wanting to measure up to your sister's prestige, beauty, status, or whatever, can often lead to your acquiring habits which in the long run you could better do without.

Like many youngest children (see Chapter 8), you have learned how to grab the limelight and hold onto it for dear life. In your love relationships this can create special problems insofar as your love partners also want to have 'equal time' and find that they rarely get it. The greatest difficulty for you in this area is your enormous need to feel important and worthy of other people's respectful attention. Thus you require too much of center stage, and are apt to be too grudging when you finally permit your love partners to express all of the thoughts and feelings which they have been sitting on while you were holding forth. Added to which you can often feel quite put upon when your nearest and dearest appear to be giving too much of their attention to other people. You have an excessive need to be number one in the life of your beloved – but for quite a different reason. The first-born considers it his or her birthright to be first because that's how it always was during the growing-up years – whereas you demand it as a consequence of having been 'runner-up' daughter or 'substitute son' during the very same period. Empathy for the viewpoint of others is not your strong suit. But – unlike the first-born – you are an astute listener (once you decide to give ear) and can learn to collaborate more readily than you perhaps believe possible. Otherwise you tend to talk when you should be listening. We think that with some diligent self-application you can learn to modify this trait. It won't be easy, but we invite you to make the effort; you won't regret it.

In connection with all the things we've been talking about – your mobility, your facility in creating and relinquishing friendships, and your unusual degree of acquired independence – we would like to point out that you have an ability to live alone and like it second only to that of singletons (see Chapter 1). Along with this, your mobility gives you a rare capacity to create a cozy home for yourself wherever you go. One thing which makes this possible is your propensity for investing your emotional attachments into a few favorite *objects* (rather than people) – a vase here, a painting there, a statuette, a small rug, a favorite kitchen or workroom appliance, etc.

What differentiates you from singletons is that, while they tend to create their own home base over a period of months and years, and to stay put for months, years and even decades, you have learned, as a consequence of your mobility, to pare your possessions down to the bare essentials. You know exactly which possessions have stood the test of time and now spell 'home' to you, no matter how far you roam. To the best of our knowledge, yours is the only birth order to fully develop this particular gift, although the younger of two boys displays the same capacity to a much lesser degree.

By this we don't mean that we consider you a lonely or isolated person. Being able to enjoy one's own company in solitude without being estranged from the rest of humanity is a rare art indeed. Your capacity for acquiring numerous friends over a seemingly limitless geographical area keeps your membership of the human race very active. At the same time, your difficulty with truly close love relationships may subject you to an occasional dark night of the soul during which you stop and wonder what life and love are really all about. While you often disdain the idea of being dependent on any one individual, you may sometimes feel that you are being passed by in a world which expects every person to find and live intimately with one true love.

Some researchers say that during childhood you may not display the kind of independence we have emphasized in this chapter, and instead may tag along after your sister's pursuits as well as her friendship circle. But we have found that in adulthood, you are apt to be a very independent person indeed. This, combined with your considerable array of social skills, makes you one of the best functioning of all ordinal positions, and the third least likely to appear in the caseloads of mental health professionals. This, we make haste to add, is not meant to imply that your adjustment is all that much better than anyone else's – rather that your special talents (a certain glibness of speech, nonbinding 'close' relationships, and freewheeling lonerism) also happen to be traits which our particular culture holds in high esteem at the time of this writing. For this reason you do not seem to fight society as often as the other birth orders, and are therefore less likely to be subjectively aware – or to make other people aware – that you may, in fact, be in a less than ideal place psychologically speaking.

Meanwhile you take genuine pleasure in your daily activities, your many acquaintances, and your unusual capacity for flexibility – for trimming your sails and charting your course in accordance with whatever the changing seasons and other worldly circumstances require. Wherever there is a safe port for you to drop anchor, rest assured that you will probably find it. Meanwhile, bon voyage to you and all your endeavors!

CHAPTER NINETEEN

Twins

We have often heard it said by twins that nobody who is not a twin is in a position either to understand or make pertinent remarks about this relatively unusual and somewhat awe-inspiring ordinal position. In our opinion this is a little like saying that if one is not an omelet, one has no right to claim any knowledge about omelets – or even eggs, for that matter. Granted that twinship is the most birth-order conscious of all ordinal positions (with the possible exception of singletons – who are also apt to feel different, on account of their sibling deficiency), we shall nevertheless plunge ahead to share whatever insights we have been able to glean about this traditionally fascinating birth order. If you are a twin, you may appreciate the feeling of being better understood than you had imagined you could be. On the other hand you may also resent what you experience as our brash intrusion into areas which you have always regarded as private property between you and your twin. We hope that you will take comfort in the fact that the avowed purpose of this book is to examine the 'secrets' of every birth order we deal with, and you are therefore not exempt from our scrutiny. You certainly have that much in common with other ordinal positions!

About ninety-eight percent of us came into the womb alone, and began our existence in that universe of warm liquid whose temperature was perfectly adjusted to our needs: oxygen, hormones, nutrients, and other substances necessary for development were obligingly piped in via the umbilical cord. Despite whatever hazards we may have encountered during our stay in the womb (and there can be many, as any obstetrician will tell you), the environment belonged to us and us alone. We hovered at the very center of the known universe; we were the Sun King, the Virgin Queen; master/mistress of all that surrounded us. Our finger was firmly planted on the bellybutton of the cosmos. Once we were born, the magic came to an end. Our circulation grappled with the shaky task of warming or cooling our skin; lungs gasped in an alien element; we squirmed and belched and gulped and defecated. Rough situation. From then on each of us, in his or her own way, has cherished a dim dark memory that once upon a time the living was easy, and maybe – someday, somehow – we will once again retrieve our Land of Milk and Honey (at the racetrack, or by winning a contest, or by mastering an esoteric skill, or by joining a religious group or political party or social movement aimed at remaking this faulty and flawed world of ours). Most of us have our own (often buried) hopes of regaining the Promised Land.

But how must it have been for you who were one of twins back in the 'first spinning place,' as poet Dylan Thomas called it? What must it have been like to have had a companion every step of the way? How must it have felt to be gradually pushed closer and closer to one another? Was there some vague sense of camaraderie, or a vague discomfort about having some intruder muscle in? Or were these feelings not vague at all, but increasingly acute as your time for being born drew near?

Are you who are one of twins more likely than 'single-borns' to be claustrophobic, or did that early experience have the opposite effect and you have a greater tolerance for cramped quarters? Did you compete in the womb as to which of you would be born first? Are you consequently more competitive by nature than most single-borns?

Obviously such thinking raises more questions than we can answer in our present state of knowledge. All we can hope to do in this chapter is to scan some of the findings and observations which have been made by those who have experienced and/or studied this fascinating and least understood of all birth orders.

If you are one of twins, it is quite possible that every observation we will be offering in this chapter is already well known to you. And yet . . . unless you have personally known quite a number of other twin pairs and compared notes with them, or have acquainted yourself with literature on the subject, there is the possibility that we may offer you some interesting food for thought along the way.

We must define two types of twinship at the outset: identical and fraternal. Identical twins are brought about by the division of a single fertilized ovum (called a zygote, which is why the term 'monozygotic' is used for such twins in the scientific literature). Each half of the divided single cell has precisely the same genetic inheritance as the other; their physical inheritance is identical. Fraternal twins, on the other hand, were each the product of a separate sperm and a separate ovum. The two eggs just happened to be in the uterus and got fertilized at approximately the same time. We say 'approximately' because one ovum could have been fertilized anywhere from hours to days or weeks after the first one began its existence as a zygote. Nowhere is this more dramatically evident than when the twins belong to distinctly different races. Which is to say that fraternal twins need not look alike, and sometimes even a family resemblance is hard to spot. The fraternal form of twinship is known as 'dizygotic.'

Whether mono- or dizygotic, and no matter how different your growing-up experience would be, certain things must have been similar about your intrauterine existence.

Although we can't speculate about the first several months, there is no doubt that things got pretty crowded as the moment for your birth drew nigh. You both had to learn to accommodate another human being in extremely close quarters, while every fiber of you was longing to stretch and be able to move freely in a space of your own. If, as we believe, prenatal experience affects our later life, you are apt to display an exaggerated form of the universal human conflict between a wish to *merge* versus a need to *separate* – a longing to be close to others opposed by an equally strong need to be an independent entity in your own right.

When it comes to you and your twin, the outside world has a very strong tendency to encourage the merging impulse and to feel somehow cheated by any efforts you may make to assert your independence. This dichotomy constitutes, perhaps, the most central theme in your life. We think that this phenomenon can best be explained by the fact that most people have a secret wish to have an 'alter ego' of their own – someone exactly like themselves who understands their every action; who knows and accepts their every attitude, feeling, and desire. To put it another way, virtually everyone comes into the world cherishing a deep and poignant wish for an ideal soul mate – a 'twin,' as it were. He or she may look for this fulfillment in a love partner, a friend, a teacher, a pupil, an employer, a protégé, etc. Twins, therefore, hold a powerful fascination for the rest of humanity, which is why you are so often surrounded by a strange and confusing aura – partly exotic and partly a big pain in the neck.

Popular mythology surrounding twinship further complicates the way in which the world views you. Anyone who remembers Bette Davis or Elizabeth Bergner in the movie versions of *A Stolen Life* or Olivia de Havilland in *Dark Mirror* or James Dean in *East of Eden* may recall that one twin was depicted as 'the good one' while the other was 'the bad one.' Among some primitive peoples identical twins are destroyed or abandoned at birth since one is considered to be the child of a demon – and, not knowing which is which, the elders take the precaution of destroying both. Meanwhile, twins are also commonly believed to have psychic powers which enable each of them to know what the other is thinking, etc.

In addition, there is a sense of apartness from the rest of society which your twinship imposes upon you. You are apt to feel too close to your twin and too different (as a twin) from other people. It is not as usual as one might think for a pair of twins to meet and really get to know another set of twins. Even in large urban areas it is a less common event than most people would imagine, and in rural areas it is much rarer; there are still many twins in this world who have yet to lay eyes on another pair of twins. So you and your twin grew up as a kind of unit – for better or worse – and the rest of the world is composed of outsiders whose understanding of twinship ranges from romantic fantasies about your supposed similarities all the way to grotesque dramatization of your real or imagined differences. That is why we will be referring to the rest of the world in this chapter as 'the outsiders': their subjective experience lies outside the nitty-gritty of twinhood, try as they might to bridge the gap that lies between their view of the world and your own. It is our hope that in the course of this chapter we may contribute something toward the closing of that gap. Let's begin by addressing ourselves to the subject of fraternal twinship.

FRATERNAL TWINS

Fraternal twins are faced with a paradox. If you are not really too much alike, the world seems to want to emphasize your similarities: you are twins, after all, and therefore you 'should' look, act, and feel alike. If you do have a strong resemblance to each other, the world can then go ahead and exaggerate the differences: 'After all,' they tell themselves, 'it is necessary to tell the twins apart!' Even if you were the opposite sex from your twin, the world you grew up in may have had a puzzling and burdensome yen to assume and promote all sorts of similarities which simply didn't exist.

Possibly because each of us seeks that ideal soul mate, we take it for granted that twins with a ready-made alter ego must really love each other. But the rock-bottom fact is that just because your birth coincided with your twin's is no reason for anyone – including yourselves – to assume that you must like each other any more than any other pair of siblings. Unfortunately, this bit of reality is apt to be overlooked by outsiders who cast their envious gaze upon you and your twin. We don't need to tell you how hard they push for merger. Even when your twin is of the opposite sex, they can often lay their vicarious alter-ego trip on you by dressing you in identical outfits. This is especially apt to happen during your early years when such experiences carry a lifelong impact. Unisex apparel (identical sailor suits and such-like) was, in that case, familiar to you and your twin long before it became a trendy innovation in the fashion world. To be sure, your family may have confined such exercises in similarity to special occasions like weddings, funerals, bar mitzvahs, and other public events. 'There go the twins – aren't they cute together? Alike as two peas in a pod!' Never mind that your twin was and maybe still is thinner or fatter than you are, and that he/she was/is a razzmatazz extrovert (or a shy introvert) compared to you. The outside world still has a maddening penchant for lumping you together as 'the twins.' Will it ever end? The answer is, 'Not likely!'

Thus yours is the difficult and arduous task of constantly sorting yourselves out from one another, and of communicating this to a world which prefers to treat you both as a single unit. If your twin is of the opposite sex or very different in looks and physique you may have a somewhat easier time of it.

Experts disagree as to the age at which toddlers become aware of gender identity, but regardless of any fine points of disagreement, it is generally conceded that a solid awareness of such matters is firmly established at around the age of three. But long before this, boys and girls are treated differently. Language alone makes a difference. (Boys are referred to in most Western languages as 'he' and girls as 'she.') Fathers and mothers both have different expectations for boys and girls. (Boys are expected, and allowed to be, rougher, more exploratory, and even dirtier than girls.) Even very little children are given sex-differentiated toys – e.g., doll 'babies' for girls and toy trucks for boys.

The sex difference between you publicly legitimizes your right to be different from your twin at a far earlier age than is generally permitted to twins of the same sex.* Having thus established 'separateness' to your mutual satisfaction, it is then much easier and safer to experience areas of genuine closeness to one another. Of all twinships yours is the one most likely to achieve a realistic and healthy balance between genuine intimacy and genuine individuality. Needless to say, there is also the possibility that you two do not share the same sets of interests (and, later in life, sets of

---

* In this connection, we would like to make note of the fact that same-sex non-twins separated by an age gap of eighteen months or less and who happen to bear a close resemblance to one another are often treated more like twins than like regular siblings.

values), and were in fact not terribly close. If such has been the case, you probably were made to feel more than ordinarily guilty on this account. Outsiders cherish the notion that *any* set of twins is actually one person who somehow got artificially separated into two individuals, and so they find it particularly threatening when the two of you do not seem to be getting along in the perfect harmony which the world has predetermined for you. Consequently you grew up feeling that any refusal on your part to play along with such nonsense constituted a violation of the rules which society had set down for the two of you. Depending on your respective personality make-ups, you may have tried very hard to hide your differences behind a façade of artificial harmony, or you may have become determined rebels who fought tooth and nail to offset society's naive brainwash. Note our use of the phrase 'respective personality make-ups.' One of you may have been characterologically inclined to act out the role of Peacemaker while the other played that of Rebel.

What we said in the foregoing paragraph holds particularly true if you are a same-sex twin – especially if you resemble one another in even superficial ways. If you don't look like twins, then you were allowed to behave like ordinary siblings. But no matter what your physical differences, if you and your twin resembled each other more than either of you resembled any other family member, then your twin-ship was probably emphasized by the outsiders. Being treated as one person is the bane of your existence as a twin, and it all started the very day you were born. Logically enough, when you stop to consider it, you were fed at the same time, burped at the same time, put on the potty at the same time, sent out to play at the same time, called home at the same time, put to bed at the same time (possibly in the same bed) and so forth. Unless your folks were wise enough to encourage activities independent of one another, about the only time you got to be on your *own* in the world was at the doctor's or the dentist's surgery (emergencies only; you got your routine checkups together) or when one of you stayed home sick in bed while the other trotted off to school. But even then you weren't truly alone because people would invariably cast worried looks in your direction and inquire solicitously as to the whereabouts of your twin, almost as though you had been physically cut in half and had no right to parade such an embarrassing amputation in public.

If you were lucky enough to bear scant physical resemblance to your twin, the chances are that your twinship was played down, especially as you grew older and strangers found it almost impossible to believe that you were twins (let alone members of the same family) even after they'd been informed of the fact. Your parents may even have arranged for you and your twin to attend different schools or to be in separate classes. Under such circumstances you were permitted to establish a clearer sense of your own individual identity than is vouchsafed to the majority of twins throughout the world.

There remains, however, one more major theme which dogs the footsteps of same-sex fraternals throughout their growing-up years. That is, which one of you was designated as the 'older' and which the 'younger'? This holds particularly true if you happen to look alike. While outsiders may take pleasure in your exotic status as twins, at the same time they need to sort you out in their own minds by accentuating any distinguishing factors. Even though you and your twin may have been born a scant five minutes apart, the first one out is known forever as the older while the other goes through life as the younger one. With most same-sex twins there is considerable rivalry – as there is apt to be between any pair of brothers or sisters close in age. Often enough (but not invariably) one of you takes over the leadership for both, deciding what games to play and when to play them (or what mischief to make and when to make it). Among ordinary siblings, the older of two brothers usually sees leadership as his prerogative, and the older of two male twins is no exception (for identicals as well as for fraternals).

In opposite-sex twins, this is far less common, owing to the fact that the sex difference takes precedence over the relatively forced concept of 'age difference.' Forced or not, it exerted an impact of incredible magnitude upon each of your lives – so much so, in fact, that you stand to learn a considerable amount about yourself and your fraternal twin if you read the appropriate chapters in Part Two of this book, wherein we discuss the psychological profiles of the older and younger child in single-born (non-twin) two-sib combinations. There is an old Polish saying that 'if you call a person a pig often enough, he or she will end up saying "oink, oink".' In the same vein, if you were told ever since you could understand speech that you were the 'older' or 'younger' twin, it's a pretty good guess that you accepted that role heartily enough for it to shape your relationship: it wasn't until much later that you and your twin realized you had been parties to what can only be described as a gross exaggeration.

Last but not least, there is the lifelong struggle to deal with the dual problems of closeness and merging versus independence and separation. Granted, all of us must come to terms with these issues throughout the course of our lives, but it is more emotionally loaded when you are a twin. Your inborn capacity for closeness can make you more comfortable with intimacy than most people, and this factor can be experienced as threatening by those with whom you wish to be close. At the same time your fierce (and sometimes inappropriate) insistence upon establishing your own identity can run counter to what most outsiders consider – rightly or wrongly – prerequisite to genuine and viable intimacy. Thus to them you come across as a contradiction in terms; you can be overly intimate when a non-twin seeks privacy, and you can be excessively private when he or she yearns for togetherness. Small wonder that you relate best to other twins when the opportunity affords itself; they, after all, understand these things. Meanwhile, you should do all in your power to articulate for yourself and then explain to others as much as you possibly can about what it means to be a twin. Human intuition is capable of grasping many things which lie beyond the realm of one's personal experience, and if you can manage to step outside of your lifelong perception of yourself as an exotic rare bird you will find that you have more in common with the outsiders than you would ever have believed possible. They have much to learn from you, and you can learn a lot from them.

IDENTICAL TWINS

Odd though it may sound at first, individual human beings can be likened to snowflakes. Scientists who have devoted many years to the study of snowflakes have devised ingenious photographic methods which have enabled them to photograph thousands upon thousands of flakes as they land on a blackened microscopic slide. Never – repeat *never* – have they found any two flakes that are exactly alike. To be sure, each one is approximately the same size and weight, contains about the same amount of hydrogen and oxygen, and has exactly six points to its characteristic 'star.' Thus they share many 'species traits' in common, but each flake is a unique individual none the less. The same holds true of people; barring birth defects, each of us is born with identical endowments – head, torso, arms, legs, organs, chemical composition, and a brain. Yet each person is a unique individual regardless of whatever he or she has in common with the rest of humanity. Like snowflakes, no two humans on the face of this planet are exactly alike, *and you are no exception.* As an identical twin you know more than anybody else what twinhood involves. And yet, unless you have read extensively on the subject or have spoken with many other pairs of identicals, there is probably a good deal that you don't know about your birth order. For instance, did you know that:

1. In many cases one twin is right-handed and the other left-handed. But in a number of instances both twins are born right-handed or left-handed. Researchers think it may have to do with the stage at which your single cell performed its self-division into separate individuals.

2. The southpaw twin tends to be smaller than the partner. This goes for fraternal twins as well, by the way.

3. You are apt to have speech problems more often than single-borns.

4. Your and your twin's handwriting rarely bear the remotest resemblance to each other. Since another of the authors' specialties happens to be graphology, our hunch is that this derives from right- or left-handedness – i.e., right or left brain 'hemisphere dominance.' We haven't run into any research on the subject as it relates to identical twins.

5. Psychological and personality measures often find that you and your twin differ markedly on such variables as introversion/extroversion, levels of anxiety, originality,

and style of thinking. Again, these may be related to hemisphere dominance.

6. Mothers around age forty are three to four times more likely to produce twins than women half that age. At the same time it is most likely that your mother gave birth at least one time before you came along. Therefore it is probable that you and your twin grew up with at least one older sibling and parents who were aged forty or older when you were born.

7. Most twins are premature and underweight at birth.

8. Twins often develop a special and secret language between themselves and usually drop it around age five.

9. Owing to the extreme intimacy of your relationship (partly voluntary, partly enforced by the environment), twins are apt to have sexual knowledge of each other more often than other sibling pairs. Call it 'incest' if you will, but we think it's more akin to masturbation – since it is at the physical level that you are both most subjectively inclined to consider yourselves as 'one person.' In any event, when it does happen it's a secret which you rarely reveal to outsiders. Furthermore, it doesn't seem to bear much relationship to later homosexuality, either, although one of you may grow up to be heterosexual while the other adopts a homosexual lifestyle.

10. Twins derive most of their own opinions concerning their alikeness and/or differences from parents and other important people in their environment.

Then, of course. there are all sorts of legends and superstitions about identical twins that stretch back to the earliest beginnings of history. Some cultures have been convinced that you were 'bewitched,' and so they did away with you at birth. Others worshipped you as gods while still others believed that you were endowed with special and occult powers. One thing is certain, however: you are almost universally regarded as being quite special and out of the ordinary, no matter how hard the outsiders may try to treat you 'just like ordinary human beings.' The only possible exception we can think of is those extremely rare instances in which a family contains two or more sets of twins – a phenomenon most likely to occur when either or both parents are themselves one of twins.

More often than not, you are the subject of secret envy and admiration on the part of outsiders who probably have seen movies where twins (played by a non-twin thespian) managed to fool everybody into thinking that one person could be in two places at once, and had wonderful romantic adventures into the bargain. As we pointed out at the beginning of this chapter, the vast majority of single-borns regard you as an embodiment of their own deep-seated yearnings for a soul mate. Just stop and think how often they have asked you with that far-off look in their eyes 'Tell me, what's it like to grow up with another *you* at your side?' or words to that effect. Aside from the fatuous assumption that you experience your twin as merely 'another you,' it's a little like saying 'I want you to sit down and tell me all about your trip across the Gobi Desert!' A special glamor is attached to identicals, and the idea of anyone having a 'double,' an identical twin, has fascinated writers back to the days of Castor and Pollux.

And yet you have to admit that there have been many moments in your life when you had cause to wonder whether perhaps you were indeed inhabiting a dream world of double identity from which you might one day awaken to find yourself blessedly free and independent of your counterpart – but at the same time dreadfully forsaken, bereft, and helpless. There may even have been a period in your early childhood when both you and your twin shared the fantasy that every outsider had also originally come into the world fully equipped with a twin – who had subsequently perished. Fear of undergoing a similar fate can constitute a lifelong preoccupation when you are one of twins – a nagging fear which you rarely share with outsiders.

Or, you may have looked into a mirror one day and suddenly realized that the image staring back at you was your twin's. This can cause a lot of confusion for both of you, especially when you are very small. Little children have enough difficulty sorting themselves and each other out without having the waters muddied further by the existence of an ever-present look-alike. As if things were not already complicated enough, outsiders are apt to enter the situation in ways which only add to the confusion. Either they push your identicalness for all it's worth – referring to you as 'the twins' and asserting proudly that they often can't tell you apart, or else seizing upon any and all differences (real or imagined) and blowing them up for all they are worth. Thus one of you may have been dubbed 'the leader' and the other 'the follower'; or one 'the shy one' and the other 'the aggressive one,' etc. – thereby typing you and (as the transactional analysts tell us) giving you an admonition to be forever true to type.

If your parents and others pushed too hard for similarity, you and/or your twin may have bent over backwards to assert your differences – even to the point of near estrangement or enmity. If, on the other hand, your parents pushed too hard for differences, you may have found yourself clinging that much more closely to your twin so as to stave off the specter of ultimate bereavement which you both always feared. In short, identical twins are apt to be the focus of enormous pressures from the environment, whether it be in the direction of exaggerated merging or of exaggerated apartness.

The upshot of all this is that you are likely to have grown up with highly exaggerated thoughts and feelings of your own when it comes to matters involving dependency and independence. As an adult you may have a strong inclination to make excessive gestures in either direction, or – even *more* confusing – to seesaw back and forth between the two extremes. You may distrust any kind of merging except that which goes on between you and your twin, or you may distrust any kind of merging whatsoever – so that you live the life of a loner who shrinks back from close relationships with other people. This, however, is a rare phenomenon for you. You tend to be more at home with shared intimacy than most people, and in fact are often surprised at how truly warm and close outsiders are sometimes capable of being. At the opposite end of the seesaw you may be hypersensitive to elements of distance (or apartness) which are so often characteristic of single-borns. This may set you to longing for the old familiar twinship bond, so that you experience needless feelings of defeat and hopelessness in your efforts to achieve closeness to others.

If you happen to have been known as 'the assertive one,' you stand a far better chance of working these problems through. You are, after all, accustomed to reaching out for what you want in the world. Your chances are not so good if you grew up as 'the timid one.' Why is this so? Because whatever the assertive one obtains from the world usually arrives in the form of a 'double order' of this or that – to be shared with his or her twin. When either of you asked for a cookie (or a doll or a baseball or a bicycle), the world, more often than not, produced two – one for you and one for your twin – so that nobody could be accused of playing favorites and disrupting the twinship. And so, if you were the passive beneficiary of your twin's assertiveness, it may now be very difficult for you to obtain what you want from the world on your own without your twin to intercede or to run interference for you.

Of course the foregoing has been magnified for purposes of illustration. A lot more likely state of affairs is one in which you were assertive in some kinds of situation while your twin took the lead in others. And it is in precisely this biographical history of mutual (and often symbiotic) reciprocity that the renowned (and 'spooky' in the eyes of outsiders) interdependency of identical twins has its deepest roots. For as long as you live nobody will ever be able to stand in for your twin, so you might as well get used to that fact.

If your life has put you in contact with other identical twins, the chances are great that you will marry a twin, who, after all, understands the experience of twinship that can't really be wholly communicated to anyone else. This, however, does not mean that other forms of closeness with other kinds of people are not well worth having; worth all the emotional difficulties of making a relationship work. 'Half a loaf is better than none,' as the saying goes – and when you stop to think about it, half a loaf is more than enough for anybody.

CHAPTER TWENTY

The Large Family

If we had the time, money and research facilities for studying large families, we might well discover that each of the hundreds of birth orders yielded sufficient similarities to make generalizations. We could then talk about the 'second child of six,' or 'the middle girl with two sisters and two brothers.' Unfortunately, our knowledge of birth order doesn't go that far as yet. Perhaps you came from a large family, where there were more than three children, regardless of whether the spacing between them was irregular or quite even. Glancing down through our Table of Contents, you may have decided that unless you happen to have been born first, last, or bang in the middle, you are excluded from consideration in these pages. Far from it! The fact is that you probably have characteristics of at least *two* birth orders – maybe more. It is the purpose of this chapter to explain what we mean by this. But first we would like to make some general observations about large families.

What we have said about the Youngest Child can hold true in the large family for any of the younger children. The last two in the family (or even the last three) may be considered 'the babies' and be heir to all of the rights, privileges, immunities and disadvantages that go along with that label. In a large family it is not only the oldest child but also the other older children who are given the burden of minding the younger ones; protecting them, and fighting their battles for them. We have pointed out (in Chapter 2) that in a large family, the oldest girl often plays mother to her younger siblings. Here let us add that the younger siblings often have the most loving memories of that older sister. Often enough they feel that they were closer to her than to their actual mother, whom they saw as being preoccupied with the larger issues of managing the house as a whole – the one who kept the wheels turning. The oldest sister, on the other hand, may have been seen as the one concerned for their comfort and happiness. Often enough they look for someone to fill that role in their adult lives, and usually manage to have at least one older woman friend whom they admire and respect and whose advice they seek. A man who genuinely adores his mother-in-law often does so because she reminds him of his loving older sister (rather than of his own mother).

The biggest problem that a large family faces is that of organization. Nowadays the big old-fashioned family, with the possible exception of some farm families, tends to be poverty-stricken, which makes for special difficulties. Occasionally we come across a wealthy family containing six or eight or even eleven children. In this latter instance, organization is maintained by servants, and the nursemaid, cook, or chauffeur can become a more meaningful person to the children or a particular child than their loving but often distant parents.

Under more financially strained circumstances, however, birth order effects tend to be exaggerated. In a family that can afford to send only one child to summer camp, or where there has to be a choice as to which child gets a new winter coat, jealousy and envy can build up an explosive head of steam, and childhood antagonisms based on who got the biggest piece of pie can last a lifetime. In a poor family with, say, six children, if the mother buys six apples and one of the children eats two of them, two others are forced to share. It is not unusual for a successful and affluent adult coming from such a background to be reluctant to use 'too many' clean towels in the course of a single week, because during childhood, being one towel short caused endless disputes.

In large families, organization can be the most important feature. The children learn a certain household choreography – that is, who uses the bathroom and when, etc. If water is at a premium, several children may even use the same bath water – in which case who goes first and who goes last can be a matter of no small consequence. (The unorganized large family is often described as 'sheer hell' by adults who grew up in one.) Organization may take many forms, from the played-by-ear adjustments and compromises made yearly (or monthly, or daily), to the kind of regimentation that one woman likened to 'an orphan asylum where the children were lined up and kept to an almost minute-by-minute schedule, and there was no room for personal preference in *anything*.' We have noted that adults who grew up in large families are often quite amazed at the food likes and dislikes of the only child. '*I*,' they assert almost triumphantly, 'had to eat everything that was put on my plate! Not only that, but we often had the same menu for days on end – potatoes, rice and beans,' etc.

One of the truly sad things that can happen in large families is that one of the children can get lost in the shuffle. Regardless of whether the family is in the high, medium, or low socioeconomic bracket, it is not unusual for a child to grow up with no attention paid to his or her special needs. A middle-class mother of five told her son's nursery school teacher, 'I have five children. There just isn't enough time for me or their father to spend with any *one* of them!' If you were that child, you have grown to adulthood wondering what life is all about, and probably are grateful whenever people pay special attention to you.

If you were neither the first nor the last child in a large

family, you undoubtedly paired up with one of your brothers or sisters. Such pairings are not always between the sibs who are closest in age. Very often each of the older children 'adopts' one of the younger children. The two oldest boys in a family often form a pair, even when they are separated by, say, three or four years. In a two-sib family these two brothers might be rivals or opposites, but in a large family they tend to form a united front against the world. If you were one of such a pair, you probably have felt comfortable in partnership situations ever since.

If you grew up in a large family you are probably more aware of the generation gap than others might be. You are used to being treated as part of a group, and are well aware that there can be safety in numbers. In a small family parents can more easily determine who has been into mischief and who has not. In your family, however, the youngsters were apt to be treated as a unit with perhaps a single distinction being made between 'the boys' and 'the girls', or 'the older kids' and 'the youngsters'. In such circumstances the *group as a whole* gets restricted, punished, or rewarded, as the case may be. If nothing else, this instilled in you a heightened awareness of group membership.

At school it often happens that teachers also treat large families as a group – and expect a child from such a family to act in certain ways, based on teachers' experiences with that child's brothers and sisters. If this was so in your case, you probably expended a lot of effort in proving that you were not just another one of the Jones boys or girls but were a bona fide individual in your own right. In any event, you emerged from your childhood better able to cope with group membership than any other ordinals.

One thing you have learned to prize, however, is your *privacy*. You may not require a great deal of space, but you do demand that some corner of the house be yours exclusively. You may have had to learn the hard way how to do your own thing amid the buzzing, booming confusion of your housemates – especially if you grew up in a city apartment where space is at a premium even for the wealthy. In that case you may have learned to go to bed early and then get up in the wee hours of the night to read or study during the only quiet hours available to you.

We said above that in large families children often pair off. To illustrate the kind of alliances that can come about, we would like to talk about the imaginary Morgan family. We will list all of the Morgan children in order of their birth, starting with the eldest, indicating the number of years between each child and the next:

Peter
4
Shirley
2
Tom
3
Bob
1
Nancy

To begin with, three of these – Peter, Tom, and Nancy – have clear-cut ordinal positions which we discuss in separate chapters of this book, so let's deal with them first. Peter was an only child for the first four years of his life before Shirley came along, and an Only Boy during that period. Then he spent two critical years from age four to six as the older brother of a younger sister. From then on, however, he was an oldest child and an Oldest Boy. Peter was primarily an oldest boy, but to really understand how birth order affects his personality one should carefully read all five of the chapters referred to.

Nancy, of course, is the youngest child and a youngest girl. Since she came along only a year later than Bob, he and she were probably treated as a pair, making her very much a younger sister of an older brother if not his 'twin.' It would be our guess that this pairing is just as important as being the youngest, but it would depend on how the *other children* in the family paired off. The same goes for Tom – clearly the Middle Child but having been youngest with both an older sister and brother.

Pairing off or 'bonding' between children makes it interesting, difficult, and challenging to evaluate the role of birth order in large families. Technically speaking, the term 'bonding' is used by modern social scientists to describe the way in which infants focus their need for nurturing on a particular figure (or class of figures) in the environment. We say 'figure' because an infant (human or animal) may bond to almost any one or any *thing* – mother, father, male, female, dog, cat, or even a teddy bear or a security blanket. While it follows that a human infant may (and probably often does) form this particular kind of bond with a sibling of either sex, we are using the term here in a broader sense: we are using it to refer to that element of *emotional importance* which one sibling can have for another. It may be one-sided or it may be mutual; it may be characterized by affectionate devotion or chronic hostility. It is never indifferent. Siblings can admire, nurture, and love or they can despise, deprive, and hate one another.

By and large, the bondings tend to be mutual, for when somebody loves us, we tend to love them in return. Similarly, if they dislike us we also reciprocate in kind. But – and this is important to remember – it is by no means a hard-and-fast rule when it comes to *sibling* interactions. It often happens that a younger child has a very positive bonding toward an older sib who is either indifferent or even downright hostile. The reverse is, of course, a lot less common; the younger children seldom resist the attentions of an older brother or sister – even when such attentions are of a negative sort. (A small child will usually put up with almost any kind of abuse rather than be totally ignored.) It should also be added that, in families where open demonstrations of affection are frowned upon, much of the backbiting and squabbling which goes on can be a disguise (albeit a pretty convincing one!) for underlying feelings of love which the children in such a family find too embarrassing or threatening to cope with.

The point we wish to make is that the larger the family, the more an individual's primary sibling bond may outweigh his or her chronological position in the family. We would also like to note here that an adult who grew up in a large family often remembers only that specially bonded sibling well; other siblings are often like vaguely known relatives. This is especially true when the children are numerous and widely spaced so that the oldest sibs are out of the house during the formative years of the youngest.

Alliances also have greater relevance in large families than in small ones. Alliances are distinguished from bondings in that they serve a practical purpose, and may or may not coincide with bondings, which are more emotionally based. Take the Morgan family, for instance. Shirley might have an affectionate bond with her older brother Peter but she could form an alliance with Nancy, the other girl in the family. Or, she might bond with Tom to whom she is closest in age, etc. But she might form an alliance with her older brother because they are both the oldest children in the family and feel a mutual need to defend their prerogatives against parents and/or other siblings.

The larger the family the more alliances a child may form, even though one or more of the children may have only one alliance or perhaps none at all (see Chapter 7 on the middle child – for whom this particular situation is most likely). In other words, it is not beyond possibility that any one of the Morgan children could form an alliance with every one of his or her siblings – each alliance having its own particular function, and each varying in strength and duration.

It therefore behoves us when assessing birth order in large families to take into account all three of the above factors: chronological position, emotional bonding, and the existence (or non-existence) of unilateral and/or bilateral alliances.

Whatever the relative weighting of these three factors for you, if you came from a large family you are no doubt comfortable in groups and possess that rare blend of easy intimacy and sensitivity to privacy that is very hard to come by among people from small nuclear families.

Postscript

Now that you have finished reading about the various primary birth orders, you may want to know something about how we make use of such data to enhance our understanding of human personality. Needless to say, assessing the impact of a given individual's ordinal position upon the sum total of his or her lifescript is not always an easy task. For when the person whom we wish to understand doesn't seem to fit into any of the categories we have discussed, it may be helpful to consider that person's parents and *their* birth order. Parents, after all, are human beings too, and their relationships to their brothers and sisters affect (either obviously or subtly) the manner in which they relate to their own children.

Parents can – and often do – treat their own children more like brothers and sisters than offspring, despite the generation gap and the obvious age differences. What's more, grandparents can do the very same thing, often treating a grandchild like a sibling/conspirator against the parents. The reason for this is that the subconscious part of our mind always evaluates the world in terms of resemblances, and doesn't really pay much attention to 'minor' factual differences like age or sex.

Because of this phenomenon, a mother who was herself a youngest child may unknowingly treat her first-born like a big sister or brother and demand the same protection, care, and even inclusion in activities which characterized her own sibling universe, with all of its bondings, rivalries, alliances, and wary truces. In the same way, a man who felt close to his father during childhood may fall in love with a woman who subconsciously reminds him of Dad. There's nothing wrong or 'crazy' about any of this – it's just a part of what makes us tick. We only seem to land in real trouble when we establish a relationship with a person whose emotional agenda runs counter to our own, or who reminds us of a parent (or sib) who caused problems for us: then we tend to feel betrayed, or to be extra touchy, or to magnify each minor offense. In the same vein, a person with a stony parent can often seek out a stony spouse – and spend a lifetime trying to wring milk from such a stone.

As we have pointed out throughout this book, a special problem can develop when children in a family are – both or all – of the same sex, and one or both parental hearts had been set on having either a boy or a girl. Instead, not one but *two* (or more) of the *less*-wanted sex appear, and, without being aware of it, one or both parents may select one of the children to stand in for that much-wanted son or daughter. In most cases it is a *younger* child who gets picked for this role. This is not to say that such a child will necessarily grow up as an imitation of the opposite sex, but the child often enters adulthood with exaggerated self-doubts as to whether or not he or she is adequately living up to the gender and sex-role stereotypes which our society still assigns to males and females.

With what we've been saying as background, let's look at one example – a model, if you will, for assessing birth order and its influences upon character formation. Our example may appear somewhat involved, but most analyses of family relationships are, by nature, complex. Our subject is Tony, and we will attempt to come to an understanding of him in terms of his birth order – taking into account not only the birth orders of his parents but also those of his four grandparents as well. Here's how the lineup of Tony's

immediate forebears looks on a 'genogram' (short for
'genealogical diagram': circles represent females, squares
depict males, and sibs are arranged from oldest on the left
to youngest on the right):

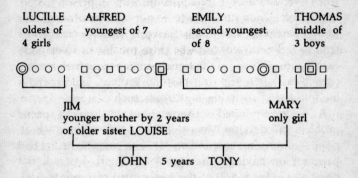

LUCILLE   ALFRED   EMILY   THOMAS
oldest of   youngest of 7   second youngest   middle of
4 girls   of 8   3 boys

JIM
younger brother by 2 years
of older sister LOUISE

MARY
only girl

JOHN   5 years   TONY

In order to understand Tony, we wish to consider what
contributions his parents and grandparents probably made
to the kind of person Tony grew up to be. Our evaluation,
in fact, will depend on how accurately we can spot what
was going on with each of them.

Let's start with Tony's grandparents and work our way
down the generations until we get to our hero. If you look
at the genogram, you will discover that Lucille, Tony's
paternal grandmother, was the oldest of four sisters. You
will also notice that Alfred, the paternal grandfather, was
the last of seven children. The two sisters who preceded him
were seven and nine years older and they took him over,
fighting his battles, seeing that he got to school on time,
and teaching him manners and morals. In other words,
both of these grandparents came from homes where
females predominated – where they were sources of
companionship and support. In Lucille's case, this was by
default. She grew up knowing and acknowledging the love

and support to be got from sisters – she knew nothing of freewheeling masculine camaraderie or male expectations, good or bad. She tends, in fact, to look on men as pretentious and even unrealistic.

Grandfather Alfred also grew up in a woman-oriented household, since he was much younger than his four eldest siblings – so much so that he scarcely knew the older children in the family and was closest to his two sisters. It was small wonder, then, that when their daughter Louise was born, Lucille and Alfred were overjoyed, and each saw in her the potential for being like the sisters they had grown up with. They 'adopted' her in the way that parents can adopt or treat as special any one of their own children. They simply didn't know what to make of Jim when he arrived, two years after Louise. They welcomed his birth, but they had no built-in positive attitudes toward him as they had toward Louise. They expected great things from Louise – she was the Heir Apparent, and they could not understand why Jim did not share their enthusiasm for this female paragon. The secretive and rebellious qualities of this type of boy were pronounced in Jim as he felt himself outranked and outsmarted by his older sister. His attitudes were, in fact, exaggerated because of his parents' experiences in their own families (whereby each came to parenthood with good preparation for bringing up girl children, but scant understanding of boys).

On the other side of the family tree we find Emily and Thomas. Emily, you will note, was the seventh of eight children. She was three years younger than the next child up the ladder, but only a year older than her brother Ralph. As in many families, the children were encouraged to pair off in a kind of buddy system so that she and Ralph were encouraged to be close and to take responsibility for one another. Emily was too near to Ralph in age to pull rank on him, and they both had fond memories of all the good times they had shared together.

Thomas was the middle of three brothers. Consequently when Mary, Tony's mother, was born he felt himself at a loss. He knew very little about a young girl's needs, and let himself be guided by what Emily thought was right and proper in Mary's upbringing. He tended, in fact, to treat her more as a son than a daughter (taking her to football games, praising her for being a good sport, teaching her maths puzzles and setting up a netball ring in the driveway). Both he and Emily were enormously proud of her when she was elected president of the pupils' council in secondary school, and between them they encouraged her in the direction of further public responsibility and achievement. Emily's only regret was that she was unable to provide her daughter with a younger brother. In an effort to compensate for what she felt as a lack, she constantly pushed Mary to be a joiner. She wanted Mary to have the companionship of other children and to be as involved with other people as she imagined that she and her brother had always been.

It comes as no surprise, then, to learn that Mary became a teacher of mathematics and went straight up the professional ladder all the way to university president. She met Jim in college and was attracted by his fun-loving qualities, his ability to do take-offs of all the professors and the more pompous of their fellow students. She found a serious, perplexed quality in him too that brought out the 'big sister' in her. In some sense she looked upon him as the little brother whom her own mother had grown up with but she herself had been deprived of – a kind of playmate whom she would love and protect and with whom she could forever be a child. Jim, on the other hand, found in Mary a woman who never tried to upstage him, never pulled intellectual rank, and who listened respectfully to all his ideas.

Jim was not the success that Mary expected him to be, however. He entangled himself in one off-beat business venture after another, often with unfortunate financial results from which his in-laws (Emily and Thomas) invariably rescued him – often over Mary's (not very strenuous) protests. Jim, in fact, was closer to Mary's parents than he was to his own. His father-in-law, Thomas, was impressed by Jim's knowledge of football (anyone able to tell you who won the World Cup back in 1930 could not be considered a failure). Emily, like her daughter Mary, loved his impish humor and his ability to make light (in public) of even his most bitter defeats.

So the stage was set for Tony's generation. Jim had felt threatened when Mary became pregnant with Tony's elder brother, John. Mary's independence had always been hard enough for him to cope with, and he certainly didn't want any rivals for her attention. Consequently, he resisted for several years the idea of having any more children, on the grounds that his financial picture was not yet secure. He tended to ignore his first-born son, and Mary reacted by protecting John in the only way she was familiar with – that is, encouraging him to be a joiner and to start climbing the success ladder as she had done. Jim felt left out, and as a result he drew closer to Mary's ever welcoming parents in an effort to balance out the neglects – real or imagined – that he was experiencing at home.

When Tony was born, five years after his brother, Jim promptly 'adopted' him and identified with him as a 'neglected' younger brother. Tony returned the compliment by rejecting his mother's and brother's plodding ambitiousness. Tony and his father did quite a lot of mutual snickering and nose-thumbing at the other two behind their backs. Tony's elder brother John became known as 'the serious one,' while Tony staked out a reputation for being a carefree maverick and was lots of fun at parties. All Jim asked in return for his devotion to Tony was that Tony not compete with him.

When all of these parental and grandparental birth orders are taken fully into account, we can now see that Tony is best described as a combination of younger brother of older brother (Chapter 17) and younger brother of older sister (Chapter 13), since John's alliance and identification with his mother was in some ways more like that of an older girl. Each of his parents latched onto one of their children in a way that echoed their own upbringing. Mary gradually shifted her 'beloved little brother' transference from her husband Jim to her first-born son, John, because John was becoming more her idea of what a little brother should be – that is, sharing her deeper intellectual and career interests. Jim's and Tony's alliance, which was deeply supportive and gratifying for each of them, was more like that of an older brother/younger brother setup, so that during early childhood Tony's role as younger brother of an older brother was greatly reinforced.

It came to an end, however, when Tony reached the age of six, at which time his father died in an auto accident and his father's older sister Louise (whose husband was killed in the same accident) moved into the household on a 'temporary' basis and remained there for the rest of her life. Tony was now left without an ally in a household dominated by two women who had been accustomed to knowing how to 'handle' a younger brother. Add to this the fact that his older brother John was closely aligned with his mother, and a picture emerges wherein a confused and embattled Tony found himself in a very tight spot. Having been closely bonded and allied with his father, he set about trying to fill the terrible vacuum in his life by embarking on a search for an older male who could provide the emotional sustenance he had received from his father. From that point until the age of twenty-nine his biographical profile reads like that of the younger brother of a sister at his most rebellious (see Chapter 13), and while he did make alliances with males considerably older than himself, he was often exploited by them, accustomed as he had been to fulfilling his father's hidden agendas during the first six years of his life. Upon graduation from high school he ran away from home and joined various and sundry protest groups which he served with dedication and gusto. Soon after he joined (as a 'sympathizer') a gay activist group aimed at countering the influence of Anita Bryant, he fell in love with a man twenty-two years his senior, 'came out' to his family, and has enrolled at a nearby college where he is majoring in anthropology. So far he is living 'happily ever after.'

Finally, we want to fulfill the promise made in our introduction – to reveal our *own* birth orders. First let us say that we both belong to the same general category. Then we suggest that you try to guess which one it is – on the basis of anything and everything you have learned about the topic so far from reading this book. When you are ready with an answer, simply turn to the next page . . .

George Edington and Bradford Wilson are both youngest
children.

GE is the youngest of four:
    Sister
    [24 months]
    Sister
    [36 months]
    Brother
    [21 months]
    GE

BW is the youngest of three:
    Brother
    [17 months]
    Brother
    [31 months]
    BW

Suggested Readings

Alder, A.: *Understanding Human Nature*, Premier Books (Fawcett Publications), New York, 1959; G. Allen & Unwin, London, 1928.

Ansbacher, H., and R. R. Ansbacher: *The Individual Psychology of Alfred Adler*, Basic Books, Inc, New York, 1956, pp. 376–382. Edington, G. and Wilson, B.: 'Children of Different Ordinal Positions,' *Basic Handbook of Child Psychiatry*, vol. 1, Chapter 44, Basic Books, Inc, New York, 1979.

Forer, L. B.: *Birth Order and Life Roles*, Charles C. Thomas, Springfield, Illinois, 1969.

– with Still, H.: *The Birth Order Factor*, David McKay Company, Inc, New York, 1976.

Kammeyer, K.: 'Birth Order and the Feminine Sex Role among College Women,' *American Sociological Review*, 31:508–515, 1966.

Koch, H. L.: 'Children's Work Attitudes and Sibling Characteristics,' *Child Development*, 27:289–310, 1956.

– *Some Personality Correlates of Sex, Sibling Position, and Sex of Sibling among Five- and Six-Year-Old Children*, Genetic Psychology Monographs, vol. 52, pp. 3–50, 1955.

– 'The Relation of Certain Family Constellation Characteristics and the Attitudes of Children towards Adults,' *Child Development*, 26:13–40, 1955.

– 'The Relation of "Primary Mental Abilities" in Five- and Six-Year-Olds to Sex of Child and Characteristics of His Sibling,' *Child Development*, 25:209–223, 1954.

Konig, K.: *Brothers and Sisters*, St George Books, Blauvelt, New York, 1973; Floris, Edinburgh, 1980.

Smith, E. E., and J. D. Goodchilds: 'Some Personality and Behavioral Factors Related to Birth Order,' *Journal of Applied Psychology*, 47:300–303, 1963.

Sutton-Smith, B., and B. G. Rosenberg: *The Sibling*, Holt, Rinehart, and Winston, New York, 1970.

Sutton-Smith, B., J. M. Riberts, and B. G. Rosenberg: 'Sibling Association and Role Investment,' *Merrill-Palmer Quarterly*, 10:25–38, 1964.

Toman, W.: *Family Constellation*, 2nd edn, Springer, New York, 1969.

Wilson, B.: 'A Clinical Portrait of M-1-F, the Elder Brother with One Younger Sibling, a Sister,' unpublished manuscript, 1966.

– 'The Personality of M-1-F as Seen in an Out-Patient Population: A Pilot Study,' unpublished manuscript, 1968.

The best in biography from Panther Books

To order direct from the publisher just tick the titles you want
and fill in the order form.   **GB281**

The best in biography from Panther Books

David Cairns (editor and translator)
The Memoirs of Berlioz   £3.95 ☐

Ronald Taylor
Richard Wagner   £2.50 ☐

Alfred Einstein
Mozart   £2.95 ☐

Louis Fischer
The Life of Mahatma Gandhi   £2.95 ☐
Handel   £1.25 ☐

F E Halliday
Thomas Hardy   £1.50 ☐

Alan Kendal
Vivaldi   £1.50 ☐

Jack Lindsay
Turner   £2.50 ☐
Gainsborough   £1.95 ☐

Bryan Magee
Aspects of Wagner   £1.95 ☐

Ted Morgan
Somerset Maugham   £3.95 ☐
Churchill 1874-1915   £3.55 ☐

Graham Reynolds
Constable: The Natural Painter   £1.95 ☐

Maynard Solomon
Beethoven   £2.95 ☐

Adam Zamoyski
Chopin   £2.95 ☐

Mona Wilson
The Life of William Blake   £1.95 ☐

To order direct from the publisher just tick the titles you want
and fill in the order form.   **GB381**

Modern society—now available in Panther Books

To order direct from the publisher just tick the titles you want
and fill in the order form.   **GM881**

All these books are available at your local bookshop or newsagent, or can be ordered direct from the publisher.